KEEPING THE PEACE

Marine Fighter Attack Squadron 251 during the Cold War 1946–1991

STEVEN K. DIXON

CASEMATE

Philadelphia & Oxford

Published in the United States of America and the United Kingdom in 2023 by
CASEMATE PUBLISHERS
1950 Lawrence Road, Havertown, PA 19083, USA
and
The Old Music Hall, 106–108 Cowley Road, Oxford OX4 1JE, UK

Hardcover Edition: ISBN 978-1-63624-193-7
Digital Edition: ISBN 978-1-63624-194-4

A CIP record for this book is available from the British Library

Printed and bound in the United Kingdom by CPI Group (UK) Ltd, Croydon, CR0 4YY.
Typeset by DiTech Publishing Services

For a complete list of Casemate titles, please contact:

CASEMATE PUBLISHERS (US)
Telephone (610) 853-9131
Fax (610) 853-9146
Email: casemate@casematepublishers.com
www.casematepublishers.com

CASEMATE PUBLISHERS (UK)
Telephone (0)1226 734350
Email: casemate-uk@casematepublishers.co.uk
www.casematepublishers.co.uk

Cover images: Flight line, Cubi Pt, Republic of the Philippines, October 1977; insignia. (both author's collection)

Contents

Acknowledgements

I could not have completed this book were it not for the help of others. The personnel at the National Archives in College Park, Maryland, were most helpful in locating squadron documents as well as other documents requested during the course of writing this book. Despite this, there are years which simply could not be found. It did not help matters that Marine squadrons, if they were not engaged in combat, were not required to file Command Chronologies. This was the norm until 1965 when regulations were changed to require all squadrons to file a report, usually in a semi-annual format.

A special thank you to the following organizations: the USMC History Division for their help in locating documents on hand in their archives and sending me copies; the USMC Heritage Foundation for providing a grant to help see this project through to completion; and the Naval Air Museum for their help in locating aircraft history cards for the F-8 Crusader.

A special thank you to those who served with the squadron during the years covered and answered my questions or contributed to the book: Neil Cummings, T. H. McAllister, Charlie Pitarys, LtCol. Josephus Mavretic USMC, Ret., LtCol. Myrl Allinder USMC, Ret., Bill Houser, Jay Cluelow, Robert Dwyer, Herbert G. Bibbee, Ken Hanson, Ralph Sabroe, Dan Shinabery, John Cummings, H. L. Logan, and Robert Pospischil.

Family members of veterans who served with the squadron also contributed photos for the book. My thanks to Dianne Cline, Anne Sayles, and Aaron Sumner.

Thank you to Steven Albright, who sent me many items concerning the squadron's early history, and to Peter Greengrass, who sent me a master list of all squadron accidents. The list, along with aircraft accident reports obtained from Naval History and Heritage Command, and Naval Safety Command, allowed me to compile a nearly complete record of all squadron mishaps and incidents.

Lastly, to my wife Lisa who put up with my long hours in front of the computer as I wrote the book.

If I missed anyone, my apologies. Your contributions are appreciated.

Preface

On 13 May 1952, the weather was warm with scattered clouds, typical for Marine Corps Air Station (MCAS) El Toro, California, and perfect flying conditions for four pilots of VMF-251. Their mission this day was to perform a ground control intercept and camera gunnery exercise with four bombers of the 102nd Bombardment Squadron, 106th Bombardment Wing of the New York Air National Guard flying out of March Air Force Base, California.

The F4U-4 Corsairs took off without any problems. At approximately 1220, the Marines intercepted the four B-29A Superfortresses 30 miles off the coast of California while flying at 15,000 feet. Shortly after the interception, for reasons unknown, the bombers requested the Corsairs initiate head-on runs.

The first three executed their head-on runs flawlessly and reformed to allow the last Corsair to make its pass. The fourth Corsair (BuNo 81218), piloted by 2ndLt. Joe K. Jensen, maneuvered to begin its run against the bombers. The until-then-uneventful training mission quickly turned into a nightmare. Jensen's Corsair collided with the left wing of his targeted B-29A (44-62119). His aircraft spun violently into the Pacific Ocean while the B-29 was quickly engulfed in flames. Several of the 17 crewmen bailed out before the bomber plunged into the ocean. Six were rescued, the remaining 11 were killed. Jensen's body was also recovered, and was laid to rest in Whitney, Idaho.

While the country was involved in the Korean War at the time of the incident, not all military units were participating in that war. As indicated by the loss of Jensen and the 11 crewmen of the B-29, training was not without risk. This was the price many aviators paid to keep the ideological enemy—communism—in check. The Cold War was in full swing, having been born from the ashes of World War II.

While the squadron eventually served in Korea, during the closing weeks of the war there, constant training exercises and deployments sum up the squadron's duty from 1946 to 1991. The exercises and deployments brought their own dangers—Jensen's loss serving as an example. Maintenance crews had their own set of problems. Vigilance had to be maintained but in doing so complacency often reared its ugly head. Aircraft were damaged, aircraft were lost, and some men died. These losses were classified according to the amount of damage sustained. The system of classification changed over the years. To avoid confusion, Appendix 7 lists aircraft as either destroyed or damaged. I do not differentiate between the amount of damage.

What follows is an operational history of VMFA-251. This history is based on available documents that were located in the National Archives and the USMC History Division. It is as complete as the documents allow.

When VMF-251 was reactivated as a Marine Reserve squadron in 1946, it had no aircraft and only a cadre of personnel. Stationed at NAS Grosse Ile, Michigan, it may have used the naval air station's Corsairs for flight training. There are no records of where the aircraft may have come from to bring the squadron up to strength. Getting the squadron up to strength in personnel was an effort, and it took a few years to reach full strength. Throughout the period covered in this book, manpower was an ongoing issue—there was never enough. Some of the issues that may have affected manpower likely included competition with other services, a lack of retention, and pay.

Pilots had to maintain their proficiency with their aircraft, and this changed through the years depending on the aircraft types flown. As a pilot completed his training, he received a mark in his training syllabus. Examples of these training exercises included navigation, air intercept missions, escort duty, air-to-air combat, air-to-ground support, radar intercepts, aerial refueling and, if necessary, carrier landing qualifications.

Supply was also an issue throughout the years covered. It seems parts were always lacking which forced the squadron to have a "hangar queen" that was used for spare parts to keep other aircraft flying. This problem was not confined to the squadron, many others had to contend with the ongoing lack of spare parts.

The squadron's record during the Cold War was stellar, completing every mission assigned to it, often away from home and despite the issues mentioned above. It is a tribute to the Marines of the squadron, as well as the families of those Marines who had to endure the long separation during deployments.

The military makes prodigious use of acronyms. To aid the reader in comprehending the acronyms used in the book, a list of acronyms and their meanings may be found in Appendix 4.

When mentioning a time, 24-hour military time is used. What would be 2:00 pm in civilian time is 1400 in military time; 9:00 am is 0900. The use of the 24-hour system avoids any confusion with am and pm.

CHAPTER I

Birth of a Squadron[1]

Marine Corps aviation grew at an exponential rate during World War II; odds are it will never see that kind of growth again. At the end of December 1941, there were 13 squadrons. At its peak strength at the end of September 1944, there were 145 squadrons. Manpower grew at the same time; at the end of December 1941 Marine aviation had 6,467 officers and men. Manpower had reached its greatest strength by the end of January 1945: 125,162 officers and enlisted men.

On 1 December 1941, VMO-251 was activated at Naval Air Station (NAS) San Diego, California. The squadron was designated to perform a photo-reconnaissance role (the "V" designates the squadron as heavier than air-fixed wing, the "M" stands for Marine, and the "O" stands for Observation). However, the squadron did not fly any such mission during the war. The only exception was a lone F4F-7 Wildcat and pilot attached to Marine Air Group 23 (MAG-23) during the battle for Guadalcanal in 1942. The F4F-7 was an unarmed version of the Wildcat with added internal fuel tanks. While it had a greater range, it was sluggish in the air. It was not a popular aircraft with the pilots.

By the time the Japanese attacked Pearl Harbor, the squadron still had no aircraft. Debate between the Navy and Marine Corps went on for months as they tried to pin down which aircraft to use. Several types were considered: floatplanes, the SBD Dauntless dive bomber, and the PBY Catalina flying boat to name a few. Finally, in the spring of 1942, the Navy and Marine Corps agreed on the aircraft: the Grumman F4F-3 Wildcat. VMO-251 began receiving its first Wildcats soon after the decision was made. By mid-April 1942, the squadron had in its possession at least 12 used Wildcats from the Navy. The aircraft were in poor shape and needed maintenance. Most importantly, however, the Wildcat was a fighter and not designed to be a photo-reconnaissance aircraft. Modifications to the aircraft had to be made.

At a modification facility at North Island, NAS San Diego, half the Wildcats had cameras installed and the much-needed maintenance on the aircraft was performed. A Fairchild F-56 aerial reconnaissance camera was added by removing one of the fuel tanks in the fuselage, located behind the pilot. He controlled the camera with a series of switches in the cockpit. The aircraft were redesignated F4F-3P. Fortuitously, the fighter's machine guns were not removed during the modifications.

While the first batch of aircraft were undergoing modification, VMO-251 became involved in the 1942 Hollywood movie production of *Wake Island*. Apparently, the film's star, Brian Donlevy, and the squadron's current commanding officer, Major (later lieutenant colonel) John Hart, knew each other from their Naval Academy days in the 1920s. Whatever tricks Donlevy and Hart used seemed to have worked. The squadron was given permission by the United States Marine Corps (USMC), but the USMC wanted complete control of publicity when it came to the squadron. Paramount Pictures accepted the request. Pilots from the squadron spent at least two weeks flying their Wildcats from an improvised airstrip near Salton Sea in California and another near Salt Lake City, Utah. After filming was completed, the rest of the aircraft were modified and repaired.

The picture was released near the end of the year, but squadron personnel were not able to catch the premiere. By then, VMO-251 was involved in the invasion and the months-long campaign to capture Guadalcanal in the Solomon Islands.

The Solomon Islands saw increased activity by Japanese forces in 1942. Of concern to the Allies was the airfield under construction near Lunga Point on the north coast of Guadalcanal. If the airfield was completed by the Japanese, it would put their air forces within range to strangle Australia by cutting off its supply route to the United States. It could also attack Australia itself. To counteract this threat, plans were quickly drawn up and the invasion of Guadalcanal—dubbed Operation *Watchtower*—was established. U.S. forces set D-Day for 7 August 1942.

In late April, the squadron was assigned in direct support of the 1st Marine Division. The division was packing up for a move from the United States to New Zealand, and on to Guadalcanal. VMO-251 received its orders on 18 May and began the arduous task of packing. The squadron departed for New Zealand on 17 June on board USS *Heywood* (AP-12), a troop transport.

Sailing with the squadron were elements of the 1st Marine Raider Battalion and a battalion of the 22nd Marines. Supplies declared not necessary for the squadron's mission were loaded aboard a different ship which set sail two days before *Heywood*. A month after the squadron arrived in theater, the supplies on this ship were finally delivered.

USS *Heywood* made its first stop at Samoa. There, the squadron received a change in assignment; it was now headed for New Caledonia. The ship anchored at Noumea—the capital of New Caledonia—on 10 July 1942. The squadron disembarked and was sent to Tontouta Airfield to await further instructions.

While at the airfield the Wildcats were reassembled, and pilots began to test fly them. As work progressed, the squadron finally found out what it would be doing. Its primary responsibility would be the air defense of the New Hebrides (now Vanuatu), an island chain several hundred miles northeast of New Caledonia. It would do so while stationed on Espiritu Santo. The squadron also had to install two radar stations: one on the north end of Espiritu Santo, and the other at the Turtle Bay Airfield near the southeast coast of the island. In addition, the Marines were to lend all possible assistance to the 11th Bombardment Group (BG) since that unit had yet to receive its ground echelon. Men from the squadron's photo section flew photo missions on 11th BG B-17 Flying Fortresses out of Tontouta and then Espiritu Santo. Other squadrons staging through the airfield on their way to Guadalcanal were also to be assisted as required. With these assigned duties, the squadron could not perform the role for which it was created: photo reconnaissance. In short, it functioned as a fighter unit rather than a photo-recon squadron.

By August 1942, the squadron was established on Espiritu Santo. As the radar stations were not yet up and running (they were finally completed in September), patrols were flown from dawn to dusk. With the squadron trying to complete multiple missions at the same time, the pilots were pushed to their limits. Pilots from VMF-212, a Marine fighter unit, based on Efate (more than 150 miles to the south) were temporarily assigned to VMO-251 to help with the load.

Prior to the invasion of Guadalcanal, five of the squadron's pilots were temporarily assigned to the heavy cruisers USS *Vincennes* (CA-44) and USS *Astoria* (CA-34). Second Lieutenants Carl Scheussler and William P. Kirby were assigned to *Vincennes* while Major William P. "Soupy" Campbell, and Second Lieutenants Roy Spurlock and Robert T. Whitten were sent to *Astoria*. Their primary job was to fly spotter planes from the ships to help direct shore bombardments of targets on Guadalcanal.

Beginning in late July, four photographers from the squadron's photo section were temporarily assigned to the 11th BG to fly two missions to provide up-to-date photos of Guadalcanal and Tulagi. Two B-17s took off from New Caledonia but encountered heavy rain and thunderstorms along the way. Precious fuel was used flying around the bad weather before the islands were reached. Once over Guadalcanal, they began to take pictures of the invasion area, but were intercepted by an unknown number of Japanese aircraft. The Japanese, after several firing passes with no damage to the bomber, disengaged and returned to their bases. The B-17s completed their photo mission and turned for home. Unfortunately, they did not have enough fuel to make it back.

The bombers put down on an island along the route home. With the radios still operational, they managed to contact the seaplane tender USS *Curtiss* (AV-4), the first purpose-built seaplane tender for the United States Navy and an only-just-repaired veteran of the Pearl Harbor attack, and requested a PBY Catalina flying boat be sent to pick up the film. The first PBY arrived but ran into rocks while maneuvering to shore. A second PBY was called for; it was able to get by the rocks safely. The film was taken to New Caledonia for processing. Once that was finished, the images were delivered to the invasion force and distributed.

The second mission was flown on 2 August. The target was Tulagi where the Marines' 1st Raider Battalion was to land on the 7th and wrest control from the Japanese. The mission was successful, and after processing, the images were again delivered to the invasion force. These two missions provided badly needed visual intelligence of the Japanese-held islands.

Guadalcanal

On 7 August 1942, U.S. forces launched Operation *Watchtower*. With naval forces providing a pre-invasion bombardment, and air cover, Marines stormed ashore with little to no resistance from the Japanese. Caught by surprise, what Japanese forces were in the area fled into the jungle. The Marines quickly captured the airfield and consolidated their positions. The airfield was not complete and needed extensive work—quickly—to be of use.

The Japanese recovered from the initial attacks and counterattacked by sea and air later in the day and into the next. During the night of 8/9 August, Japanese naval forces engaged U.S. naval forces near Savo Island. The Japanese soundly defeated the Americans. Several ships were sunk, including *Vincennes* and *Astoria*. Scheussler and Kirby were lost when *Vincennes* went down, becoming the first squadron casualties of the war. Spurlock, Campbell, and Whitten survived the sinking of *Astoria* and later made it back to the squadron.

Vice Admiral Frank Jack Fletcher, the task force commander, withdrew his carriers from the area, not wanting to risk his valuable ships to Japanese attack. Without air support, supply ships halted the flow of supplies to shore and withdrew from the area. The Marines on Guadalcanal were left without air support and limited supplies.

Getting the captured airfield operational—now known as Henderson Field[2]—became a priority. Vice Admiral Robert Ghormley, commander of the South Pacific Area, ordered Vice Admiral John McCain, Sr.—Commander, Aircraft, South Pacific—to round up transport aircraft, supplies, and men and send them to Guadalcanal to get the airfield operational. VMO-251's executive officer, Lieutenant Colonel Charles "Fog" Hayes, along with Second Lieutenant Oscar P. "Curly" Rutledge, Jr., with other men from the squadron, an Australian coast watcher, and engineers from construction battalion CUB-1, boarded the transports and arrived on 15 August. Hayes had overall command of the task, with squadron personnel to set up communications. The engineers would get the field ready for use.

Marines from the invasion force were already hard at work on the field to extend its 2,000-foot runway. The CUB-1 engineers jumped in with their gear to take over construction. The field was finished three days later, but Japanese bombers made sure its use was delayed.

The determined Japanese scored several hits on the runway. Once the bombers left, the engineers immediately went back to work to fill in the bomb craters. The work ended on 21 August and the first Marine air units, VMF-223 and VMSB-232, arrived from the escort carrier USS *Long Island.*

After two weeks without air cover, the Marines finally had aircraft on the island to help alleviate the pressure they were under.

From September 1942 to January 1943, the squadron supported the Cactus Air Force[3] in many ways. The Cactus Air Force was a mixed bag of Army, Navy and Marine aircraft designated to defend the air over Guadalcanal. VMO-251 trained personnel from non-fighting squadrons as fighter pilots. These pilots eventually ended up cycling through Guadalcanal. The squadron also sent several of its aircraft and pilots to Guadalcanal on a rotation basis. In January 1943, the unit was transferred to Guadalcanal and remained there until May. By late February, pilots were posted to other squadrons or sent back to the United States. What officers and men remained, aided the Cactus Air Force until the squadron was transferred home.

Disease, constant combat, and poor living conditions took a toll on VMO-251. Squadron documents for the period are incomplete but an approximate number of casualties can be determined. From August 1942 to May 1943, the squadron suffered 20 casualties: eight killed in action; seven wounded in action; two injured (non-battle); and three accidental deaths. The last death was a tragic one. On 10 May, Technical Sergeant[4] Robert L. Andrews, Jr. was electrocuted while working on an aircraft just days before the squadron was to ship home.

Squadron pilots contributed to the demise of the Japanese empire by downing 32 enemy aircraft of all types. Second Lieutenant Herbert A. Peters was the squadron's top scoring pilot with four confirmed kills and two others probably shot down. Two future Marine Corps aces, Second Lieutenants Mike Yunck and Henry McCartney scored their first kills with the squadron. Several went on to command their own squadrons during the war, including Spurlock and First Lieutenant Charles P. Weiland.

What remained of VMO-251 boarded the attack transport USS *George Clymer* (APA-27) on 12 May and sailed for Espiritu Santo. The ship arrived two days later and after a 48-hour layover, USS *Kitty Hawk* (AKV-1), an aircraft transport that had delivered aircraft to *USS Long Island* (AVG-1) for subsequent delivery to Guadalcanal, set sail to take the squadron back to the United States.

Converting to the Corsair

The ship arrived at San Francisco in early June. Squadron personnel were granted a 30-day leave pass. When they returned to their unit, VMO-251 began a massive reorganization. Many of the squadron's combat veterans were transferred out to provide needed experience to new squadrons being activated. After all the transfers, all that remained were four officers and about thirty enlisted men. The Marines who remained passed on their experiences in combat to the new officers and enlisted personnel who joined the squadron at its new duty station outside of Mojave, California: Marine Base Defense Air Group 44, Marine Corps Air Station Mojave.

Training began in earnest as the squadron geared up for its return to the Pacific Theater. The pilots were pushed hard: from September 1943 to January 1944, the squadron lost 12 aircraft, 27 damaged, and four pilots killed. They trained in Wildcats until October 1943 when new aircraft were finally delivered.

The squadron received the F4U-1 Corsair. It was designed as a fighter, not for the photo-reconnaissance role. As the pilots gained experience in the powerful Corsair, they became comfortable with its quirks. Training emphasized fighter and bombing tactics. When the squadron returned to the Pacific, it would be flying bombing missions nearly every day. It is interesting that the squadron kept its "observation" squadron designation (VMO) despite the fact it was flying a new fighter aircraft.

From August through September, maintenance men were sent to several schools to learn the workings of the Corsair's systems: F4U School in Bridgeport, Connecticut; the Army–Navy School for Pratt & Whitney Aircraft in Hartford, Connecticut; Oxygen Equipment School at NAS San Diego; Goodyear Aircraft Corporation in Akron, Ohio; and the Propellor School at Hamilton Standard's Propeller Division in East Hartford, Connecticut, to name a few. When not in school, men performed maintenance on the aircraft or pulled duty in firefighting details.

Training concluded in February 1944 and the squadron began preparations for another tour in the Pacific. Aircraft were returned to aviation authorities at the base, and the unit was brought up to combat strength with an influx of personnel. The Marines of VMO-251 boarded the seaplane tender USS *Tangier* (AV-8) at NAS North Island, San Diego, on 20 February 1944 and departed for Espiritu Santo the next day.

A Second Tour of Combat

After nearly a three-week cruise, the squadron arrived at Espiritu Santo on 9 March 1944. The next day they left the ship and set up at Luganville Bomber Field where they would operate while on the island. Unfortunately, they had no aircraft to fly.

Marine Air Group 11 was responsible for delivering the aircraft to the squadron. After waiting a month, the squadron received 20 F4U-1 Corsairs on 6 April. The next day, the pilots took to the air on familiarization and training flights which included division tactics, gunnery training, oxygen system testing, blind flying (reference to cockpit instruments only), radar training and problem solving, and bombing practice. The training period lasted several weeks.

The squadron received orders to send its pilots, the flight surgeon, intelligence officer and intelligence clerk to Green Island[5] on 6 June. There, under MAG-14 control, they would be flying combat familiarization flights over the Rabaul area. Transport aircraft took the men to their new home. VMO-251's ground echelon and its aircraft remained at Espiritu Santo, more than 1,100 miles to the southeast. Operations began on 18 June when they received 13 F4U-1s and three FG-1s[6] from MAG-14. The pilots flew several fighter sweeps and bombing missions while at Green Island. These types of missions would be flown by the squadron until it departed for the Philippines at the end of December 1944.

In early July, the squadron received orders to move about one hundred fifty miles south to Piva Airstrip, located near Torokina on Bougainville. Except for 20 pilots, led by squadron commander Major William C. Humberd, the flight echelon was transported by South Pacific Combat Air Transport Command aircraft on 27 June. Humberd and his 20 Corsairs flew to Bougainville on 28 June. VMF-223, undergoing a refit, sent its ground echelon to Piva to provide maintenance for VMO-251 until the squadron's own maintenance personnel arrived from Espiritu Santo. Almost a month later, on 24 July, an indication of the vast distances encountered throughout the Pacific Theater, the squadron's ground echelon arrived at Piva and took over maintenance duties from VMF-223.

From 28 June and until 8 December, the squadron flew several missions a day. Anywhere from four to 18 aircraft flew on a mission. The larger ones were usually flown in coordination with other squadrons. Areas targeted were Bougainville, Buka Island, New Britain, and the Duke of York Islands. An example of a large mission was the multi-squadron attack on Vunakanau Airfield, near Rabaul on the island of New Britain, on 18 August. Squadrons from Torokina, Piva and Emirau—seven in total—armed their aircraft with a 1,000-pound bomb each. The Japanese put up a stiff resistance at Vunakanau: five planes were lost and several damaged. VMO-251 was one of the squadrons that lost an aircraft, but its pilot was rescued. Patrols were flown by two to four aircraft and attacked targets of opportunity: convoys, coastal vessels, suspected camps, and Japanese troops left behind as their units retreated towards Japan. The squadron lost 16 Corsairs while at Bougainville, with four pilots killed in action, four wounded, and three killed in accidents.

The End of the War

In early December, the squadron halted all attacks and began its preparations to move to Guiuan Airfield on the southern tip of the island of Samar in the Philippines. The squadron took off for its new assignment on the 30th.

Led by PBJ Mitchell bombers to help with navigation, and flying via Emirau, Hollandia, Owi, and Peleliu, the journey covered nearly two thousand miles before touching down just past 1700 on 2 January 1945. Late that same evening, Humberd located an Army signal station and reported to the commanding general of the Fifth Air Force that the squadron had arrived and was ready for operations. All Marine aviation units fell under the command of the Fifth Air Force since the Philippines was in General Douglas MacArthur's area of operations.

The field was not in the best shape. It was crowded with other aircraft and construction gear. The ground echelon of the squadron put together a makeshift line area so the pilots could park their Corsairs. There were no taxiways, no hard buildings—just tents, no stockpile of supplies, and daily torrential rains tore into the runway, creating huge potholes that were a danger to aircraft taking off and landing. The lousy weather kept Navy engineers busy resurfacing the field on an almost daily basis. Accidents were numerous and the conditions made maintaining the Corsairs difficult.

VMO-251 was MAG-14's first squadron to arrive in theater; the day after arriving, the unit began combat operations from Guiuan. Different types of missions were flown: combat air patrols, convoy cover, and close air support for Army units and Filipino guerilla operations. The squadron flew this mix of missions until May 1945.

The Marine flyers suffered their worst month for losses in January. Four pilots were killed in action within eight days. Two were lost on the 20th. The aircraft were on a strafing run south of Manila when they collided head-on. Eight days later, the squadron lost two more pilots due to possible anti-aircraft fire while flying missions near Taytay and Neilson Auxiliary Airfield.

The squadron was finally redesignated as VMF-251 on 31 January. Two months later, the gull-winged octopus patch, which the squadron had worn since its Bougainville days, was retired and a new one adopted. The new patch featured a caped red devil riding a gull-winged general-purpose bomb with "Lucifer's Messengers VMF-251" written in the background.

The last mission the squadron flew was on 1 May. It sent 12 Corsairs to Leyte in support of advancing Filipino ground forces in the vicinity of Sulpa. The Corsairs hit the target located near the front lines and well within view of the Filipino forces, earning a well done message from the commander on the ground. The aircraft turned for home and arrived back at Guiuan unscathed.

By 1 June 1945, only three officers remained with VMF-251. The pilots had been transferred to other squadrons or sent home; the same applied to the members of the ground echelon. After nearly four years of service, the squadron was deactivated. The acting squadron commander—First Lieutenant Glen F. Keithley—signed the papers, officially ending the unit's participation in the war.

The squadron received several awards for its service during World War II. These were the American Defense Service Streamer, the Presidential Unit Citation, the American Campaign Streamer, Asiatic–Pacific Campaign Streamer with one Silver Star and one Bronze Star, the World War II Victory Streamer, the Philippine Liberation Streamer, and the Philippine Presidential Unit Citation. It was also recommended for the Army's Distinguished Unit Citation as well as a Navy Unit Commendation. Unfortunately, the squadron did not receive these two well-deserved awards.

CHAPTER 2

Reactivation

Shortly after 0900 on 2 September 1945, World War II officially ended. Japan had been beaten. The surrender ceremony was held on board the battleship USS *Missouri* (BB-63) anchored in Tokyo Bay with Allied ships representing the United States, Britain, Australia, and New Zealand in full view. It was witnessed by high-ranking generals and admirals, as well as sailors in their dress uniforms. After Allied and Japanese representatives signed the instrument of surrender, General Douglas MacArthur concluded the historic event with these words: "Let us pray that peace be now restored to the world and that God will preserve it always. These proceedings are closed."[1]

Unfortunately, there would be no peace. A different kind of war began to take root, one that saw two opposing ideologies—democracy and communism—struggle in a quest for international domination. Out of the ashes of a world war that saw nearly sixty million people killed, grew the seeds of the Cold War.

During the latter stages of the war in Europe, the race was on to get a jump on the Soviets. The Soviet Union, allied with Great Britain and the United States, was not trusted and the feeling was mutual. Allied teams, as well as Soviet, raced behind their advancing forces to gather technology that would give them the edge in a post-war world. In this they were successful. For both sides, German technological advances in such fields as nuclear research, aerospace, and chemistry, as well as some of its key figures, provided the foundation for the development of weapons in the early days of the Cold War. Perhaps the most well-known of these German scientists, who were brought to the United States despite their Nazi background, was Wernher Von Braun—the man who guided German rocket technology and "the chief architect of the Saturn V launch vehicle, the super-booster that would propel Americans to the Moon."[2]

At the Yalta Conference in February 1945, the Allies pledged to establish democracies in liberated countries. However, Soviet actions following the conference as it moved west into Poland and south into the Balkan states, dispelled any idea they would follow through with that pledge.[3]

Europe became the main theater of the Cold War; the Soviets perceived it as the primary threat. Ironically, the two nations never engaged one another in direct combat. Instead, both nations backed regimes in other countries to thwart moves by the other, or to gain a foothold in an area dominated by their opponent.

Once the Japanese were defeated, disagreements put on hold to fight a common enemy picked up once again in China. Chinese communists under Mao Zedong and Chinese Nationalists under Chiang Kai-shek resumed their bloody war to control China. For other nations in greater Asia, the Japanese had shown them the colonial powers could be beaten. Conflicts for independence soon began to spring up, most notably in the Dutch East Indies (now Indonesia), a colony of the Netherlands, and in Vietnam, a colony of France.

In early 1946, Soviet leader Joseph Stalin delivered a speech to voters in Moscow, stating that "capitalism and imperialism are permanent enemies to communism, and will inevitably cause war."[4] Soon after, Winston Churchill, the former prime minister of England, delivered his famous "Iron Curtain" speech at Westminster College in Fulton, Missouri:

> From Stettin in the Baltic to Trieste in the Adriatic, an iron curtain has descended across the Continent. Behind that line lie all the capitals of the ancient states of Central and Eastern Europe. Warsaw, Berlin, Prague, Vienna, Budapest, Belgrade, Bucharest, and Sofia, all these famous cities and the populations around them lie in what I must call the Soviet sphere, and all are subject in one form or another, not only to Soviet influence but to a very high and, in many cases, increasing measure of control from Moscow.[5]

The course of history had been set. As to who would prevail, only time would tell.

The future was uncertain, and it was under this uncertainty that VMF-251, deactivated in June 1945, was reactivated as a Marine Air Reserve squadron at U.S. Naval Air Station (NAS) Grosse Ile, Michigan, on 1 July 1946 per a dispatch from MARTCOM (Marine Air Reserve Training Command) in June 1946. Its authorized strength was established at 57 officers and 164 enlisted men. Why VMF-251 was chosen to be reactivated is not known. There are no set guidelines to determine if a squadron is reactivated. While the USMC History Division is sometimes consulted, in most cases HQ USMC chooses who they want, without consultation, according to the needs of the Marine Corps.[6] The squadron's first commander was Major Ralph G. McCormick, USMC Reserve. He was a veteran of World War II, having served with VMF-311 at Okinawa.[7] The squadron's mission upon reactivation was to "provide training facilities for aviation personnel in the Detroit area to maintain flight proficiency."[8]

As was customary for the time, training was held every weekend. Starting in 1947, the squadron deployed during the summer months for two weeks of training at Marine Corps Air Station (MCAS) Cherry Point, North Carolina.

Lack of manpower was a constant problem for the squadron in the months following its reactivation as it built up its strength. This was compounded by the uncertainty of available aircraft. The squadron was dependent on NAS Grosse Ile for its aircraft, which was usually a mix of Chance Vought (F4U-4D) and Goodyear (FG-1D) built Corsairs. To take advantage of available aircraft, two divisions were formed by the squadron—Division One and Division Two. The pilots of each division met on separate days to earn their hours in the cockpit. But it was not enough; squadron pilots were urged to fly on non-scheduled drill days to meet flight-time goals. During August, just after the unit's reactivation, 46 pilots flew slightly over 88 hours; 83 were flown in September. In addition, a group of 16 volunteers got in more flight time than the pilots assigned to the squadron. McCormick kept a list of these 16 men with the aim of replacing squadron pilots when slots became open due to attrition.[9]

To make up for the lack of enlisted strength, the squadron initiated a recruitment drive during the last three months of 1946. The drive ultimately proved successful. Every trick in the book was used to recruit: newspaper ads, radio advertisements, a sound truck that cruised neighborhoods, and speaking tours at nearby colleges. When the drive started, there were only nine enlisted men assigned to the unit. By the end of March 1947, 132 had been sworn in and were serving with the squadron.[10]

Weather was also a factor in the lack of training. There were several periods where flight hours were reduced or cancelled due to the severe winter weather that occasionally hit the area.

The training regimen varied for the pilots. Classroom instruction included the use of movies, lectures, mock-ups, plotting board problems, Link[11] time, and instruction on ground control intercept and ground control approach procedures. Flight time was taken up with gunnery practice, tactics, rocket firing, bombing practice, and instrument training. Of course, the enlisted men received hands-on practice maintaining the Corsairs. Training also served to ready squadron personnel for the two-week active-duty deployment to Cherry Point.

The number of accidents involving squadron aircraft during this time is unknown, and it is unclear if the squadron lost any aircraft between 1946 and 1949. Of the available documents, only one incident was noted. On 25 August 1946, three pilots were briefed for a practice bombing exercise to an ordnance area located on Lake Erie, several miles east of Toledo, Ohio. The aircraft were armed with 3-pound practice bombs. The floating target they were assigned to hit was painted white. Naval patrol boats were assigned to the area to keep any civilian boats away from the range.

Despite the precautions taken, one civilian boat—painted white—managed to enter the range area undetected. They were there to fish but were in for the shock of their lives. Apparently, the VMF-251 Corsairs mistook the fishing boat for their target and began their bombing runs.

The Corsairs made three passes at the boat. The first two bombing runs were ineffective, but the third severely damaged the boat. "One of the bombs struck at the waterline near the gas tank. Several of the men jumped overboard," said Charles Desmond, secretary of the nearby Ottawa Yacht Club, who spoke to the men when they were brought ashore.[12]

The near miss caused a fire in the engine room which quickly spread through the boat. All but one of the men jumped overboard. The owner of the boat, Albert Reisig, remained aboard to fight the fire but he was unsuccessful. It burned to the waterline, causing nearly $5,000 in damage. The men were rescued by a nearby naval vessel; Reisig was the only one injured, receiving minor burns.

A preliminary investigation determined one of the pilots was at fault for not positively identifying the target. Commander F. A. Brossy, executive officer of NAS Grosse Ile, noted the incident occurred about twenty miles east of Toledo and 10 miles from the Ohio shore, and was in the danger zone, but two miles from the actual target.[13] A thorough investigation began soon after the fiasco. Unfortunately, the final report could not be located. It appears the name of the pilot held responsible for the incident may never be known. Many of the reports for this period in the squadron's history are missing.

In August 1947, the squadron, joined by a fellow Grosse Ile resident unit, Marine Ground Control Intercept Squadron (MGCIS) 19, participated in its first Marine Air Reserve maneuvers held at MCAS Cherry Point, North Carolina. The exercise served a dual purpose—to see how well reserve squadrons performed in a variety of situations and to see how quickly they could deploy

Marine Corps Air Reserve Mobilization, 1947

in case of a national emergency. Squadrons east of the Mississippi River (with a few exceptions) held their exercise over the period 15–30 August, while squadrons west of the Mississippi held their exercise over the period 8–20 September at MCAS El Toro, California. The following squadrons were deployed (see map for location of stations):

Marine Air Reserve East Squadrons to MCAS Cherry Point

Squadrons	*Station*
VMF-321	Anacostia
VMF-224	Columbus
VMF-121, MGCIS-22	Glenview
VMF-351, MGCIS-15	Atlanta
VMF-251, MGCIS-19	Grosse Ile
VMF-144	Jacksonville
VMF-142	Miami
VMF-132	New York
VMF-233	Norfolk
VMF-217, VMF-235, MGCIS-21	Squantum
VMF-451, MGCIS-17	Willow Grove

Marine Air Reserve West Squadrons to MCAS El Toro

Squadrons	*Station*
VMF-241, VMF-123, MGCIS-18	Los Alamitos
VMF-236	Denver
VMF-213, VMF-234, MGCIS-16	Minneapolis
VMF-216	Seattle
VMF-112, MGCIS-20	Dallas
VMF-124	Memphis
VMF-143	New Orleans
VMF-221	St. Louis
VMF-215	Olathe
VMF-141	Oakland

Within 24 hours, squadrons east of the Mississippi River flew their aircraft to Cherry Point and had their mechanics and ground personnel transported there.[14] In VMF-251's case, 33 pilots and 71 enlisted men participated in the training. On average, each squadron sent 14 aircraft—all Corsairs. The total number of hours flown by the squadron during the two-week training period was 365.[15] No fatalities or accidents were reported by any of the 12 participating units. The squadron kept slightly over 87% of its aircraft at operational readiness during the exercise.

Pilots flew a variety of missions—gunnery, bombing, rocket firing and tactical exercises supporting ground troops from Camp Lejeune. During these exercises, pilots took turns flying missions. One day they would observe from the ground, then fly missions the next day.[16]

Apparently, the squadron did well. In fact, it received a glowing write up in several articles published by newspapers in Detroit, Wyandotte, and Dearborn, Michigan, as well as Chattanooga, Tennessee. Radio stations in Detroit and Toledo, Ohio, also spread the news of the squadron's good showing.[17]

Following the end of the sojourn at Cherry Point, the squadron returned to Grosse Ile and resumed its weekend training schedule for the remainder of the year and into 1948. When weather curtailed flying operations, pilots attended classes.

By June 1948, the Marines once again focused on training to help it get through another two weeks at MCAS Cherry Point. Mid-summer, the squadron sent 15 Corsairs, 31 officers and 74 enlisted men. The pace of the exercise was set at wartime requirements and did not let up. The squadron flew nearly five hundred seventy-six hours during the two-week period.[18] The highlight of the training was a "two-day battle problem in close support of Fleet Marine Force infantry regulars from Camp Lejeune."[19] Squadron personnel were also able to view displays of the newest jet aircraft as well as the latest propeller-driven machines such as the AD-1 Skyraider, AM-1 Mauler and F4U-5 Corsair.[20] The trip back to Grosse Ile after the conclusion of the training exercise was without incident.

As 1949 rolled around, the jet age was in its infancy and VMF-251 had yet to get a detailed look at any of the new jets the Marine Corps had in its inventory. Early in the year, the squadron designated two pilots for training in the upcoming deployment to MCAS Cherry Point in July. Also, the Marine Corps Institute (MCI) began offering a course on gas turbines and jet propulsion to all members of the reserves; about fifteen men applied for the course.[21] Since none of the ground personnel had any training in jet engines, this exposure via the MCI represented the squadron's total experience with the new technology up to this point. However, it was expected some of the ground crew would get practical training on the new jet engines at Cherry Point.[22]

In mid-July,[23] the squadron sent 24 Corsairs, 38 officers and 80 enlisted men to Cherry Point for the year's two weeks of active-duty training. It was one of 14 fighting squadrons and two MGCIS units participating.[24] After the squadron arrived, the officers and men located their quarters, lockers, and the all-important mess facility. Apparently, they found all the facilities "inadequate."[25] The squadron's commander at the time, Major William A. Carlton, did not give any specifics concerning the state of the facilities in the squadron's report for the period.

Once the Marines were settled in, staff officers held meetings in which details of the coming operations were passed out. A brief summary was given to all personnel as to what was expected of each squadron. Work in various sections began immediately.

The high point of the exercise was the two-day air-to-ground assault undertaken with units of the 2nd Marine Division from Camp Lejeune. Reserve aircraft were assigned to give close air support to the Leathernecks on the ground as they destroyed the "enemy" dug in along the coast 25 miles east of Cherry Point.[26]

Pilots selected from all reserve units, based on their annual record, were given their initial checkouts in jet aircraft assigned to regular Marine squadrons. Each of the pilots logged 12 hours of flight time and 40 hours of classroom instruction in the McDonnell FH-1 Phantom.[27] The pilots of VMF-122, commanded by Lieutenant Colonel Paul J. Fontana, served as instructors.[28]

VMF-122 was the first Marine squadron to operate the FH-1 Phantom. The pilots had the experience in the aircraft to instruct the reserve pilots.

The squadron did well during the two-week training period. It flew close to 982 hours across 561 flights. Based on its performance, it was runner up for the Herman Ridder Marine Reserve Trophy which was won by VMF-142 out of MCAS Miami.[29]

The return to Grosse Ile was made without any incident. However, one of the squadron's Corsairs was left behind at Cherry Point due to mechanical problems. Upon return, the men resumed their standard weekend training routine: a mix of flight time and classroom instruction.

By December 1949, the squadron finally reached its full strength—45 Naval Aviators, 12 Air Ground Officers and 160 enlisted men. With a good showing during the two-week maneuvers, a full complement of men, and morale high, the squadron was well placed to meet the new decade.

CHAPTER 3

The Korean War

Lousy weather, as well as a shortage of aviation fuel, hampered squadron operations from Grosse Ile for the first half of 1950. Despite the lack of flight time, VMF-251 still managed to fly over 1,000 hours from January to June. The figure was 63% of the possible hours based on what the squadron considered ideal conditions (that each assigned pilot fly six hours per drill).[1]

On 25 June 1950, the North Koreans launched an attack on South Korea. Within weeks of the attack, the North Korean People's Army had overrun most of South Korea. Despite the United States, along with countries fighting under the United Nations (UN), committing air, land, and sea assets already in the Far East, by late July UN forces were pushed back to Pusan. General Douglas MacArthur, appointed commander of all allied forces, clamored for a full-strength Marine combat division. He was already planning the Incheon counterstroke. Unfortunately, the Marines did not have such a force available. "The ground forces in the entire Fleet Marine Force were insufficient to field an entire 22,000 war-strength Division."[2] On 19 July 1950, to make up for this lack of strength, Congress gave President Truman permission to call up and mobilize reserve units, as well as individuals, to active duty.[3]

For the time being, VMF-251 remained in reserve. It continued with its training program, but with a new urgency. Inclement weather continued from the previous six months and, for the period July–December 1950, the squadron flew close to 680 hours. From 5 August to the 15th, the unit participated in its annual active-duty deployment to Marine Corps Air Station (MCAS) Cherry Point, providing 53 officers and 120 enlisted men. Total hours flown were 1,054.8 during the two-week exercise.[4]

By late summer MacArthur had built up his forces and, on 15 September, landed troops at Incheon and soon after captured Seoul. With their main supply routes cut-off or threatened, North Korean forces began a disorganized retreat.[5]

By 25 October, UN forces had established positions south of the Yalu River, which bordered China.

With the success of the Incheon landing, and with the possibility of the war ending, the call up of reserve air units did not keep pace with the call up of reserve ground forces. That changed on 25 November when China sent its troops across the Yalu River and engaged UN forces.[6]

On 3 January 1951, the Joint Chiefs of Staff authorized the Marines to increase the number of their fighting squadrons from 18 to 21. A week later, nine Marine Reserve fighting squadrons were ordered to report for active duty. Six of the squadrons mobilized with personnel only, while three others—VMF-131, VMF-251 and VMF-451—were mobilized as units.[7]

Eleven days later, with its Corsairs grounded due to low visibility, the squadron received a telegram from the commander of Marine Air Reserve Training ordering it to prepare for mobilization on 1 March. The squadron remained at Grosse Ile and continued its reserve training.[8]

When 1 March arrived, the Marines were kept busy. Barracks were assigned, physicals were performed, and clothing issued. The squadron also learned it would be giving up its famed Corsairs for the Douglas AD-1 Skyraider. The aircraft had been introduced at the 1948 Cherry Point exercises.[9] It was a change many in the squadron were not looking forward to. A change of duty station was also in the works. The squadron would soon move from Grosse Ile to MCAS El Toro in California.

The Skyraider was born during World War II, designed as a replacement for the venerable SBD Dauntless, the Grumman Avenger, and the Curtiss Helldiver. The Avenger and Helldiver had largely replaced the Dauntless in the final two years of WWII. The Skyraider was originally designated as the Douglas XSB2D-1 Dauntless II. The propeller-driven aircraft had gull wings and a tricycle landing gear. It flew for the first time on 8 April 1943. Because of specification changes ordered by the Navy, Douglas had to alter the design. With the changes made, the aircraft was redesignated as the BTD-1. The BTD-1 made its maiden flight on 5 March 1944. With the war progressing well by this stage, the Navy cancelled the contract three months later, leaving Douglas with no new Navy design for the foreseeable future. In their hotel rooms in Washington, D.C., the talented engineers at Douglas quickly came up with a design based on the BTD-1. They removed the gull wings and the tricycle landing gear, making it a 'tail dragger' like the Corsair, and incorporated a host of test results and other information then available. The engineers met with BuAer (Bureau of Aeronautics) officials at the Pentagon and made their case for the new design, now designated as the

XBT2D-1. The officials were impressed. They gave Douglas permission to build a prototype, but they had to be ready for an upcoming competition against companies that had a half-year head start! The Douglas engineers finished ahead of schedule. The aircraft made its maiden flight on 18 March 1945. Officials were so impressed the Navy placed an order for nearly six hundred aircraft. The end of the war saw the contract reduced to nearly four hundred. In February 1946, the aircraft was renamed Skyraider, with the AD-1 designation coming in April. In December, the first Navy squadrons began to receive the aircraft. Over 3,000 Skyraiders were built by the time production ended in 1957.[10] With its 1,500-mile range and the ability to carry a heavy payload—6,000–8,000 pounds of ordnance—more than the Corsair carried during the WWII and as much as the famed four-engine bomber, the B-17 Flying Fortress. The Skyraider became a workhorse in the ground-attack role. The AD-1 was powered by Wright R-3350-26W Cyclone radial engine, a slightly modified version of the engine used in the B-29 Superfortress during WWII. The Skyraider's engine had a nasty habit of leaking oil which may have led to engine fires and the loss of several aircraft while in use with VMA-251.

On 6 March 1951, the squadron sent eight pilots to El Toro to pick up the first of its Skyraiders. The first four pilots returned to Grosse Ile on the 16th with their AD-1s. The remaining pilots arrived four days later. For the remainder of the month, and on into April, the squadron began acceptance checks on its newly acquired aircraft.[11]

The squadron began its move to El Toro on 15 April. An advance echelon consisting of 33 officers and 48 enlisted men departed to prepare for the arrival of the rest of the unit, which left on the 21st. The movement was made in two parts: the first to leave were men authorized to drive their own vehicles while the remainder of the squadron were flown from Cherry Point to El Toro in six R5C transport aircraft (the Navy designation for the Douglas C-54 Skymaster). By the 23rd, all squadron personnel were established at their new home.[12]

Three days later, the squadron received General Order number 58, dated 26 April, from Aircraft, Fleet Marine Force, Pacific, redesignating VMF-251 as VMA-251.[13] No longer a fighter squadron, it was now an attack squadron. During the coming months before the unit departed for Korea, training shifted focus to close air support for ground forces.

Aircraft acceptance checks continued in May. Five additional Skyraiders arrived, raising the squadron's strength to 13 AD-1s. Along with the checks, the pilots flew slightly over 400 hours for the month.

More personnel joined VMA-251 to bring the squadron to its full complement. By the end of May 1951, the unit reported 36 officers, 220 enlisted men and three Navy medical corpsmen attached. Along with training in the Skyraiders, inspections, acceptance checks, award ceremonies, and an Armed Forces Day airshow, volunteers and others from nearby units participated in a search for a missing girl.

On 19 May, 10-year-old Patricia Hull and her two younger brothers went to the matinee at the Valukis Theater in Buena Park. At some point between 1730 and 1800, a man known as Henry Ford McCracken was seen to lure a girl resembling Hull into his rented cabin. When she did not return home, her parents became worried and called the authorities. A massive search to find her began the following day. Volunteers from all over the area participated.

Authorities quickly homed in on McCracken and he was taken into custody the day after Patricia disappeared. A search of his cabin revealed evidence of a struggle. Among the items found were blood-stained clothes worn by the suspect the day of the incident.

The day after McCracken was detained, Marines from VMA-251 and other nearby units joined the search but had no luck finding the girl. On 24 May, authorities found her body in a shallow grave in Live Oak Canyon, nearly thirty-five miles from Buena Park. The next day, McCracken was charged with child stealing, kidnapping and murder.

After two trials, McCracken was found guilty of Hull's murder and sentenced to death. McCracken and his attorney fought the verdict. After nearly three years of legal wrangling to no avail, McCracken was finally put to death on 19 February 1954.[14]

The squadron continued adding personnel and aircraft during June. By the end of the month the squadron had 21 Skyraiders, 37 officers—32 of which were pilots—and 215 enlisted men. The highlight of the month was a two-week training exercise at nearby Naval Auxiliary Air Station (NAAS) El Centro. During the exercise, the squadron concentrated on ground attacks with rockets and bombs.

In July, the squadron ran into a roadblock in its continual struggle to build up to full strength. It received one Skyraider during the month, bringing the total to 22 aircraft. Unfortunately, it lost nearly half its pilots due to transfers or discharges. At the end of the month, VMA-251 had 21 officers (18 pilots) and 212 enlisted men—including one enlisted pilot (Naval Aviation Pilot). Training during the month consisted of air support missions, field carrier landing practice, navigation, day and night tactics, and instrument flying.

The flying and training continued into August and September. It was in September that the unit's first known accident was recorded since its reactivation in 1946. The squadron had departed El Toro to head back to El Centro for another two weeks of training to hone their skills at dropping bombs, firing rockets, and providing close air support. On 12 September, Second Lieutenant Frank L. Leister was in his take-off roll when the aircraft dragged a wing, cartwheeled, and ended right-side up. His AD-1 (BuNo 9320) was destroyed in the mishap, but Leister escaped without injuries. Training at El Centro ended on 15 September and the squadron returned to El Toro the same day.[15]

Routine operations continued in October. More than 700 sorties were recorded, accumulating nearly one thousand one hundred seventy-five flying hours. The training for the month did come with a cost, though. On 4 October, NAP (Naval Aviation Pilot) Sergeant Leo C. Adlon,[16] while conducting a night landing with his AD-1 (BuNo 9202), overran the aircraft in front, causing him to nose over and chew up the rudder of the aircraft. Adlon's prop was also damaged. Both aircraft were eventually repaired. Near the end of the month, on the 28th, the unfortunate Leister damaged his propeller while landing his AD-1 (BuNo 9294). No injuries were sustained in any of the incidents.[17]

In November, the mission of the squadron was spelled out in detail, as were the tasks it was expected to perform. First, it was to conduct flight operations in support of the Fleet Marine Forces and Naval Forces afloat in amphibious operations; and second, to augment or replace Naval air units aboard carriers and to provide air defense of advanced Naval bases. As for the tasks assigned, it was to:

- Provide close air support using dive bombing, glide bombing and strafing.
- Provide adequate air defense by intercepting and destroying enemy aircraft.
- Assist in defending against enemy surface attack.
- Operate from either a land base or carrier.
- Support offensive operations.
- Provide anti-submarine defense.
- Spot for Naval gunfire and shore artillery.
- Provide visual aerial reconnaissance.

For reasons unknown, the squadron was ordered to transfer 11 of its Skyraiders to FASRON (Fleet Air Service Squadron) 701. In exchange, it received 12 F4U-4 Corsairs. For the time being, the squadron had to maintain two types of aircraft. One can only imagine the maintenance headaches this may have caused. These transfers occurred prior to the squadron departing for Operation *Lex III*, a training exercise under simulated combat conditions to be held at Camp Pendleton.

On 6 November, the squadron received orders for the exercise, scheduled to begin on the 13th. Preparations began in earnest. The logistics section issued field gear, crated supplies and equipment, and readied vehicles for sea transport. The Operations Section prepared flight schedules for pre-D-day combat air patrols and close air support sorties in accordance with the operation order. Personnel and the intelligence sections prepared field desks, safes, and files for movement into the field.

At 0715, 13 November, the forward echelon consisting of eight officers and 103 enlisted men departed for the designated port of embarkation, Seal Beach, with four vehicles and nearly twenty tons of supplies. At Seal Beach, they embarked aboard the Haskell-class Attack Transport USS *Mountrail* (APA-213).

They set sail at 1330 and made way for the Pendleton beach area. Two days later, the ship arrived and the squadron's Marines were landed. Supplies and equipment were transported ashore. In the afternoon, a tent camp was erected by the landing party at the Pendleton airstrip.

For the period 12–16 November, VMA-251 flew combat air patrol (CAP) and close air support sorties out of El Toro in support of the amphibious phase of *Lex III*. Just before noon on the 16th, the squadron flew to the Pendleton airstrip while the remainder of the personnel and equipment were airlifted in. To keep the squadron's Marines on the ground at readiness, many air raids on the strip were flown and "enemy" guerillas used infiltration tactics among the aircraft and line areas.

Shortly after noon on 19 November, *Lex III* was concluded. VMA-251 flew 39 CAP sorties and 147 close air support sorties for a total of 331 hours. Sergeant Herb Bibbee, who joined the squadron in 1947, was a mechanic pulling guard duty near the airstrip when he witnessed the squadron's only mishap during the exercise.[18] One aircraft was damaged on 18 November when the landing gear of the AD-1 flown by Captain Herschal A. Watson collapsed on landing; the Skyraider was repairable, and Watson was not injured. Following the end of the exercise, the squadron remained in the field to conduct routine operations. Five days later the camp was secured, and all gear and aircraft returned to El Toro.[19]

The loss of Skyraiders continued into December. Five were transferred to VMAT-10 (an attack training unit), and five to FASRON 701. To make up for the loss, 12 Corsairs arrived. The squadron now had two Skyraiders and 23 Corsairs.

Despite the change in aircraft, flight operations continued. In accumulating 680 hours for the month, three Corsairs were damaged: two in a morning pre-flight accident and another in a landing accident. No one was injured, but these incidents reduced the number of Corsairs available to 20.[20]

January 1952 had the squadron trading Corsairs with VMF-235, VMF-451, and Naval Air Station (NAS) San Diego. It was not an even trade, however, as 20 were transferred and 15 received. This put the number of Corsairs assigned to the squadron at 18.[21]

Adorning the squadron's cover for its semi-annual report covering the period of January–June 1952, was a squadron insignia that has been forgotten over time. It features a flying "duck" carrying a bomb and a rocket over a red/white roundel in the background. Above the waterfowl is a thunderbolt. It is a mystery as to who designed the insignia and when. The thunderbolt would go on to appear in future squadron patches and in time would become the unit's nickname, the "Thunderbolts."

The highlight for February was another amphibious training operation, *Lex Baker I*. On the 20th, the squadron sent personnel, aircraft, and supplies to Camp Pendleton, and flew missions like those flown during *Lex III*. The Marines returned to El Toro on 28 February.[22]

March was a relatively quiet month with pilots gaining experience through numerous ground lectures and sorties. The squadron was still understrength: 59 officers were authorized, but it only had 46, 39 of which were Naval Aviators. As for enlisted men, only 141 filled the rolls—nearly 25% below authorized strength. On the aircraft front, one AD-1 Skyraider and 20 F4U-4 Corsairs were on hand.[23]

The squadron participated in ordnance training when it deployed to NAAS El Centro on 6 April. Pilots had the opportunity to fire live ammunition, bombs, and rockets during the day and night. The first three days went by with no incidents reported.

At approximately 0730 on 10 April, however, Second Lieutenant Douglass R. Annand took off in his F4U-4 Corsair (BuNo 81151) as part of a five-plane detail to execute a strafing exercise. Soon after the wheels were up and locked, his engine quit at 150 feet altitude. With a speed of 75 to 80 knots, the aircraft hit the ground straight ahead at what appeared to be a very nose-high, fully stalled attitude. The fuselage broke in half at the cockpit just forward of the pilot's seat and armor plate.

The rear section, with the pilot, traveled through the air, flipping before coming to rest facing the opposite way approximately one hundred fifty feet from the initial point of impact. The forward section, with the wings and engine, made one complete flip, ending up on the propeller with the left wing broken off at the wing root. The forward and aft sections of the Corsair were found 25 feet apart.[24]

Annand was still strapped in the cockpit alive but severely injured. He recovered from his injuries but was medically discharged from the Marine Corps, having lost the use of his legs. Annand was in a wheelchair for the rest of his days but did not let this stop him from living a full life.

Despite his disability, Annand eventually earned his pilot's license. He loved to travel and visited destinations throughout the United States, Europe, and Africa. Leading by example, he published a magazine to help others who travelled with disabilities. While living in New Hampshire, Annand served on the Governor's Commission for Disabilities, assisting in the creation of the new Americans with Disabilities Act, which passed into law on 26 July 1990. If that was not enough, he served as director of several New Hampshire organizations and the Greater Nashua Transportation Service.[25] He passed away in 2006.

The training at El Centro ended on 18 April, at which time the squadron returned to El Toro. For the next three days, no flying was scheduled. On 21 and 22 April, VMA-251 flew close air support missions for an exercise held at Camp Pendleton. The rest of the month was spent flying test and cross-country flights, practicing division tactics, and instrument hops.

May was marred by the death of a pilot, the first recorded fatality since the squadron was reactivated in 1946, when 2ndLt. Joe K. Jensen collided with the wing of a B-29 Superfortress on the 13th. Eleven men on board the B-29 were also killed.[26]

Despite the death of Jensen, training did not stop. For the rest of May and into June, pilots continued with their flying, accumulating needed hours. June saw another exercise at Camp Pendleton. From the 16th to the 21st, the squadron participated in Operation *Amlex I*.[27]

The period from July to December 1952 saw numerous training deployments made by the squadron. The continual manpower problem—especially pilots—made meeting the demands of the training for the period difficult. The number of pilots ranged from 15 to 47, but in October 1952 the squadron had just seven effective flyers. Despite the continual turnover, pilot readiness remained between 25 and 40%. All departments found it difficult to maintain their own training syllabus while experiencing a rapid turnover of officers and enlisted men due either to transfers to other units or discharges. The commanding officer, Lieutenant Colonel Sumner H. Whitten, believed the performance of the squadron could be improved if it was maintained as a tactical unit (perhaps implying it was being utilized as an ad hoc training unit for other squadrons) and that pilots be sent through a refresher program in service-type aircraft before reporting to a tactical squadron for permanent duty. Despite these problems, Whitten credited his engineering officer and his staff of enlisted men for working long hours to meet the requirements of the flight schedules.

The one major training exercise the squadron participated in during the six-month period was *Air Lex I*, held at NAAS Fallon from 2 to 8 September. The mission for the exercise was to provide tactical support for an amphibious landing. The squadron deployed via airlift, leaving behind a rear echelon of four officers and 20 enlisted men. It provided 24 aircraft, flying 196 sorties and accumulating nearly four hundred ten hours in 3½ days. Sorties consisted of close air support missions, smoke missions and combat air patrols. While considered a good training evolution, any benefit the squadron may have gained was nullified by the large number of TAD (temporary assigned duty) personnel with the squadron. When training was over, most left the squadron for other assignments.

VMA-251 was scheduled to participate in another large exercise, *Phibex I*, but due to lousy weather conditions the squadron was unable to take part. It was prepared to go, and briefings were given to all personnel. At least it may have benefitted from the preparation for use in future deployments.

While flying out of El Toro, training continued to consist of familiarization flights, section and division tactics, ground-controlled intercepts, cross-country flights, and instrument checks. Most of the rocket, bombing, strafing, and close air support was flown from NAAS El Centro. Deployment dates to El Centro were 24 July to 2 August, 16–26 November, and 7–12 December.

Only one accident was reported during the period. On 15 August, Second Lieutenant Leonard C. Weatherwax made a crash landing at El Toro in his F4U-4 (BuNo 81040) when he could not get his main landing gear to lower properly. Fortunately, the aircraft suffered minor damage and Weatherwax escaped uninjured.[28]

For most of January 1953, the typical training regimen continued. Early in the afternoon of 15 January, however, Second Lieutenant Edward M. Belford had his landing gear collapse during his landing roll. The F4U-4 Corsair (BuNo

80871) suffered minor damage and Belford was slightly injured. Despite the Corsair undergoing a thorough inspection by mechanics, what caused the landing gear to collapse could not be determined.[29]

Eight days later, six pilots and enlisted men were temporarily detached from the squadron to Marine Training Group 10 for carrier qualifications aboard the escort carrier USS *Sicily* (CVE-118). One of the pilots, Captain Paul F. Kurfess, flying an F4U-4 Corsair (BuNo 81578), was involved in an accident during the qualifications.

Thirteen officers were detached from the squadron on 25 January to attend the Tactical Air Support School at the Naval Amphibious Base at Coronado, California. The men returned to El Toro five days later.

The squadron also flew missions for a close air support training exercise at Camp Pendleton on 27 and 29 January. No deployment was necessary as the missions were flown from El Toro.

The manpower situation did not improve despite the increasing flying tempo. Nine officers and 11 enlisted men were transferred during the month and sent to Service Squadron AIRFMFPAC (Air Fleet Marine Force, Pacific) for assignment to an overseas replacement draft. No personnel were received to make up for these losses.[30]

February kicked off with another deployment to El Centro. On the first day of the month, five more officers were sent to the Tactical Air Support School at Coronado. In addition, 24 officers and 95 enlisted men were sent to sharpen their skills in rockets, strafing, and bombing. While at El Centro, an unusual accident occurred that could have been prevented. While parked in a F4U-4 (BuNo 97125), Captain Stanley H. Carpenter was struck in the left temple by a valve from a CO2 fire bottle. The fire bottle was standing upright in the middle of the taxiway leading into the magazine loading area when it was struck by the propeller of a Corsair (BuNo 80871) piloted by Robert J. Barbour. Both aircraft were slightly damaged. Carpenter was wearing his protective helmet which cracked on impact from the force of the valve's impact. The helmet no doubt saved his life. The CO2 bottle should not have been left in the middle of the taxiway. It was a serious lapse of awareness by ground personnel and an incredibly lucky escape for the pilots involved. The squadron returned from El Centro on 7 February as did the five officers sent to Coronado.

The squadron received dispatches from the Chief of Naval Operations and the Commandant of the Marine Corps, dated 4 February and 5 February respectively, ordering it to be ready to deploy to Korea in early June.[31]

Once again, the unit began the long process of turning over its Corsairs for Skyraiders; personnel were sent to specialized schools to get back up to speed on their new aircraft. The transition began on 8 February when 23 enlisted men were sent to NAS San Diego for a maintenance school on the Skyraider. Three days later, the squadron received two Skyraiders from NAS Alameda. More trickled in during the rest of the month and into March.

On 14 February, Lieutenant Colonel Arthur N. Nehf gave a lecture to the unit's pilots on the situation in Korea. Nehf had seen service in Korea as executive officer of VMF-115, flying the Grumman Panther jet.[32]

On the same day, 14 officers were sent to the Indoctrination School for the Skyraider. Following successful completion of the school, they returned on 20 February. While they were detached from the squadron, two Corsairs participated in *Airlex II* at Camp Pendleton by laying a smoke screen.

Another lecture was presented by Captain William H. Bortz on 21 February. Bortz earned the Distinguished Flying Cross during combat in May 1951. The subject was the situation in Korea and the problems encountered during his recent tour with Marine Air Group (MAG) 12.

Two days later, the 23 enlisted men on the Skyraider maintenance course returned to the squadron having successfully completed their training. Also, nine officers and one enlisted pilot (NAP) left to attend an indoctrination course on the Skyraider at NAS San Diego. They returned on 26 February.

Another 18 enlisted men were detached from the squadron on 27 February to attend the Skyraider maintenance course at NAS San Diego. The following day the chief Douglas test pilot for the Skyraider program, Laverne Brown, gave the pilots of VMA-251 a lecture on the flight characteristics of the aircraft.[33]

During the first week in March, all pilots were assigned flights consisting of familiarization and section tactics. Also, the last Corsairs were transferred to VMAT-10 on the 4th, and on the 5th, a representative from Douglas Aircraft, W. L. Pheiffer, was assigned to the squadron. Orders were received that day ordering commanders of attack squadrons to accelerate pilot training. To that end, each pilot was to complete 113 hours (ground classes and in the air) following a syllabus listing the types of training the pilot was to receive. It was broken down into three phases. Phase one consisted of familiarization flights, basic tactics, instruments, navigation, and night familiarization for a total of 27 hours. Phase two consisted of weapons training in gunnery, strafing, bombing, rockets, night navigation, and close air support for a total of 44 hours. Phase three consisted of training in MPQ drops (a radar-controlled bombing sortie), night intruder interception, night and instrument navigation, and the use of flares during attack missions for a total of 42 hours. Ending the first week, two representatives from the Curtiss-Wright Corporation gave a lecture on the performance and capabilities of the twin-row, supercharged, 18-cylinder R-3350–26 Duplex-Cyclone engine, the Skyraider's powerplant.

Due to limited facilities and targets available for use by the squadron at El Toro, 29 officers and 112 enlisted men, with 14 Skyraiders, deployed to NAAS El Centro from 8 March to the 28th. During the intensified training at El Centro, all assigned pilots received a minimum of 45 hours of flight time in the Skyraider. This included night bombing and strafing missions. Unfortunately, the squadron lost one of its aircraft during this period. On the 25th, the engine of Captain Kenneth A. Lund's AD-3 Skyraider (BuNo 122754) quit while on a night-bombing exercise. Lund was forced to bail out of his aircraft, sustaining serious injuries when he did so. He parachuted to the ground and was quickly picked up by a helicopter from El Centro and flown to the infirmary at the base. After an examination, he was immediately transferred to the Naval Hospital at San Diego. Lund's AD-3 was a total loss. The cause of the engine failure could not be determined.

While at El Centro, the Skyraiders were put through angle-calibration hops. Pilots went through dives at angles of 30, 50 and 70 degrees. The 70-degree dives were discontinued due to excessive oil leaks, believed to be caused by the steep dive angle.

For those that did not go to El Centro, flight operations were confined to familiarization flights, and section and division tactics. The enlisted men who left on 27 February to attend the maintenance course returned on 15 March. On the 30th, pilots either qualified or requalified in ground-controlled approach by making five successful approaches each.

At the end of the month, the squadron had 39 Naval Aviators, 2 Air Ground officers, and 170 enlisted men, including two enlisted pilots. Twenty Skyraiders were now assigned to the squadron—a mix of AD-2s, 3s and 4s.[34] The AD-3 and AD-4 were improvements over the AD-2. The AD-3 had an improved propellor design and its landing gear was completely re-designed to provide less shock to the wings while landing. The AD-4 had an improved engine, a strengthened landing hook assembly, and the ability to use the AN/APS-19A radar unit. Both the AD-3 and the AD-4 were also adapted for night fighting, getting the designation AD-3N and AD-4N respectively.[35]

April Fools' Day had personnel from the squadron getting a brief from a World War II veteran of the squadron. Lieutenant Colonel Mike Yunck, who served with VMO-251 during its Guadalcanal days, gave a lecture on the MK-7 nuclear bomb to 14 officers at El Toro's station theater.[36] The weapon was the first tactical nuclear bomb to be adopted by the U.S. military.[37] Concurrently,

Douglas Aircraft had produced a variant of the Skyraider capable of carrying the MK-7, the AD-4B.[38] The bomb was to be delivered by the "Toss Method."[39] The Marines of the squadron did not know it, but they would be practicing this delivery method by 1954.

During the month, the squadron received seven Skyraiders: four AD-3s, two AD-4Bs and one AD-4. At the end of the month, with 27 Skyraiders on hand, the unit finally had more aircraft than was authorized (24).

Pilots attended several lectures on a diverse range of topics during April: procedures and operations of MPQ (radar-controlled bombing from the ground); recognition; the E6B flight computer; the R-3350–26 engine; close air support; and ADF/MDF direction-finding operations. The E6B was basically a manual, circular slide rule capable of computing time, speed, distance, altitude, true airspeed, and a host of other variables.

The highlight of the month was beginning a five-week deployment back to El Centro, where the pilots continued their training by following the syllabus handed down the previous month in preparation for combat in Korea. On 12 April, 35 officers, 157 enlisted men, and 19 Skyraiders departed for El Centro. The squadron flew many night missions: bombing, strafing, navigation, division tactics, familiarization, flare drops, and flare bombing. The Marines returned to El Toro on 19 May.

The use of flares brought up a potential problem. The squadron's current commander, Lieutenant Colonel Harold A. Harwood, pointed out in a letter to the Commanding General, Fleet Marine Force, Pacific, that "it was obvious to observers that the standard, glossy blue aircraft paint with white markings on fuselage and wings are undesirable for night operations. Reflection from these surfaces is great particularly when the aircraft makes any turns below flares."[40] Harwood wanted permission to change the paint scheme from glossy blue to a dull black and to paint markings red.

Apparently, permission was not granted. When the squadron finally reached Korea in July 1953, its aircraft still had the glossy blue paint scheme with white markings.

There were a few incidents at El Centro during April. The first occurred on the 15th when Captain James R. Blunt experienced a loss of power and a rough-running engine in his Skyraider (BuNo 122790). He landed safely and made it to the squadron flight line. Mechanics began checking the engine and found the cause of the problem. Paint—zinc chromate—was found in the fuel strainer. An investigation determined the strainer in a fuel truck at the air station had been painted with zinc chromate. All aircraft in the squadron were checked after the discovery. As a result, personnel found four aircraft with paint in their strainers. The next incident occurred the following day when Second Lieutenant Waldo R. Reynolds experienced an engine failure in his Skyraider at about fifty feet altitude soon after take-off. He was able to bring his plane down onto the runway without further incident. A ground test and a test hop the following day failed to turn up any problems. It was believed paint in the fuel may have also caused the failure. On 25 April, the third incident occurred. Captain Milton A. Wilson made a wheels-up landing in his Skyraider (BuNo 122762). Wilson aborted his first attempt at landing when clearance was not received from the air traffic controllers. He retracted his landing gear and rejoined the circuit to make his second attempt. Unfortunately, he forgot to lower his landing gear during the second approach and ended up sliding down the runway. Wilson was not injured, although his ego might have been a little bruised, and the aircraft was repairable.

Apparently, the few AD-4 Skyraiders the squadron had in its inventory were prone to engine problems. On 28 April, the cowl flaps were wired off to remain open. The automatic cowl flap regulators were not working as advertised, forcing the pilots to closely monitor them to prevent the engines from overheating.

On the last day of April, a potential disaster was prevented by a quick-thinking enlisted man. While maintenance personnel were loading a sonobuoy dispenser, a one-million-candlepower flare was released and ignited under the wing of an AD-4. Staff Sergeant Daniel E. Blaszak pulled the burning flare to a clear area away from the aircraft. Fire crews from El Centro were called to the scene but were not able to extinguish the flare. They had to let it burn itself out. It is not known if Blaszak was recommended for an award.[41]

The squadron returned to MCAS El Toro on 19 May and by 1 June was preparing to head off to war. Squadron officers and pilots were given a lecture on what facilities were available at their new duty station—K-6 Pyeongtaek, Korea. Over the next two days, all the squadron's aircraft—24 Skyraiders—were flown to NAS San Diego, to be prepped and loaded aboard USS *Windham Bay* (T-CVE-92), a World War II-vintage escort carrier now serving as an aircraft transport. In addition, 30 enlisted men were sent to the air station to aid in the preparation and preservation/protection of the aircraft for loading on to the carrier. These men would rejoin the squadron on 9 June, just prior to the ship shoving off. An advance echelon, commanded by Major James W. Merritt and consisting of three officers and eight enlisted men, left by air for Marine Air Group 12. MAG-12 was headquartered at K-6.

On 9 June, the remaining squadron personnel left El Toro and arrived aboard the escort carrier an hour before noon. Along with the 30 enlisted men previously sent, the squadron soon departed for Yokosuka, Japan. Two days later, *Windham Bay* docked at Pier No. 3 at the naval air station at Alameda, California. Officers and staff non-commissioned officers were granted overnight liberty. At 1600 hours on 12 June, the ship departed for Japan.

While the ship was on its way, a new squadron patch approved by the squadron was forwarded to Headquarters Marine Corps for approval on 18 June. The patch depicted a black shield with a thunderbolt cutting across in a diagonal direction, the "big dipper" in the lower right section of the patch and a crescent moon in the upper left portion of the shield. A banner was to be placed across the top of the shield with the squadron designation VMA-251. The nickname for the squadron became the "Black Patchers."

After eight days at sea, the ship docked at Ford Island, Oahu, in the Territory of Hawaii, to refuel and replenish supplies before making the final run to Japan. During its two-day stay, all squadron personnel, except those assigned to shipboard duty, were granted liberty until midnight 21 June.

Early in the morning of 22 June, *Windham Bay* departed Oahu for its final leg to Japan. Since they began the voyage, squadron pilots attended several lectures covering a variety of topics on Korea, including close air support operations, evasion and escape techniques, VT (variable-timed) and anti-withdrawal fuzes, and types of bombs available for use.[42]

At 2015 hours on 2 July, USS *Windham Bay* docked at Yokosuka. Immediately upon arrival, VMA-251 was assigned to MAG-12 and plans went into effect to get the squadron to Korea as quickly as possible.

Twenty of the pilots were designated to fly the aircraft to K-6. The Skyraiders were offloaded and sent to Kisarazu Air Force Base (AFB) to be de-preserved and prepared for flight. Along with the aircraft, two officers and 18 enlisted men were detailed to do the work on the Skyraiders. Four enlisted men were detached and assigned as guards over the squadron gear still on board the ship.

The remaining officers and enlisted men of the squadron boarded a train for Itami AFB. They arrived the following day and awaited air transport to Pyeongtaek. On 5 July, they were flown to Pyeongtaek where the advance echelon sent in June rejoined the squadron.

The unit received an influx of personnel over the next several days. The largest number of personnel was received on the 6th when 11 officers and 45 enlisted men were transferred from VMA-323 (a Corsair unit being sent home) and assigned to the squadron, as well as 18 enlisted men from the June replacement draft.

On 9 July, the 24 Skyraiders of VMA-251 were de-preserved and flown to Itami. At the base, they were joined by four pilots from MAG-12 who would lead them to K-6 at Pyeongtaek. The detail assigned to de-preserve the Skyraiders was flown from Kisarazu AFB to K-6 to rejoin the squadron. The following day, 37,400 pounds of squadron gear brought from the United States was sent by air from Tachikawa AFB.

Finally, on 12 July, 23[43] of the squadron's aircraft left Itami for Pyeongtaek. The Skyraiders would have been in Korea sooner if not for an admin glitch. The flight was required to file and fly as a ferry hop. Weather below the minimum requirements for ferry hops was a common occurrence in the area for most of July and August; thus, the flight was delayed. If the flight had been classified as operational, the Skyraiders could have flown to Korea despite the less-than-ideal weather conditions.

By the time VMA-251 began operations, the war had progressed to a stalemate with both sides taking up positions roughly along the 38th parallel—Communist forces to the north and UN forces to the south. As these opposing forces kept each other at bay, politicians worked to bring about a truce. An end to the conflict was close, but the business of war continued. Following a spat between North Korea and the United Nations Command after a breakout of North Korean POWs, enemy forces launched an attack on 13 July. Communist forces drove a:

> … wedge eight miles deep in the Eighth Army's central sector. General Taylor deployed units to contain the shoulders and point of the wedge, then counterattacked. But he halted his attack force on July 20 short of the original line since by that date the armistice delegations had come to a new accord and needed only to work out a few small details. Taylor's order to halt ended the last major battle of the war.[44]

It was within the context of this attack that VMA-251 began flying combat missions.

K-6 was situated on a flat piece of land near the village of Pyeongtaek, with rolling hills and mountains visible to the north and the Yellow Sea a short distance to the west. The area was mostly dirt which turned to mud with heavy rains and melting snow. Quonset huts made up most of the buildings on the facility. The front line was approximately seventy miles north of the base, easily within range to the squadron's Douglas Skyraiders.

The type of missions the squadron was assigned to fly in the coming two weeks varied. The most frequent were "Interdiction" and "MPQ" (radar-controlled). Other mission types flown were "RESCAP" (Rescue Combat Air Patrol) and "Close Air Support." Procedures to fly these missions varied slightly according to MAG-12 documents.

When scheduled for close air support missions, the assigned pilots would stand-by in the MAG-12 briefing room until alerted by the Joint Operations Center in Seoul (callsign *Godfrey*). The pilots were then briefed on the latest target area weather conditions, time of rendezvous and coordinates where the air controller was to be met, the radio frequency for contacting the controller, and the identity of the target if known.

As soon as the flight was airborne, the flight leader directed all pilots to change from the tower frequency to the proper frequency of the "Report In and Out" (RIO) net, also known as Channel Blue. Contact was then established with the Tactical Air Direction Center (TADC, callsign *Newport*) on the RIO net. The TADC was given the following information: mission number, callsign, number of aircraft in the flight, the type of mission, the identity of the air controller, and the estimated time of return to K-6. If the mission was not aborted, the flight continued to the rendezvous point. As the formation neared this point, the flight leader ordered the pilots to change radio frequency to contact the designated air controller.

Once communication was established with the air controller, he relayed the position of the target, the type of target, and proceeded to lead the flight in. When the target was reached, the air controller marked the target with a strafing attack. The flight leader then initiated the attack and maintained control until all ordnance was expended.

After all aircraft had delivered their ordnance, and as the flight was retiring from the target area, the air controller estimated the damage caused by the attack and reported his findings to the flight leader. After the report was received, the flight leader ordered his pilots to change frequency back to the RIO net in preparation for relaying the strike assessment to *Godfrey*, or to *Newport*, who would then send it to *Godfrey*.

As the flight approached K-6, the strike report was given to *Godfrey* along with the number of aircraft returning, the latest area weather, and the estimated time of arrival at K-6. The flight was then cleared to continue to K-6 with instructions to change frequency and contact the tower only after the airfield was in sight.

Rail targets usually fell under "Interdiction." In both cases, assigned pilots were briefed in the MAG-12 briefing room and received information on weather conditions, target coordinates, scheduled time over target, the identity and radio callsigns of friendly aircraft hitting the same area, and other items. Once airborne, the designated flight leader ordered all pilots to change radio frequency to Channel Blue. At this time, *Newport* was contacted and given the following information: mission number, callsign, number of aircraft inbound to target, and estimated time of return. Newport would then order the flight to either continue to the target, divert to another one, or return to base.

If the flight continued to the target, the aircraft involved would climb to the altitude from which the attack would be made. Once at attack altitude, the aircraft continued flying in level flight until the target area was reached. In most cases, participating aircraft were deployed in either echelon or in a column, with the leader at approximately 11,000–12,000 feet and the other aircraft nearly level with him.

Aircraft attacking the target would go into a dive, usually at an angle of 45 degrees. The altitude at which the bombs were released was left to the discretion of the individual pilot. In most cases, airspeed when pulling out of the dive was nearly three hundred knots (345 miles per hour).

Following the attack, all aircraft climbed to a prearranged rendezvous altitude and rejoined the flight leader. The last aircraft, which carried survival gear and did not dive during the attack, was designated to observe and give his report to the flight leader.

Once the rendezvous was complete and the flight reached friendly territory (implying an attack in enemy territory), the strike report—consisting of the mission number, callsign, number of aircraft outbound, damage to rail lines, area weather, and estimated time of arrival at K-6—was transmitted to *Godfrey*. The flight would then continue to within 40 miles of K-6 where the TADC was contacted and clearance to continue to base was received.

When approximately ten miles from K-6, all pilots switched their radios to the tower frequency at which point the flight leader requested landing instructions and clearance to land.

Radar-controlled MPQ missions were flown during the day and at night. For an MPQ mission not designated as a close air support mission, pilots assigned were briefed to contact *Newport* when inbound to the target by giving the mission number, callsign, number of aircraft in the flight, the type of mission and the estimated time of return to K-6; in other words, the usual information. They were further briefed to proceed to 15,000 feet altitude and contact the Marine Ground Control Intercept Unit serving as the TADC, codename *Anaconda Baker*, en route to obtain a magnetic heading to its position. The magnetic heading was maintained to help with coordination between the flight and *Anaconda Charlie*, the callsign of the Air Support Radar Team (ASRT) attached to the 1st Marine Division. The ASRT was the controller for the attack if the strike was in the 1st Marine Division's area of operations. Radar teams changed depending on where the strike was taking place.

Upon arriving over *Anaconda Baker*, the flight leader contacted the TADC and received the designated radio frequency for controlling the flight. This frequency was often referred to as the MAG-12 "group common" frequency and known as Channel Violet. Once the frequency was received, the flight leader contacted *Anaconda Charlie*. The ASRT then took over control of the aircraft by directing their attack as a result of observing the unit's radio-electronic equipment. The desired speed, direction, altitude, point of ordnance release, and the proximity of one aircraft to the other was carefully controlled by the MPQ operator in the ASRT.

Since the MPQ operator had the aircraft dropping their ordnance from 11,000 to 12,000 feet, getting an estimate of the damage by the participating pilots was impossible. In this case, the MPQ operator received the results from an observing forward air controller and relayed the results to the flight leader. The flight was then cleared to return to K-6, first reporting to the TADC and then *Newport* with the results of the mission.

After receiving the strike report, *Newport* requested the flight contact the K-6 Tower only after the airfield was in sight. The pilots in the flight complied and switched to the tower frequency as per other types of missions. Landing instructions were requested after which landing was completed.

MPQ missions were also employed in the use of close air support. These were usually flown during the day. The missions made use of the radar and radio gear of a Marine Ground Control Intercept Squadron and its ability to control aircraft equipped with the necessary electronics for a level bomb run. The target was usually within five miles of friendly lines, but on a few occasions more distant targets were hit.

The pilots took off from K-6 and climbed while heading on a course to *Anaconda Baker*. The climb was usually through cloud cover and required instrument flight procedures (blind flying) to maintain orientation. The pilot reported to *Newport*, stating his mission, type of aircraft and estimated time of return to K-6.

The same information was repeated to the Joint Operations Center (JOC) in Seoul. It was at this time the final clearance for the mission was either granted or rejected by the JOC through the TADC, callsign *Shirley*. As the pilot neared 15,000 feet over *Anaconda Baker*, and after an identifying pattern for radar was flown, radio control was passed to *Anaconda Charlie*. This station monitored the aircraft, assigning the tactical speed and altitude (usually 160 knots and between 10,000 and 12,000 feet) for the level bomb run.

Once the aircraft was flying straight and level and on autopilot, azimuth control was turned over to the radar unit while the pilot continued to control speed and altitude by use of the autopilot. At the command of "Armstrong" by the ground controller, the ordnance was armed by the pilot and, at the pre-calculated moment, dropped by remote control from the ground unit. The routine was repeated for as many runs as necessary until the job was finished and all ordnance expended.

The bomb runs were made in level flight along a path that ran perpendicular to the front lines—from friendly position to enemy positions. When a run was completed, control of the aircraft was returned to the pilot while ground radar contact was maintained, or the mission aborted.

When the last run was completed, the results of the mission were transmitted by a ground observer to the pilot. The pilot passed the results to the JOC via *Godfrey* as he checked out of the target area. The checkout procedure was repeated for *Anaconda Baker* and *Newport* control. *Newport* then guided the pilot in his approach to K-6.[45]

The weather was not the best for flying. The MAG-12 Command Diary for July 1953 noted the weather was "comparatively poor for combat operations. The weather breakdown for the month of July was as follows: 6 operational, 9 non-operational, 1 operational to non-operational, 1 operational to marginal, 4 marginal to non-operational, 2 non-operational to marginal, 1 marginal to operational, 1 non-operational to operational and 3 marginal days."[46] Temperatures ranged from a high in the 90s to a low in the 50s (Fahrenheit). The average temperature was in the 80s.[47] July was a wet month, raining 22 days out of 31.[48]

With squadron aircraft and personnel now established at K-6, VMA-251 prepared to fly its first combat mission since the early days of World War II. That day came on 16 July 1953. Four missions were flown. The first was assigned a target approximately six miles south of the North Korean town of Sariwon in the province of North Hwanghae (YC-4356).[49] The target was approximately one hundred twenty-two miles to the northwest of K-6. Seven aircraft in two divisions—a mixed bag of AD-3, AD-4 and AD-4B Skyraiders—were loaded with 1,000-pound and 250-pound bombs. Flying in the first division were Captains George F. McLaughlin, Ward L. Hooper and Austin C. Fitzgerald, and Major James W. Merritt. Flying the second division were Captain Dail D. Fine, First Lieutenant Irwin Feher, and Captain Albert V. Aaron.

The seven Skyraiders were wheels up at 1221. Nearly 50 minutes later they were over the target. In the ensuing attack, 10 buildings were claimed as destroyed. No enemy anti-aircraft fire was noted, and all aircraft had returned safely to K-6 by 1355.

The second mission also consisted of two divisions. The target was a series of buildings (YC-255017) nestled in mountains located approximately eleven miles east of the North Korean town of Ongjin in South Hwanghae Province, about one hundred five miles to the northwest of K-6. Flying in the first division were Captains Melvin E. Locke, McLaughlin, Aaron (both having returned from their first mission), and Second Lieutenant Reynold M. Olson. The second division consisted of Captains Charles Friend III, Hooper and Fine, and Major Merritt (the latter three also back up for their second mission of the day). The AD-3s, -4s and -4Bs were loaded with napalm.

The eight Skyraiders took to the air at 1533. After slightly more than 30 minutes in the air, the Marines were over the target. They dropped their napalm canisters, damaging eight buildings. No enemy fire was encountered, and all aircraft returned to K-6 undamaged at 1645.

The third mission for the day once again consisted of two divisions, this time flying four AD-3s and four AD-4Bs. Pilots in the first division were Fitzgerald, Captain Dewey M. Mark, Jr., Major LeRoy C. Barton, and Captain Stanley E. Free; in the second division were Feher, Captain William J. Foster, Major Kevin Cochrane, and Captain James R. Blunt. The target (YC-433266) was located about six miles south of Ayang in South Hwanghae Province, slightly over one hundred eight miles to the northwest of K-6. The eight Skyraiders were armed with 1,000-pound bombs.

The aircraft took off at 1809, reaching the target 36 minutes later. The Skyraiders dropped their bombs and made a few strafing runs before turning for home. The pilots were unable to assess the damage they may have caused. Once again, there was no enemy response, and all had returned safely to K-6 by 1930.

The last effort of the day was an interdiction mission, but the specific target type is not known. Fine, Locke, McLaughlin, and Merritt flew the first division while Hooper, Olson, Friend, and Aaron brought up the rear. With the eight Skyraiders armed with a mix of 2,000 and 1,000-pound bombs, they took off by 1853. Before reaching the target area (YC-387412), Friend and Aaron had to abort due to unspecified mechanical problems. The remaining six Skyraiders were over the target at 1937. After dropping their bombs and executing a few strafing runs, the pilots headed home. Damage to the target was not assessed. All planes returned safely to K-6 by 2023. Rounding out the near-perfect first day of operations, the enemy again did not offer any resistance.

For the first mission of 17 July, six Skyraiders flying in two divisions were to hit suspected enemy positions (YC-285017) 13 miles east of the town of Ongjin, not far from targets attacked the day before. The target was approximately one hundred thirteen miles northwest of K-6. Assigned to the first division were Friend, Barton, Feher, and Blunt. Fitzgerald and Foster made up the second division.

Carrying 780-pound napalm canisters, the Skyraiders took off at 1023. Following a 40-minute flight, the Marines were over the target and dropped their napalm, firing their 20-mm cannons while doing so. Smoke from the fires created by the napalm obscured the pilots' vision, which did not allow an assessment of the damage. The pilots met no enemy resistance and had landed safely at K-6 by 1127.

Four minutes after the first strike mission took off, another six Skyraiders departed to return to a target hit by the squadron south of Ayang the day before (YC-433266). Hooper, Cochrane, Olson, and Mark flew the first division while McLaughlin and Free completed the formation. Arriving over the target at 1105, the pilots dropped twelve 780-pound napalm canisters and expended 1,000 rounds of 20-mm ammunition in strafing runs against the target. In what was becoming the norm, the enemy put up no anti-aircraft fire. Damage could not be assessed due to the smoke covering the target area as a result of the napalm; the pilots had returned to K-6 by 1124.

The last two missions for the day were flown in the late afternoon and early evening. At 1705, two divisions consisting of Locke, Merritt, Olson, and Aaron in the first division and Fine, Cochrane, Feher, and Barton in the second division, flew northwest from K-6 to hit a group of buildings, this time approximately six miles west of Ayang (YC-323351). Reaching the target at 1745, the first division let loose seven 1,000-pound bombs and expended another 1,400 rounds of 20-mm ammunition. One aircraft had a hung bomb and could not release it. The second division dropped eight 1,000 bombs as well as 16 2,000 pound bombs. Once again, the enemy put up no resistance. The pilots could not assess the damage they may have inflicted and returned to base by 1818.

The last mission flown consisted of two divisions of four aircraft each. McLaughlin, Blunt, Hooper, and Foster were in the lead, while Mark, Friend, Free, and Fitzgerald followed. Each of the Skyraiders was armed with one 1,000 and two 2,000-pound general-purpose bombs. The target assigned (YC-378578) was located six miles south-southwest of Sariwon in North Hwanghae Province.

The aircraft took off at 1826, reaching the target after a 44-minute flight. With no resistance encountered, the pilots released their ordnance and used up another 1,300 rounds of 20mm. As with the previous missions during the day, the pilots could not assess the damage inflicted. The Skyraiders were back at K-6 by 1950.

Combat missions started early on 18 July. The first of eight missions for the day consisted of six Skyraiders: three AD-3s, one AD-4, and two AD-4Bs. Assigned to the first division were Fine, and Captains Albert G. Webbeking, Jack W. Robbins, and Keith O'Keefe. Flying the second division were Feher and First Lieutenant Ralph M. Euwema. Ordnance for the mission consisted of a mix of 1,000 and 250-pound general-purpose bombs.

The target was an area approximately twelve miles east of Kangryong in South Hwanghae Province, and 104 miles northwest of K-6 (YC-264011). The six aircraft took off at 0612, reaching the target within 40 minutes[50] only to find the area covered in fog. The pilots dropped their ordnance, smothering the area with 10 1,000-pound bombs and 34 250-pound bombs. Because of the fog, and debris thrown up by the explosions, damage to the target could not be determined. The enemy put up no resistance. All aircraft had returned safely to K-6 by 0849.

The next mission saw another six Skyraiders—three AD-3s and three AD-4Bs—go after a railroad bridge (YC-387578) located approximately five and a half miles southwest of Sariwon and 126 miles northwest of K-6. Flying in the first division were Locke, Carpenter, and Captain Elree G. Barr. Captain Jack R. Merkle, Olson, and First Lieutenant Charles R. Kucharski were assigned the second division.

Taking off just 13 minutes after the first mission, the six Skyraiders reached the target at 0708. After dropping twelve 1,000-pound bombs, twenty-two 250-pound bombs, and expending 1,500 rounds of 20-mm ammunition, the bridge was left damaged. There was no resistance to the attack and the aircraft made it back to K-6 by 0823.

The third mission of the day was airborne at 1123. According to Elree Barr, Intelligence had gathered information that the North Koreans were digging tunnels to allow their troops to infiltrate the area near Haeju in South Hwanghae Province.[51] The target would be the suspected tunnels about ten miles west-southwest of Haeju and 103 miles northwest of K-6 (YC-287011). Flying his second mission of the day, Locke led Second Lieutenants Francis E. Martin, Duane H. Albert and Frederick H. Clapp in the first division, while Olson and Barr, also on their second sortie for the day, rounded out the formation. Each Skyraider—three AD-3s, one AD-4 and two AD-4Bs—carried two 780-pound napalm canisters. Napalm seems to be an odd choice for a strike against tunnels.

Upon reaching the target at noon, local time, each aircraft made a run to the target, coming in as low as 400 feet to drop its load. No enemy flak was present. As Barr was making his run, a woman and child crossed a road in front of his flight path. He held off dropping his ordnance and proceeded to a nearby area to dispose of it before heading home. As it turned out, both bombs "hung up," not releasing when Barr wanted them too. However, after a few maneuvers, he was finally able to shake them loose.[52] When the runs were completed by the other aircraft, three buildings were claimed destroyed. As for the tunnels, it is not clear if they were damaged or destroyed. All aircraft returned to K-6 safely at 1234.

A few hours before take-off time, Friend, Hooper, Merritt, McLaughlin, Barton, Fitzgerald, and Blunt received a briefing for their mission, scheduled to depart K-6 at 1203. They were assigned to attack caves, bunkers, and supplies about a mile east of the south end of the Rimjin River, six miles north-northwest of Chorwon in Kangwon Province (CH-139552) and approximately one hundred two miles from K-6. Flying the usual mixed assortment of AD-3s, AD-4s and AD-4Bs, each aircraft carried three 1,000-pound and eight 250-pound general-purpose bombs.

The seven Marines of VMA-251 took off as scheduled, reaching the target 48 minutes later. With no enemy flak interfering with their attack, the pilots covered the target area with most of their ordnance, damaging some of the installations before turning for home and landing back at K-6 at 1251.

While the pilots of the fourth mission were receiving their briefing, pilots flying the fifth mission for the day were receiving theirs. Scheduled to take off at 1229, Fine, Reynolds, Feher, and Master Sergeants Raymond J. Delacqua, Walter L. Simpson, Jr., and Harvey L. Bearden were ordered to hit buildings, troops, and supplies located about seven miles east-northeast of Haeju in South Hwanghae Province (YC-512215). For the attack, each of the Skyraiders carried two 1,000-pound and four 250-pound general-purpose bombs.

The six Skyraiders took off on time and reached their target at 1305. They dropped their bombs and expended over 1,300 rounds of 20-mm ammunition. The North Koreans did not interfere with the attack; they put up no resistance. Unfortunately, damage to the target could not be assessed. All aircraft returned to K-6 at 1344.

For the sixth mission, Marines of VMA-251 returned to strike the tunnels near Haeju. Flying in the first division were Fine, Carpenter, Reynolds, and O'Keefe. In the second were Hooper and Kucharski. Once again, for an attack on tunnels, the six Skyraiders were armed with 780-pound napalm canisters.

The two divisions took off at around 1600 and were over the target about a half hour later. Despite no resistance, only two buildings were assessed as destroyed. All aircraft were back at K-6 by 1700.

At 1609, six Skyraiders—piloted by McLaughlin, Albert, Captain Robert A. Steinway, Second Lieutenant Kenneth D. Peck, Fitzgerald, and Clapp—took off to strike a rail bridge approximately one hundred eleven miles north-northwest of K-6 in the province of North Hwanghae (BT-433521). Each of the Skyraiders carried two 1,000-pound and four 250-pound general-purpose bombs.

Upon reaching the target at 1635, the aircraft began their individual runs on the target. After dropping all their bombs and expending 5,000 rounds of 20mm, the rail bridge was destroyed. It no doubt helped that the North Koreans offered no resistance. All aircraft had returned safely to K-6 by 1722.

The last mission of the day had the squadron attacking a group of buildings approximately nine miles south of Ayang in South Hwanghae Province, 103 miles northwest of K-6. The five Skyraiders—two AD-3s, one AD-4 and two AD-4Bs—each carried two 780-pound napalm canisters. Assigned to fly the mission were Friend, Euwema, Webbeking, Merkle, and Olson.

The aircraft were in the air by 1730. They had arrived over the target by 1808 to find no resistance welcoming them. After completing their attack, four buildings were assessed to be destroyed, and a secondary explosion was noted. All aircraft made it back to K-6 by 1834.

Combat started bright and early for the pilots of VMA-251 on 19 July. Facilities in the northern end of South Hwanghae Province about ten miles south of Nampo were the target for the first two missions of the day (YC-073781). The first mission consisted of six Skyraiders: three AD-3s, one AD-4 and two AD-4Bs. The ordnance carried by the aircraft was a mix of 2,000, 1,000, and 250-pound bombs. The pilots assigned for the mission were Hooper, Barr, Webbeking, Euwema, Feher, and Kucharski.

The Skyraiders were wheels up at 0610. It took a bit longer than usual to get to the target; it was the longest distance the squadron had flown to date, and the large weight of ordnance carried by each aircraft slowed them down. The six Skyraiders were carrying at least 17 tons of bombs between them.

Following a 50-minute flight, much to the surprise of the pilots, the North Koreans let loose with automatic weapons fire. Despite damage to the right wing of one Skyraider, the Marines pressed their attack and dropped their bombs. Unfortunately, damage to the target could not be assessed. The pilots turned for home and had made it back by 0753.

The next mission was to the same target, but the five Skyraiders—three AD-3s and two AD-4s—each carried two 1,000 and eight 250-pound general-purpose bombs. Along with Hooper and Feher flying their second mission for the day, Peck, Steinway, and Merkle were assigned to the mission. The heavily laden Skyraiders took off at 0912 and reached the target at 1100, an unusually long time based on the other missions flown. It's possible the flight had to be re-routed to avoid bad weather en route to the target. Unlike the early morning raid, the enemy did not put up any resistance, but despite dropping another 10 tons of ordnance on the target, damage to the targeted buildings could not be assessed. The Skyraiders turned for home, reaching K-6 at 1150.

An area approximately six miles south of Ayang was the target for the next two missions. For the first strike, the squadron assigned 12 Skyraiders, mostly AD-3s, armed with a mix of 1,000-pound and 250-pound bombs. The pilots scheduled to fly were Locke, Barton, Fitzgerald, Cochrane, McLaughlin, Merritt, Fine, Mark, Friend, Free, Olson, and Foster. Barton and Cochrane aborted prior to take-off, possibly due to mechanical failures. The remaining Skyraiders headed out at 0920.

Following a 45-minute flight, the pilots spotted the collection of buildings they were assigned to hit. After dropping 20 tons of ordnance, 20 buildings were assessed to have been destroyed, and a secondary explosion was noted. The North Koreans offered no resistance and the Marines arrived home at 1052.

The second strike to the same location took off at 1330. Six Skyraiders—piloted by LtCol. Harold A. Harwood (the squadron commander), McLaughlin, Friend, Major William A. Lamont, Fine, and Martin—carried two 1,000 and four 250-pound bombs each for a combined total of nine tons. No problems were encountered during take-off.

Following a 35-minute flight, the aircraft were in the target area and proceeded to attack the designated target. After all ordnance was expended, five more buildings were destroyed; a secondary explosion was again observed. No flak met the attackers and all Skyraiders had returned to K-6 by 1450.

It was back to South Hwanghae Province for the fifth mission of the day. The squadron was assigned to strike buildings approximately four miles northwest of Kangryong (YC-258017). Eight of the Skyraiders—seven AD-3s and one AD-4—participated in the mission. Each was loaded with two 780-pound napalm canisters. Piloting the aircraft were Locke, Bearden, Robbins, Peck, Olson, Delacqua, Reynolds, and Simpson. They were wheels up at 1430.

Following a 30-minute flight, and meeting no resistance, the pilots dropped their ordnance, resulting in 20 buildings destroyed and another secondary explosion. The aircraft then reformed and turned for base. All made it home safely.

Buildings eight miles south of Nampo were the recipient of VMA-251's sixth mission for the day (YC-073789). Six Skyraiders—one AD-3, one AD-4, and four AD-4Bs—were assigned, as were Fitzgerald, Lamont, Feher, Harwood, Hooper, and Aaron. As in the previous mission, the six aircraft each carried two 780-pound napalm canisters. The Marines took off as scheduled at 1550 and, following a flight lasting slightly over 50 minutes, reached the target area. The ordnance was dropped without interference from the North Koreans; their guns remained silent. Despite this, damage could not be assessed. Once all the aircraft rendezvoused at a prearranged point, they turned for K-6, making it back at 1733.

The last mission of the day consisted of eight Skyraiders, flown by Fine, Robbins, O'Keefe, Clapp, McLaughlin, Martin, Olson, and Albert. Flying northwest to hit buildings southeast of Chaeryong, the aircraft carried approximately twenty tons of ordnance between them. They took off at 1824, reaching the target nearly forty minutes later. Once again, the enemy offered no resistance. The Marines dropped their ordnance, creating several fires that remained burning as they turned for home.

The fifth day of combat operations began with an interdiction mission to hit a group of buildings approximately six miles south of Ichŏn-ŭp in the Kangwon Province of North Korea, 102 miles due north of K-6. An impressive 15 Skyraiders—consisting of nine AD-3s, two AD-4s, and four AD-4Bs—each carried three 1,000-pound and eight 250-pound bombs, a massive 37.5 tons to be delivered to the North Koreans. Assigned to fly the mission were McLaughlin, Foster, Friend, Aaron, Locke, Hooper, Blunt, Fitzgerald, Cochrane, Olson, Mark, Fine, Barton, Barr, and Merritt. Each of the pilots had one or more combat missions under his belt.

The 15 Marines took off at 0840; after nearly an hour, they reached the target area. With no anti-aircraft fire thrown up by the North Koreans, the pilots of VMA-251 dropped their ordnance unimpeded. The bombs wreaked havoc on the target area; damage was assessed as 20 buildings destroyed. The 15 aircraft reformed and turned for home, arriving safely at K-6 at 1025.

The second mission of the day took several of the squadron's Skyraiders to the east coast of South Korea, near Goseong, approximately eleven miles northwest of the town and near the front lines defended by the Korean 15th Division (DT-410600). The type of target was not identified in the squadron reports. The pilots participating in the mission, some on their second of the day, were Friend, Barton, Hooper, Merkel, Harwood, Fine, Lamont, and

Cochrane. The four AD-3s, two AD-4s and two AD-4Bs carried nearly twenty tons of explosives—a mix 1,000 and 250-pound bombs.

The eight Skyraiders took off at 1321. As they made their way to the target, Hooper and Cochrane developed problems which forced them to abort and head back to K-6 (the second abort in two days for the latter). The six remaining aircraft continued with the mission. When they reached their designated target, they found it had already been destroyed. They were given a new target—road bridges—by their controller which took them 13 miles north into North Korea near the town of Kosong on the east coast (DT-411818). As was the norm, the North Koreans put up no resistance. Unhindered by the lack of AA fire, the pilots dropped their ordnance, damaging two bridges in the process. After the six Skyraiders regrouped, they turned for K-6, touching down at 1450.

At 1415, the next mission took off to strike a railroad bridge near Hwangju, located in the province of North Hwanghae, North Korea. Flying this mission were McLaughlin, First Lieutenant Donald R. Stiver, Fitzgerald, and Second Lieutenant Burrel E. Sumner. Each of the Skyraiders—one AD-3, two AD-4s and one AD-4B—carried 1,000-pound and 250-pound bombs. Following a flight of about a half-hour, the four Marines reached the target area.

No flak greeted the flyers. The four aircraft made their bomb runs, leaving the railroad bridge damaged. The Marines regrouped and changed course to head to K-6, touching down at 1620.

Shortly after 1700, 10 Skyraiders—six AD-3s, two AD-4s and two AD-4Bs—took off to attack an unspecified target about eight miles south of Nampo in South Hwanghae Province (YC-054794). Between the 10 aircraft they carried 21.5 tons of ordnance (a mix of 1,000-pound and 250-pound general-purpose bombs). Assigned to the mission were Fitzgerald, Bearden, Cochrane, Delacqua, Fine, Stiver, Sumner, Reynolds, Hooper, and Simpson. Of these men, Fitzgerald, Fine, Hooper, and Cochrane were assigned to their third mission of the day (albeit the latter two had to abort an earlier sortie), Sumner and Stiver were on their second.

Arriving over the target by 1805, the aircraft dropped their ordnance without enemy interference. If any damage was done, it was not noted. They regrouped and turned for home, arriving by 1850.

While their colleagues were nearing the Nampo area, four more Skyraiders took off at 1750 to strike a railroad bridge approximately seven miles south-southeast of Hukkyo in North Hwanghae Province (YC-470887). Each aircraft was armed with three 1,000-pound and eight 250-pound bombs for a total of 10 tons. Flying their second missions of the day were Locke, Lamont, and Harwood, while Friend was on his third.

They arrived over the target at 1818. With no flak encountered, the aviators ended up damaging the railroad bridge and cutting a rail line. They turned for home and arrived at K-6 by 1918.

Two combat missions were flown on 21 July. The first, designated Mission 21, was close air support in the rugged, central area of North Hwanghae Province (YC-7373). Initially the target was YC-405613, an area a few miles south of Sariwon, North Korea.[53]

Eight Skyraiders—a mix of AD-3s, AD-4s and AD-4Bs—were assigned to hit the target. Pilots flying the mission were Friend, Kucharski, Mark, Clapp, Hooper, Martin, Barr, and Bearden. Mark's aircraft had mechanical problems so had to abort prior to take-off. The remaining seven departed at 1219. Ordnance carried by the aircraft were 1,000-pound and 250-pound bombs. While en route to Sariwon, the VMA-251 pilots were diverted by their controller—callsign *Elgin* (Fifth Air Force TADC)—to head for a new target about twenty-two miles east-northeast of Sariwon. At some point during the flight prior to reaching the new target, Hooper, Martin, and Barr had to abort and head back to K-6. The remaining four Skyraiders flew on.

They had arrived over the target by 1347. The North Koreans offered no resistance as the Marine aviators made their attack runs. After the four Skyraiders expended their ordnance, one secondary explosion was seen. The aircraft regrouped for the flight home to K-6, arriving at 1443.

The second mission (designated Mission 20) left two minutes after the first. Its initial target was to strike areas in Sariwon, but it also was diverted by *Elgin* to strike in the same general area as the previous mission—this time at (YC-7375). It too was a designated as a close air support mission. Eight Skyraiders, and Fitzgerald, Reynolds, Aaron, Peck, Fine, Albert, Foster, and Simpson, were assigned. As in the last mission, the planes carried 1,000-pound and 250-pound bombs.

Prior to take-off, Fine had to abort. The other seven took off at 1221. They reached the target area and began their run when the North Koreans opened up with small-arms fire. One of the Skyraiders took some hits, suffering minor damage to the canopy and tail section. The Marines dropped 18 tons of bombs on the target area, creating a secondary explosion, then reformed and turned for home, touching down at 1345.

July 22 saw a shift in focus regarding the missions flown. Instead of interdiction and close air support, radar guided MPQ missions dominated. These missions were flown by a single Skyraider, usually an AD-3 or an AD-4B. Unfortunately, some of the locations for the assigned target on the MPQ missions are unknown. Weather conditions for the day were not optimal for

MPQ Missions 22 July

Pilot	*T/O Time*	*TOT*	*Landing Time*	*Coordinates*	*Ordnance*	*Result*	*Notes*
Hooper	1036	1120	1149	CT-06240878 Just north of front lines—appx. 30 miles north of Seoul	3 × 1,000 lb.	One 76-mm gun position damaged	Reported to *Horseback* 1st Marine Division
Fine	1141	1320	1355	Unknown	3 × 1,000 lb.	Unknown	No controller available—free drop
Olson	1304	1450	1515	CT-046173 5 miles north of front lines in North Korea	3 × 1,000 lb.	Unknown	Possibly north of 1st Marine Division lines
Fitzgerald	1505	1551	1615	CT-046173 5 miles north of front lines in North Korea	3 × 1,000 lb.	Unknown	Possibly north of 1st Marine Division lines
Friend	1630	1703	1732	CT-1904 appx seven miles south of front lines in South Korea	3 × 1,000 lb.	Unknown	Unknown
Hooper	1700	1826	1934	CT-130272 5 miles north of front lines in North Korea	3 × 1,000 lb.	Unknown	Unknown
Fine	1825	1912	1933	Unknown	3 × 1,000 lb.	Unknown	Unknown
Simpson	1855	1931	2008	Unknown	3 × 1,000 lb.	Unknown	

standard combat missions and it may be why the MPQ missions were flown.[54] The following table gives a brief synopsis of the day's missions. In all cases, flak was either not encountered or noted. All aircraft returned safely to K-6.

In the late afternoon of the same day, four Skyraiders—two AD-3s and two AD-4Bs—were assigned to fly CAP for rescue missions in the vicinity of Chodo Island off the west coast of North Korea. Taking off at 1704, the four pilots—Harwood, Merritt, Locke, and McLaughlin—reached the area in the early evening. When relieved of their CAP duties, they struck a gun position about a half mile inland of the west coast (XC-747596) but were unable to determine the effectiveness of the attack. No flak was encountered, allowing the Marines to return home unscathed at 2012.

The following day, 23 July, the squadron flew two combat missions. Both were MPQ missions conducted at night. The first took off at 2047, Olson carrying three 1,000-pound bombs under the wings of his AD-3. The target appears to have been off the east coast of South Korea, approximately one hundred twenty-six miles east of K-6 (DT-987024). If this is correct, what exactly Olson tried to hit is not known. Of all the coordinates given in the squadron July report, this is the only one over open water. In any case, after dropping his three bombs, the result could not be assessed. Olson arrived back at K-6 at 2200.

The squadron commander, Harwood, flew the second mission. His AD-3 also carried three 1,000-pound bombs. No coordinates were given for his target, but the results were the same as Olson's—damage unable to be determined. Taking off at 2132, Harwood returned at 2246, taking just one minute longer than Olson. Based on the total time for both flights, as well as the same bomb load, Harwood may have hit the same target as Olson.

Over the next three days, the squadron flew 18 more MPQ missions (most controlled by *Romeo*, the Fifth Air Force TADC) and two interdiction missions. Damage results could not be assessed for the MPQs. A few of the reasons given were cloud cover and darkness. At least two of the MPQs were flown in support of the 1st Marine Division and the U.S. I Corps. The interdiction missions fared no better. The first was able to drop its ordnance on target, but cloud cover prevented assessment of the attack. The second mission was aborted when the weather deteriorated. The North Koreans offered no resistance during any of the missions. No losses were sustained by the squadron.

While the war continued, talks were underway to work out a truce. Since 1951, an armistice had always been a possibility. When a dedicated site for talks was finally established in Panmunjom, North Korea, in 1952, the completion of a formal truce gathered pace.[55] The day finally came when, on 26 July, word was received by the 1st Marine Air Wing (MAW) that an armistice was to be signed at 1000 on the 27th and go into effect at 2200 that same day. Until that hour was reached, the squadron continued to strike targets.[56]

The squadron flew 16 missions—MPQ and close air support—on 27 July in a maximum effort ordered by MAG-12. Weather throughout the day was marginal for flying. When the day concluded, VMA-251 had flown 60 combat sorties for a total of nearly one hundred twenty-four hours.

The first mission took off at 0934 for a strike controlled by the U.S. IX Corps. The target area was 3 miles north of the front lines and approximately twelve miles east-southeast of Pyonggang in Kangwon Province (CT-67854505). The Skyraiders—an AD-3 and three AD-4Bs—each carried three 1,000-pound and eight 250-pound bombs. Piloting the aircraft were Hooper, Barton, Cochrane, and Merritt. They arrived in the target area at 1103 and, one by one, each plane dropped its ordnance controlled by the radar operators in IX Corps' area. No flak was encountered. Damage could not be determined. The four Skyraiders had all landed at K-6 by 1138.

Twelve minutes after the first mission took off, pilots Fine, Foster, Free, and Blunt got airborne. In the face of inaccurate automatic and heavy weapons fire, they ended up dropping nearly nine tons of ordnance on an unknown target with unassessed results. No damage was sustained by the aircraft that had all returned home by 1147.

At 1001, McLaughlin, Captain John W. Andrepont, Harwood, and Carpenter took off to strike a target in the I Corps area. Their Skyraiders—two AD-3s, one AD-4, and an AD-4B—carried slightly over seven tons of ordnance. The delivery point was approximately seven miles east-southeast of Chorwon, in North Korea's Kangwon Province, and about three miles from the front lines (CT-218366). They were over the target at 1143 less one Skyraider as Andrepont had to abort due to mechanical difficulties. Each aircraft dropped its ordnance, but damage could not be determined. The aircraft had returned safely to K-6 by 1215.

Two minutes after the four Skyraiders took off for mission three, four more left to hit their target—location unknown. The four VMA-251 pilots assigned were Locke, Sumner, Webbeking, and Stiver. On the way to the target, Sumner had to abort and return to K-6. The remaining three Skyraiders pressed on and reached the target area at 1113. They dropped 7.5 tons of ordnance and, as before, the results could not be determined. They were wheels down at K-6 by 1125.

Fitzgerald, O'Keefe, Martin, and Euwema took off at 1013 to deliver nine tons of ordnance on a target less than two miles north of the U.S. IX Corps front (CT-55164543). Incredibly, this made for 20 pilots, not including aborts, airborne across five missions at the same time. The result for this fifth mission was the same as in the previous missions: damage unknown and no North Korean resistance. All aircraft had returned safely to K-6 by 1156.

The first mission of the afternoon, like the previous five, was an MPQ strike with Friend, Hooper, Mark, and Sumner directed to hit a target at an undisclosed location. Take-off time was 1216, with time over the target set at 1329. The four aircraft dropped 10 tons of ordnance, but damage could not be ascertained. No flak was encountered, and all aircraft returned safely to K-6 at 1416.

Barton, Andrepont, Aaron, and Delacqua flew the next MPQ mission to hit a target on the IX Corps front, controlled by *Marlin*. They dropped nearly ten tons of bombs on the assigned target but could not assess the effectiveness of their work. The aircraft were all back on the ground by 1510.

Four Skyraiders piloted by Fine, Peck, Harwood, and Cochrane took off to hit a target near the front lines of the 2nd and 12th Infantry Divisions, Republic of Korea (ROK), on the eastern side of South Korea. However, while en route, the flight was diverted to strike a target approximately twenty miles west of Kosong, North Korea. Reaching the target area at 1530 following a one hour, 23-minute flight, the Skyraiders dropped 10 tons of ordnance but the success of the MPQ mission could not be determined. The four pilots had returned safely to K-6 by 1624.

McLaughlin, Carpenter, Blunt, and First Lieutenant Billy D. Bouldin took off in their Skyraiders at 1415 on another MPQ although the location of their target is not known. They arrived over the target area at 1455 and, within a few minutes, had dropped nearly nine tons of ordnance. Spotters in the area could not assess the damage. The Skyraiders returned undamaged to K-6 at 1532.

Twenty minutes after the previous strike has taken off, Fitzgerald, Stiver, Foster, and O'Keefe were airborne in their Skyraiders for a close air support mission to hit North Korean positions approximately fifteen miles north of the front lines of X Corps (DT-0866). Arriving over suspected positions at 1547, they dropped five tons of ordnance. The results of the bombing could not be determined. No flak was encountered and the Skyraiders returned undamaged at 1632.

Locke, Albert, Free, and Simpson took off at 1531 to hit a target (DT-205418) just north of the "Punchbowl" near the X Corps front. The "Punchbowl" was the name given by United Nations forces to the bowl-shaped Haean Basin near the front lines. While on the way to their target, Simpson had to abort due to mechanical problems.

The remaining three pilots pressed on to the target, arriving at 1620. With no flak to worry the Marines, nearly eight tons of bombs were dropped in the target area. As usual, no assessment of the damage could be made. The three Skyraiders turned for home, arriving at K-6 by 1650.

At 1700, Hooper, Friend, Barton, and Aaron took off in their Skyraiders to strike North Korean supply dumps located a few miles north of the "Punchbowl" (DT-194430). The division of four aircraft was soon reduced to three when Barton radioed the leader that he was experiencing problems with his aircraft and had to abort. The remaining three Skyraiders continued on but were soon told weather had deteriorated over the intended target. They were redirected to the west to attack enemy positions a few miles north of Haeju in North Korea's South Hwanghae Province (YC-4018).

Hooper, Friend, and Aaron arrived over the target at 1900, two hours after taking off. They met no resistance during the attack, dropping 7.5 tons of ordnance in the target area. The three Skyraiders turned for K-6, reaching the base by 1924.

The next attack occurred just north of the "Punchbowl." Flying a close air support mission, Merritt, Barr, Merkle, and Carpenter took off at 1830. On the way to their intended target in North Korean territory (DT-235451), they too were diverted to a new target about two miles east-northeast of the original. The squadron command diary for the month of July states no flak was encountered, but Barr recalls facing machine-gun fire from the North Koreans.[57]

In any case, none of the Skyraiders were damaged. Unfortunately, after dropping nearly eight tons of bombs, damage caused could not be determined. The Skyraiders turned for home and were on the ground at K-6 by 2000.

Another close air support mission took off at 1837, just as the roar of the preceding four Skyraiders receded into the encroaching twilight. The intended target area was northeast of the "Punchbowl" (DT-275458) within a mile of the front lines of the ROK's 20th Infantry Division. Fine, Euwema, Martin, and O'Keefe arrived over the target at 1925, dropping slightly more than twelve tons of bombs with no interference from the North Koreans. A secondary explosion was observed as the aircraft turned for home, providing, at last, some measure of the effectiveness of their attack. They had arrived back at K-6, no doubt looking forward to reporting the explosion during their debrief, by 2005.

At 1850, Harwood, Bearden, Delacqua, and Simpson were wheels up as they set a course towards the "Punchbowl" area for another close air support mission, this time striking a target area eight miles northeast of the "Punchbowl" near the corps boundary of X Corps and the ROK's I Corps (DT-376458).

Arriving over the target area at 1927, they dropped five tons of ordnance unopposed. The damage could not be determined. The Skyraiders turned for home and, no doubt sharing the circuit with the previous mission, were wheels down at K-6 by 2005.

At some time between 2000 and 2030, the squadron put up another four Skyraiders on what would be the squadron's last combat mission of the war. Barton, Foster, Aaron, and Merritt were assigned to fly an MPQ attack in support of the 1st Marine Division. Where they placed their bombs is not known with certainty since the squadron's command chronology lists two different locations: they were briefed to attack a target CT-03401260 eight miles north of the 1st Marine Division's front lines. According to the command chronology, they did—dropping twelve 2,000-pound bombs. However, the same report states Foster dropped his three bombs five miles south CT-001208 at 2125, becoming the last Marine pilot of the Korean War to drop his bombs on the enemy.[58] No flak was encountered, and all the aircraft returned safely before the ceasefire went into effect at 2200. In a press release located within the 1st MAW's July 1953 Command Diary, Foster said he was "very happy to be the last Marine aviator to drop his bombs in this war."[59]

At 2200, the armistice ended the Korean War. VMA-251's involvement was short, but busy. It flew 310 combat sorties, for a total of 551 combat hours. The squadron's busiest day was 27 July, when its pilots flew 124 combat hours.[60] No aircraft were lost in expending 1,293,620 pounds of ordnance while striking their assigned targets. The Marines of VMA-251 performed their job well, earning the Navy Unit Commendation streamer, the National Defense Service Streamer, and the Korean Service Streamer with one Bronze Star.

However, the effectiveness of the missions is frustratingly hard to determine. For most of the missions, it was impossible to assess any damage. This may be attributed to the lousy weather conditions in which the pilots had to fly. Since assessment of damage had to be done either by teams on the ground or by pilots in the air, the fog, rain, low ceiling, and dark nights seems to have made this impossible to do, especially when targets were behind enemy lines and in mountainous terrain.

As for the type of targets the pilots hit, many remain unknown, especially the MPQ missions. Squadron records state 36 buildings destroyed and six damaged, five secondary explosions, three road bridges damaged, one rail line

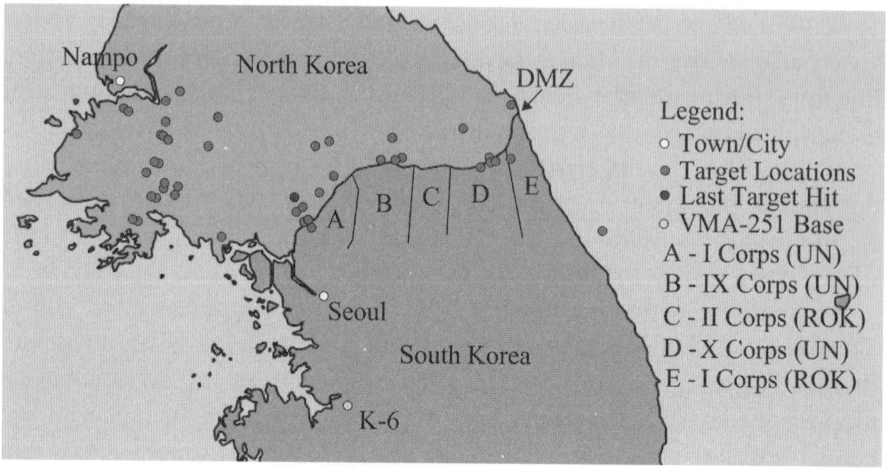

VMA-251 targets and base location (K-6) in Korea

damaged, and one railroad bridge destroyed and two damaged. As for the other missions, one can get an idea of what they may have hit by looking at the MAG-12 Damage Assessment Table in the July 1953 Command Diary, as well as the 1st MAW Command Diary for the same month: bunkers, gun positions, personnel shelters, trenches, tents, guns, supply shelters, ammunition dumps, trucks, caves, supply stacks, tanks, automatic weapons, mortars, boats, carts, observation posts, oxen, and other targets.

Over the years since the armistice was signed, tensions have risen and fallen between North and South Korea. With North Korea's nuclear program now in full swing and its sporadic test-launching of ballistic missiles, it is a matter of time when an incident will occur, forcing the United States and China to make some hard choices.

CHAPTER 4

Keeping the Peace

Following a day of rest, the squadron prepared for its new mission in a post-war Korea. The squadron was assigned the mission of night defense against possible attacks by enemy aircraft in the K-6–Seoul area, taking over from VMC-1 (Marine Composite Squadron) and the Royal Navy's 810 Naval Air Squadron[1] by early September. It was also assigned to provide close combat support at night—if needed—and would assume this duty as soon as enough pilots were trained. It did not help matters that the squadron did not have the proper aircraft for night intercept missions. To that end, one AD-4N Skyraider (a night intercept version with an AN/APS-19 or AN/APS-31 radar pod as well as an Aero 3A searchlight pod)[2] and an airborne intercept operator from VMC-1 were assigned to help train VMA-251 personnel in night interceptions.

With K-6 not having the facilities to train pilots in night-time close air support missions, Harwood sent a request in August to the Commanding General, 1st Marine Air Wing (MAW), for training facilities, suggesting the "Suwon Bomb Range[3] as well as floating targets in the Asan-Man Estuary."[4] While squadron personnel did receive training in night close air support while at El Toro, they had not flown any such missions since. Commanding Officer Harwood felt it was "mandatory that this training be continued; both in order to maintain the high degree of efficiency attained, as well as to further develop new methods of accomplishing"[5] its new mission. Harwood also believed the training would establish standard operating procedures "covering all phases of night close air support."[6]

However, there were three types of target illumination the squadron was not trained in: Cross Beam Method, Single Beam Marking Round Method, and the Crossed Tracer Method. In Korea the squadron was not exposed to any of those methods during training. Instead, the method used required one-million-candlepower flares which were dropped by a forward air controller to mark the target. This was a new procedure and one the squadron had not been exposed to. Once the target was "illuminated and the strike leader oriented, he would assume control of the flare plane."[7] Two flares would then be dropped for each run, set to ignite at 2,000 feet above the target. At that point, the aircraft would make their attack runs.

Until Harwood's recommendation was either approved or denied, the squadron instituted a training program for its officers and enlisted men to be conducted once a week. During the rest of the week, pilots accumulated hours through instructional sorties, ground control approach (GCA) sorties, test hops and cross-country flights. When the AD-4N arrived on 10 August, pilots began using it to hone their skills in night intercept work. The training continued into September.

While still in a training mode, the squadron began flying night patrol missions on 1 September. On the 6th, the British squadron was relieved of its night intercept duties. A week later, VMC-1 was also relieved of its duty of flying low-altitude night patrols. At this point, VMA-251 took over the duties of patrolling Incheon–Seoul airspace, usually under the control of *Elgin*, the Fifth Air Force Tactical Air Direction Center, as well as the low-altitude night patrol missions. By 20 September, the squadron had trained all pilots as observers under the supervision of the air intercept operator. On the same day, the squadron returned the AD-4N aircraft to VMC-1. Since the squadron still did not have the aircraft to fly the night patrols, it continued to borrow them from VMC-1. Why the first aircraft was transferred back to VMC-1 in the first place is a question that cannot be answered. The responsibility of debriefing pilots returning from night patrols was assumed by the squadron Operations Section on 24 September, taking over the job previously held by VMF(N)–513 (a specialist Marine night fighter unit), also located at K-6. By the end of September, 11 pilots in the squadron were qualified for night patrol intercept missions.

These missions were typically flown late in the evening or the early morning hours before sunrise. The area patrolled usually extended slightly west of Incheon to a point several miles east of Seoul. In some cases, squadron aircraft patrolled airspace between designated airfields. If any unknown aircraft (bogeys) were contacted, the aircraft was to intercept and identify. Fortunately, these were few. Most of the time, the night patrol intercept missions were uneventful.

The availability of aircraft to fly missions remained high until mid-September when the squadron suffered a critical shortage of tires for the Skyraiders. By 26 September, 10 of the 24 aircraft on hand were grounded as a result. Training hops were curtailed until 28 September when the squadron received eight tires, not nearly enough to prolong operations. Combined with the difficulty of obtaining gyro instruments, the average number of aircraft available for missions was 18.[8]

The night patrols continued into October: most resulted in no contacts. However, on a few missions, there was a bit of excitement for the pilots involved. On 2 October, Ralph Euwema, now a captain, developed on oil leak while on a mission. He made a forced landing at K-5 (Taejon). Upon touchdown, his right front tire blew out, forcing him to stay overnight. The next day, a mechanic and the necessary equipment were flown to K-5 to repair the aircraft. Euwema flew back to K-6 at 1030.

Seven days later, Raymond Delacqua, one of the squadron's three NAPs (enlisted pilot), was patrolling Incheon to a point 40 miles east when his aircraft developed mechanical problems. He aborted his mission, returned to K-6, grabbed another aircraft, and took off to complete his task. No contacts were made.

Albert Aaron, while flying a night patrol on 17 October aborted his mission due to mechanical difficulties. Landing at K-6, he also got into another aircraft and resumed his mission. He returned shortly after midnight.

Two days later, Walter Simpson's Skyraider had to make an emergency landing at K-52 (Yanggu) after developing a leak in the hydraulic system. He remained at the base overnight until the aircraft was repaired, then returned to K-6. On the same day, Lieutenant Colonel Frank Porter made a forced landing at K-8 (Kunsan) when the propeller control rod sheared off just forward of the fire wall. The plane was repaired, and Porter returned to K-6. The following day, he assumed the duties of squadron executive officer.

During mid-October, VMA-251 assumed the task of briefing its pilots prior to each night patrol mission. Conducting the briefings was the squadron operations duty officer. They were previously performed by Marine Air Group (MAG) 12 personnel.

Near the end of the month, the unit began night close air support training using searchlights to locate and indicate targets. The searchlights were set up at the Suwon Bombing Range and operated by a unit of the 1st Marine Division. Harwood's recommendation in August for such a practice area was apparently approved.

On 28 October, all squadron pilots attended a briefing in the MAG-12 briefing room for the *Marlex*[9] *III* exercise. The following day, as a rehearsal for the exercise, scheduled to start on the 30th, the squadron flew 22 sorties in support of the 2nd Battalion, 1st Marines (Reinforced), landing on the island of Tokchok-To west-southwest of Incheon in Kyönggi Bay.

Marlex III commenced as scheduled with the squadron flying 16 close air support sorties as the Marines landed on the island. At the same time, the Commandant of the Marine Corps, General Lemuel C. Shepherd, Jr., visited K-6 and inspected the squadron area.

Night patrols also continued until the end of the month with no contacts made. During one of the patrols, Burrel Sumner's radar failed. He returned to K-6 and grabbed another Skyraider to complete his mission. He patrolled the Incheon area and made no contacts or interceptions before returning to K-6, landing just before 0100.[10]

As November moved in, the squadron faced its first bout with cold weather and the difficulties that come with it, especially when it came to the maintenance of aircraft. The mechanics only had one "nose hangar" to use when working on the Skyraider engines. Insulation had been applied at an earlier date and four heaters had been installed to blow hot air into the hangar.

During the month, the squadron began to lose its experienced pilots as they transferred out. Pilots from VMA-332, as well as replacements from the United States, took over. The squadron's operations department immediately began checking out the new pilots on night patrol and night attack missions.

Despite the changes, the squadron continued its night patrols into December, as well as training missions consisting of bombing, check out on instruments, cross-country flights, strafing, rockets, and familiarization flights.[11] Winter weather either delayed or cancelled some of the planned missions.

The squadron suffered a serious mishap on 31 December. At 1345, Second Lieutenant William C. Durand took off in an AD-4 (BuNo 123898) for a scheduled GCA flight. After completing a few GCA landings, Durand discovered he was unable to lower his right main wheel. Every trick in the book was used to force the gear to lower, including bouncing the left main wheel on the runway. All emergency procedures failed, forcing Durand to make a wheels-up landing on the runway at K-6. The propeller, flaps, and wheel well doors of the aircraft were damaged, but Durand escaped injury.

During the month of January,[12] the personnel situation became critical. Two pilots and one enlisted man had been assigned, but six pilots and 30 enlisted men were transferred out. The squadron also lost a pilot and his AD-4B (BuNo 132279) in a fatal accident.

The accident occurred at 2345 on 4 January when the unfortunate Durand crashed while on a routine night patrol. He had just completed an intercept of a friendly aircraft while under *Elgin*'s control when he complained of vertigo and requested a steer home. Soon afterward, *Elgin* lost radar and radio contact with Durand and a nearby VMF(N)-513 aircraft reported an explosion approximately twenty-eight miles due east of K-6. Low overcast and haze in the area made an air search impossible. Early the next morning, Korean National Police found the wreckage and Durand's remains.

According to the accident report, the Skyraider "struck the ground in an 80 degree left spiral and about 450 knots. The initial contact was made with the port wingtip. The plane then cartwheeled onto its nose and exploded. The Skyraider was completely demolished, and wreckage was strewn for nearly 200 yards."[13] It was the conclusion of the accident board that Durand "made a steep, rapid, breakaway from the target plane and immediately experienced vertigo from which he did not recover. It is also a possibility that during his break away he 'tumbled' his gyro instruments and was unable to make a partial panel recovery with his turn and bank indicator."[14] It was the squadron's first fatal accident since 13 May 1952.

Flight operations were curtailed for most of the month due to severe winter weather as well as an ordered stand-down for a scheduled prisoner exchange. Normal flight operations did not resume until 25 January. Taking advantage of the downtime, the squadron exchanged some of its AD-3 Skyraiders for some of VMA-121's AD-4s, giving VMA-251 more aircraft capable of night radar intercept work. It also acquired two AD-4s from Japan. At the end of the month, a dispatch from the Commanding General, AIRFMFPAC (Air Fleet Marine Force, Pacific), was received stating that plans had been made to equip six squadron AD-4B aircraft with special weapons capabilities.[15] No details were given, but material assignments were to occur later.

Winter weather continued to hamper operations in February,[16] as did the continuing loss of personnel due to end of service and transfer home. The number of Naval Aviators assigned to the squadron stood at 32. Despite the loss of personnel, the squadron received a new Table of Organization (T/O) which increased the authorized number of enlisted personnel to 220. The number assigned at the end of January stood at 128. Where the extra enlisted men would come from to bring the squadron up to T/O strength remained an unanswered question.

A massive search for a fellow Marine highlighted the squadron's actions for the month. Herbert Peters saw extensive action with VMO-251 during the squadron's assignment on Guadalcanal during World War II. Peters, then a second lieutenant, was credited with shooting down four Japanese aircraft, making him the squadron's top gun. On 5 February, Peters, now a lieutenant colonel with Headquarters, and Headquarters Squadron, 1st MAW, took off in an OY[17] light aircraft from K-3 (Pohang) at 1310.[18] He quickly became lost in a massive snowstorm. Spending some time looking for a break in the clouds, he found one and located an airstrip to land his aircraft. When he landed, Peters no doubt realized he had made an error when his aircraft was rushed by North Korean soldiers. He came to halt as the soldiers hung on to his airplane. Peters was apprehended and became a prisoner of the North Koreans.[19]

The following day, 1st MAW squadrons, including VMA-251, as well as units of the Fifth Air Force launched a massive search operation to locate Peters. The squadron had one mishap on the first day of the search. Second Lieutenant Sidney Neblett's Skyraider (BuNo 132275) suffered an engine failure, forcing Neblett to make a wheels-up landing in a rice paddy approximately three miles northwest of Gongju and 33 miles south of K-6. The aircraft suffered extensive damage, enough to require an overhaul. Neblett escaped with no injuries.

For three days, units scoured the countryside from the air looking for any sign of Peters. None was found. At 1135 on 9 February, the commanding general of the 1st MAW called off the search for the missing Marine.[20]

It was thought by many that Peters was either missing or dead. No word of his capture was sent by the North Koreans. It came with great surprise to everyone, including Peters' family, when they were told of his return from North Korea eight months later.[21]

The lousy weather that had curtailed operations for the previous few months finally began to break in March, allowing the squadron to increase its flight hours. Training exercises and operational flights resumed with gusto. Sorties included bombing, close air support, cross-country flights, navigation problems, instrument flights, test hops, target spotting, familiarization flights, interdiction exercises, flare drops and night tactics, GCA exercises, section tactics, rocket and strafing exercises, radar training, and scrambles due to alert exercises held at K-6.

Several incidents highlighted the month for the squadron. Beginning on 6 March, the Marines flew dozens of sorties in search of South Korean Brigadier General Kim Yung Hwan, who was last reported flying a Republic of Korea (ROK) F-51 Mustang near the east coast. The search for the general continued until 9 March when it was called off. Existing documents do not indicate if he was ever found.

Two aircraft were knocked out of commission in separate incidents. On 12 March, Second Lieutenant Dennis W. Wright developed engine trouble in his AD-4 (BuNo 129008) approximately twenty-six miles east of K-6. Wright was able to nurse his ailing machine home, but the aircraft stalled out over the runway extension, shearing the landing gear. The Skyraider was severely damaged, and Wright received minor injuries. Thirteen days later, Second Lieutenant Thomas F. Miller ran off the runway in his AD-3 (BuNo 122808) while attempting a night take-off during an assigned rocket mission. Miller was uninjured, but his aircraft sustained damage severe enough to require an overhaul.

On 24 March, the squadron participated in another search for a downed pilot. Second Lieutenant Joseph R. St. Louis, a flyer with VMA-121, took off for an early morning training mission over the Yellow Sea. Unfortunately, he ended up crashing.[22] Five Skyraiders equipped with APS-19 radar took off in search of St. Louis. It was hoped they would be able to pick up a signal from his life raft radar reflector. A visual search was impossible due to fog between 600 feet and sea level. The following day, the squadron flew 10 sorties in search of St. Louis. His body was never recovered. VMA-121 carried him on their rolls as missing until 8 April when he was officially declared dead.[23]

The squadron was selected to participate in a Fifth Air Force training exercise, dubbed Operation *Candy Counter*. VMA-251 was assigned to the aggressor forces for the exercise. On 29 March, eight Skyraiders (callsign *Typhoon 7*) took off at 0435. Following completion of their flight, all returned to K-6. The next eight Skyraiders (*Typhoon 52*) were scheduled to take off at 1405, but the mission was aborted due to a fuel screw-up.

It was discovered the aircraft had been refueled with JP-4 (fuel for jet engines!) instead of 145 octane gasoline, the fuel the Skyraider needed. The mistake occurred when an inexperienced truck driver was dispatched to the fuel dump to reload. The reloading was then conducted by Korean laborers. One aircraft, an AD-3N (BuNo 122917), had departed for K-3 before the refueling error was discovered. The pilot was notified and, after landing at K-3, the fuel tank was drained and refilled with the correct fuel. The pilot had experienced popping and detonation on take-off, as well as excessive cylinder head temperatures during the flight.[24]

The month of April began with all squadron aircraft grounded for a thorough check for any possible structural fatigue. The check was made in response to the loss of the VMA-121 Skyraider piloted by St. Louis, which may have disintegrated in the air.[25] No discrepancies were found; the Marines resumed their normal flying operations the following day.

The training of squadron pilots in special weapons delivery was finally initiated. Ground training consisted of 140 hours of classroom training through a series of lectures, and nearly one hundred hours of flight time. Wiring in the five AD-4B Skyraiders assigned to participate in the training was checked and brought up to date with the required modifications. In-flight control equipment was tested as was all necessary ground-handling equipment.

On 9 April, eight squadron aircraft were used in a simulated strike on Sasebo, Japan. The mission was flown inbound without IFF (identification friend or foe) to test the readiness of the Japanese air defenses. The flight was intercepted shortly after entering the Japanese air defense identification zone.

There was only one mishap recorded for the month. On 28 April, while making a practice GCA approach to K-6, Second Lieutenant Duane H. Albert made a wheels-up landing in his AD-4 (BuNo 128989). During one of his practice runs, Albert was notified by his chase pilot that his right landing gear was twisted 80 degrees from its normal position. He decided to land his aircraft wheels-up. After remaining airborne for nearly four hours to burn off fuel to reduce the possibility of fire, Albert brought the Skyraider in. Despite his best efforts, the plane was severely damaged and required an extensive rebuild. Albert received minor injuries.

It was determined the cause of the accident was an internal failure of the right main landing gear shock strut. The strut's upper bearing nut had worked its way loose, causing the axle assembly to drop and disengage from the splines while the aircraft was in flight. This caused the main wheel and axle assembly to rotate the 80 degrees from its normal position and allowed the wheel to spin 360 degrees. It was suspected the nut had not been properly tightened when a new strut was installed by VA-65 on 16 July 1952 following a barrier crash by the aircraft carrier.[26]

As May began, training in special weapons delivery continued. The training emphasized 70-degree dive bombing on the ranges available. However, the ranges were not set up to handle the training since no dive-angle calibration equipment designed for low-altitude releases was installed. Work was in progress at a nearby range to install the equipment. Until it was complete, the current ranges had to be used.

Training in the loft-bombing technique was also begun, but no drops were made. The six AD-4Bs designated for use in loft bombing had not yet been modified to do the job. Equipment was ordered and the Skyraiders were to be modified when that came in.

On 4 May, the squadron sent 11 officers, 16 enlisted men, and six AD-4Bs to Naval Air Station (NAS) Atsugi, Japan, to participate in loading operations of special weapons. The pilots made several heavy load take-offs with the MK-7 and MK-8 tactical nuclear weapons, as well as making in-flight checks with the T-63 and T-64 practice units. Six of the pilots made low-altitude Japanese Air Defense Force penetration flights against three targets on the island of

Honshu, simulating special weapons delivery. Nearly 150 MK-76 bombs were dropped on a high-altitude bombing range on the island.

There was one incident while the detachment was at NAS Atsugi. Returning to the air station following a practice bombing hop, Second Lieutenant John H. Dunn experienced an engine failure in his AD-4B (BuNo 123309).[27] He made a successful landing at Atsugi, and a new engine was installed.

Following completion of the training, the detachment returned to the squadron at K-6 on 14 May.

On 21 May, another AD-4B (BuNo 132316) was grounded at Itami, Japan, and required an engine change. The change was necessary due to excessive use of oil. It is unclear as to how the aircraft ended up at Itami.

The squadron rehearsed for an exercise dubbed *Marlex V* on 23 May and, on the 25th, six Skyraiders provided simulated night close air support for the exercise, dropping flares to illuminate the target area. As the squadron flew one of its night missions, automatic weapons fire was observed near the target area approximately five miles west of the east coast city of Sokcho. An investigation determined the fire to be ricochet tracers from an ROK rifle range in the area.

As the squadron readied for the *Marlex* exercise, it received word that its insignia—the Black Patch—submitted before leaving for Korea in 1953, had been approved by the Chief of Naval Operations.[28]

The squadron continued its normal operations in June, flying 578 sorties, of which 249 were non-combat bombing missions. Other sorties flown were interdiction, instrument, rockets close air support, cross-country, GCA, and a host of others. Twenty-one sorties were aborted due to mechanical or equipment failures.

From 13 to 27 June, the squadron sent another detachment to NAS Atsugi for special weapons training. The detachment consisted of 14 officers, 12 enlisted men and three AD-4 Skyraiders. The Marines received checkouts on weapons and practiced loading procedures.

While flying as a tactical air observer for *Marlex VI* on 16 June, Major Leroy Barton's engine failed. The Skyraider (BuNo 123887) caught fire and began to disintegrate. Barton was forced to bail out but landed without injury. He was immediately picked up by helicopter. The wreckage of the destroyed aircraft was located 115 miles east-northeast of K-6 near the coastal town of Gangneung.

Near the end of the month, eight of the squadron's Skyraiders participated in Operation *Home Plate*, a Fifth Air Force radar defense exercise designed to test the readiness of airfields throughout the Republic of Korea. VMA-251 was assigned to the aggressor forces. However, due to bad weather, the Skyraiders were not able to reach their pre-assigned targets and returned to K-6.[29]

The squadron continued its operations out of K-6 for the next three months. The standard sorties continued as did training of the special weapons unit. On 24 August, the Commandant of the Marine Corps, General Lemuel C. Shepherd, Jr., was at K-6 for an inspection and visited VMA-251. He received a tour of the squadron's special weapons building and observed a demonstration of the relevant equipment.

On 27 August, during a late morning approach for a landing at K-6, First Lieutenant Richard M. Gessaman faced a severe crosswind and a low ceiling with light rain showers as he returned from a familiarization flight. As he made his approach using instruments, he stalled (not enough airspeed maintained) and the AD-4 (BuNo 129009) spun into the ground before he could recover. The Skyraider was destroyed as it impacted, bursting into flames and breaking into several pieces. Gessaman was alive but unconscious when he was removed from the cockpit by emergency personnel. He had suffered third degree burns over 60% of his body and his jaw was broken. A helicopter transported him to the 121st Evacuation Hospital where he succumbed to his injuries. He had joined the squadron just five days before following duty with the 3rd Marine Division as a forward air controller.[30]

Special weapons training picked up its pace during July despite lousy weather for most of the month. One hundred sorties were flown, with training in high-altitude bombing and the loft technique. Training slowed in August as preparations were made to have the special weapons detail permanently moved to Japan. On 7 September, that move was made. Six AD-4Bs were sent to NAS Atusgi along with qualified pilots and enlisted men. The special weapons detachment was placed under the command of Headquarters and Maintenance Squadron (H&MS) 11, MAG-11 at Atsugi. With the transfer of the six AD-4Bs, the squadron had 12 Skyraiders left on strength, one of which was receiving an engine change at H&MS-12, also located at K-6. This left just 11 operational Skyraiders in the squadron.[31]

The Marines flew their normal assortment of sorties from October to December: bombing sorties, instrument flights, air-to-air gunnery, reconnaissance missions over the 38th Parallel (also known as the "main line of resistance" or MLR), navigation training, and familiarization flights to name a few. During the three-month period, the squadron flew 1,694 sorties, with 36 aborts, for a total of 3,078 hours. There were no aircraft accidents for the period. After several months of construction, the engineering department received a new hangar, but perhaps the highlight of the quarter was a Christmas party held for the children from a nearby orphanage. Thirty were entertained, each one escorted by a member of the squadron. Santa Claus arrived by helicopter and gave each child a coat. Finally, each of the orphans received a meal at the enlisted mess hall on the base.

As for the special weapons detachment at NAS Atsugi, it continued its intensive training in the use of tactical nuclear weapons. During the three-month period, the detachment flew 468 sorties for a total of 848 hours, which included close air support for the 3rd Marine Division during an exercise in November. Training flights concentrated on high-altitude, high-angle dive bombing and loft bombing. Additional emphasis was placed on long-range, low-level navigation. In addition, field carrier landing practice was also carried out. Pilots also flew training flights while carrying the T-63 and T-64 practice bombs.[32]

The first quarter of 1955 saw the squadron make a move to its new duty station. Until the move was made, normal operations continued, flying a variety of missions. On 10 March, the squadron lost another Skyraider (BuNo 123810) and pilot. Second Lieutenant James F. Kunzmann was taking off in his AD-4 for a routine bombing exercise when his Skyraider veered to the left with its nose high and collided with a 16-foot embankment near the runway. The aircraft burst into flames, killing Kunzmann. An investigation determined pilot error to be the cause of the accident.[33] Kunzmann had recently joined the squadron, transferring from VMA-212 on 1 March.

From the 21st to the 28th, the squadron spent the week transferring to its new duty station, K-3 airbase near Pohang on the central east coast of South Korea. The move was made without a hitch. Squadron aircraft arrived at K-3 at noon on 28 March and immediately began operations from their new home.

The Atsugi detachment continued the same training flights, as mentioned for October, through December 1954. A 1st MAW exercise was conducted on 15 March 1955. Major Robert. L. Allen, commanding the detachment, oversaw his unit's participation in the exercise. Assigned teams loaded the MK-7 and MK-8 weapons, and pilots planned a simulated strike. One pilot flew with the T-63 practice bomb. Results showed the unit's performance was satisfactory. The unit once again flew close air support missions for the 3rd Marine Division. For the first three months of the year, the detachment flew 526 sorties for nearly eight hundred sixty-four hours.[34]

From April to June 1955, there was no change in routine as the squadron settled in at K-3. The training flights continued with the squadron racking up nearly five thousand hours across more than 2,000 sorties.

Several incidents occurred during the period that involved the squadron. The first occurred in May[35] and could have had severe repercussions for those involved. First Lieutenant Robert A. Gillon was leading an MLR reconnaissance flight along the 38th Parallel when gunfire lit up the sky, damaging his AD-4 Skyraider (BuNo 128981) in the port wing. The source of the gunfire could not be determined. Gillon was not injured; he was able to nurse his aircraft back to K-3. His wingman, Second Lieutenant John C. Olson, escorted him home.[36] The wing was replaced within 48 hours and the Skyraider put back in operation. A flash report of the incident was sent up the chain of command (MAG-12 and 1st MAW).[37] First Lieutenant Kenneth C. Sanguinetti provided more detail, revealing the incident to be much more dangerous than the squadron command diary for May 1955 indicated:

> Four ADs from VMA-251 were assigned to fly CAP[38] over the MLR (38th Parallel). The flight was led by 1st Lt. Bob Gillon; I was flying as section leader with Lt. Chauncy Clark[39] as my wingman (tail-end Charlie). We were in a racetrack pattern over the MLR when I noticed these little gray clouds appearing at our altitude directly in front of us.
>
> I got on the mic and said we are being fired on; break left. We broke left but since Chauncy Clark was hanging back he was able to spot where the antiaircraft fire was coming from and called out that he had them in sight and was rolling in for a run on the target.
>
> We were under positive radar control and under the command of the Air Force and the controller came up on the radio and told us to break off the run and return to base. Lt. Clark came up on the radio and said, "your transmission was breaking up and unclear but that he understood he was cleared in for a live run" and he continued his run.
>
> Since I was now his wingman, I followed him down in the run and watched him fire … [twelve 5-inch] rockets and drop in salvo three bombs (I think they were 500 pounders). All the while the Air Force controller was saying break off, do not drop your ordnance. Since my radio worked fine, I did not drop any ordnance but just followed Lt. Clark down in case he got hit. I saw him pull up and watched fireworks as his bombs and rockets hit.
>
> Then the flight joined up and we headed home to K-6.[40] When we landed, we found that the flight leader Lt. Gillon had an eight inch hole in his horizontal stabilizer[41] and a six inch hole in the oil cooler. And of course, the NCO in charge of fixing Chauncy's radio did find a loose wire.[42]

MAG-12 attributed the gunfire to ROK forces since the mission occurred over an area occupied by forces of the II ROK Army Corps.[43] Apparently there were no repercussions for the four pilots involved, and available documents do not indicate any investigation into the incident. The aircraft was definitely damaged but whether it was the port wing, as squadron documents indicate, or the horizontal stabilizer and oil cooler, as Sanguinetti recalls, is anyone's guess.

An accident that occurred on 3 June resulted in the loss of an AD-4 (BuNo 123900). First Lieutenant Lloyd C. Dillon was on a close air support flight somewhere over South Korea when his engine failed. He made a successful wheels-up landing. Dillon was uninjured. An investigation into the mishap determined either material failure or a malfunction. Exactly where Dillon made his wheels-up landing is not stated.

The last incident occurred on the last day of June 1955. Upon landing at K-3, Captain William D. Thayer, Jr.'s AD-4 (BuNo 123839) ground-looped, substantially damaging the aircraft. Thayer apparently did not receive any injuries.

The Marines at Atsugi continued their training in the use of tactical nuclear weapons. Under orders from the 1st MAW, the unit conducted an exercise from 9 to 13 May. They flew simulated nuclear strikes on designated targets on Shikoku Island. Three missions were completed, dropping MK-7 and MK-8 practice munitions. A third mission carrying a T-63 shape was diverted to NAS Iwakuni and stayed overnight to allow the MWSG-17 (Marine Wing Service Group 17) Bomb Disposal Team to get some practice. Four additional missions were aborted due to lousy weather.[44]

It was at this time that documents from the squadron ceased. Regulations at the time did not require squadrons to file Command Chronologies unless in active combat. The only document in the National Archives between July 1955 and June 1965 is a report of the squadron's deployment aboard USS *Shangri-La* (CVA-38) in 1962. For the rest of 1955, it can be assumed the squadron continued its mission patrolling the skies of Korea and providing ground support in case of attack by the North Koreans. The squadron had three aircraft involved in accidents between July and December 1955: an AD-4B (BuNo 132272) piloted by First Lieutenant Lee E. Blanchard suffered moderate damage in a mishap in Japan on 25 October; two days later, First Lieutenant Philip T. Smith was killed when his AD-4 (BuNo 128952) was destroyed while flying a mission near Okinawa; the last mishap occurred on 16 December when First Lieutenant Robert S. Reed's AD-4 (BuNo 123791) was damaged at K-3. Blanchard and Reed may have been assigned to the Atsugi detachment at the time. No further details of these accidents exist; the aircraft accident reports at the Naval History and Heritage Command (NHHC) could not be located.

Towards the end of 1955, the squadron no doubt received word of its change of duty station. If the Marines of the squadron were looking forward to a trip back to the United States, they were to be disappointed. After nearly three years in Korea, a trip home was not to be. VMA-251 would be heading to the naval air station at Iwakuni. While the exact reason why the squadron stayed in the Far East for so long is not known, the ongoing feud between China and Taiwan may have had something to do with its extended stay.

China and Taiwan each claimed several strategic islands in the Taiwan Strait. Jinmen was located two miles off the Chinese coast while Mazu was located about one hundred miles west of Taiwan. When Chiang Kai-shek lost control of China, his government fled to Taiwan and forces also occupied the two islands in the strait as well as the Dachens, further north. In the early 1950s, Chiang's forces launched minor attacks against the Chinese mainland from Jinmen and Mazu. These attacks had little effect except to anger China.

The United States, at one time, was prepared to let China cross the strait and defeat Chiang but, with the outbreak of the Korean War, the U.S. sent its Seventh Fleet into the Taiwan Strait to prevent the Korean conflict from expanding to the south. This move angered the Chinese government, which had transferred troops poised for the Taiwan invasion to the Korean front.

In late 1954, the U.S. led an effort to establish the Southeast Asia Treaty Organization. It was hoped the treaty would unify the region against the perceived communist threat. The U.S. was also considering a Mutual Defense Treaty with Taiwan. China viewed these developments as threats to its security, and its leadership in the region, and reacted by bombarding Jinmen, as well as Mazu and the Dachen Islands.

This act by the Chinese prompted the U.S. to sign the Mutual Defense Treaty with Taiwan. The treaty did not commit the U.S. to defend the contested islands, but it did promise support to Taiwan should it find itself in a larger conflict with China.

Tensions continued into 1955. With the passage of the Formosa Resolution, the U.S. Congress gave then President Eisenhower absolute authority to defend Taiwan and the disputed islands. Soon after, the U.S. promised to defend Taiwan from communist aggression but did not mention the islands. However, in a private exchange with Chiang Kai-shek, the U.S. promised to help Taiwan defend Jinmen and Mazu but only if Taiwan gave up the Dachens, which they did.

In the spring of 1955, China expressed a desire to negotiate with the U.S., perhaps prompted by the Soviet Union in order to ease tensions in the area. Talks began in September and dragged on with no resolution.

Instead, in 1958, China began to bombard the disputed islands. The U.S. quickly resupplied the Taiwanese forces on the two islands which caused China to halt the bombardments. Tensions eased and eventually China and

Taiwan reached an odd arrangement: they each shelled each other's garrisons on alternate days. This arrangement continued for two decades when China and the United States normalized relations.[45]

Another problem was brewing further south—Vietnam. France completed its conquest of the region in the late 1800s. Its colonial rule was harsh and led the Vietnamese to ultimately revolt. Soon after World War II ended, Ho Chi Minh sought to enlist U.S. help to establish Vietnamese self-rule by declaring an independent North and modeling his declaration on the U.S. Declaration of Independence. The U.S. opposed the move and Ho Chi Minh, a communist since the 1920s, sought help from both China and the Soviet Union. The U.S. began aiding the French, but it was all to no avail; by 1954, Vietnamese forces had defeated the French, culminating with the loss of Dien Bien Phu. Soon after, the Geneva Accords established a North and South Vietnam. Despite the agreement, Ho Chi Minh continued his fight for a unified Vietnam. The U.S. thus began to aid the South Vietnamese to shore up its democratic leanings. By July 1959, the first U.S. soldiers were killed when communist forces attacked their quarters in the capital of South Vietnam, Saigon. The spiral had begun and would soon lead to the huge U.S. commitment in the 1960s.

The squadron made the move to Iwakuni in January 1956. From 7 to 10 January, personnel and equipment were moved by government transport and began operations soon after establishing themselves at the base.[46]

Iwakuni was home for the next 15 months. It is not known if the squadron made any deployments since the relevant records do not exist. Operations continued to take their toll, however; between February 1956 and February 1957, the squadron lost four aircraft and five damaged, with one pilot killed.

On 14 March 1956, First Lieutenant John H. Taylor was scheduled to fly a practice close air support mission. Taylor was the number two man of a two-plane flight. His flight leader, First Lieutenant Floyd V. Zoch, gave the mission briefing. Pre-flight checks went well and both aircraft were wheels up at 1325. Their course was a heading of 135 degrees. They leveled off at 5,000 feet, changed course and continued to their orbit point over the town of Iyo-Nagahama, approximately forty miles south-southeast of Iwakuni.

Taylor and Zoch were near their orbit point when they were jumped by a single Skyraider—one of two from an earlier section launched before Taylor and Zoch departed Iwakuni—flown by Second Lieutenant Gerald M. Kibbe.[47] Taylor and Zoch increased power and began a climbing turn to 7,000 feet.

As Taylor was climbing, his engine exploded causing his aircraft to lose power. He switched to rich mixture, direct air, and tried to change RPM to regain power but nothing worked. Taylor notified Zoch of his problem. Zoch told him to make for an emergency landing field near Matsuyama, about nineteen miles northeast of their position.

The engine on Taylor's aircraft soon began to vibrate violently and smoke began pouring out of the exhaust stacks. Taylor determined he could not maintain altitude and an emergency declaration was made. The pilots switched IFF[48] to the emergency position and the UHF channel on their radios to the guard channel. At 1355, Zoch transmitted the Mayday message.

Taylor tried to regain power by advancing his throttle and was met with more explosions from the engine. As he did a visual check, Taylor could see his left exhaust stack glowing red. He set up a glide at 125 knots. His oil pressure was down, and his oil temperature was climbing past the 100-degree mark. As the Skyraider passed through 500 feet, Taylor knew he was not going to reach the emergency airfield, so he notified Zoch he was going to ditch. Zoch continued to broadcast the Mayday message but received no answer.

Four minutes later, Taylor, with landing gear and flaps up, cowl flaps and engine cooler doors open, hit the water at a speed of just under 100 knots in a slightly nose-up position. The water was calm as the aircraft made three impacts before coming to a halt about one hundred fifty feet from the initial impact. Taylor hit the water 10 miles south of Matsuyama and approximately three miles off the coast. Zoch transmitted a crash message and circled at low altitude to keep Taylor in his sight.

As soon as the aircraft came to a halt, Taylor released his safety harness and exited the cockpit. In the water, he watched as his plane sank nose first. It disappeared within 40 seconds. Taylor released his para-raft and inflated it. It failed to fully inflate, and Taylor struggled to lift himself into it. Exhausted, he secured himself in the raft and signaled the still-circling Zoch that he was uninjured. He also tried to contact Zoch with the emergency radio in the raft but was unable to do so; the radio was inoperative.

Shortly after Taylor went down, two VMA-251 Skyraiders arrived on the scene, orbiting between 5,000 and 6,000 feet to help relay messages. Two towers and an unidentified Air Force aircraft received the Mayday messages and alerted Air–Sea Rescue (ASR).

Taylor was in the water for about fifteen minutes when two Japanese fishing boats arrived. The fishermen recovered and cared for him until an ASR amphibian arrived on the scene. He was transferred to the rescue aircraft which then left the area for NAS Iwakuni.

The Skyraider was recovered five days later and sent to Iwakuni to be examined by investigators. Because of the long exposure to salt water, the aircraft (BuNo 127860) was written off. The engine was sent to an overhaul facility at NAS Alameda, California, to be disassembled and inspected.

An inspection of the aircraft at Iwakuni found filings and pieces of metal in the two magnetic finger strainers and the main oil sump strainer. However, no definite cause of the failure was determined. The robust Skyraider suffered negligible damage from the impact and the ensuing deceleration.

Taylor, Zoch, Kibbe, and Captain Donald P. Plante were all interviewed, as was the squadron's engineering officer and flight equipment officer, and NAS Iwakuni's base operations officer. While Taylor made it out unscathed, the interviews revealed several shortcomings.

In Taylor's interview, he revealed the para-raft did not properly inflate and, had he been seriously injured, it would have been impossible for him to get into it. He also noted that, had he needed treatment for injuries, there was no doctor or medic aboard the ASR aircraft.

During an interview with the squadron's Flight Equipment Officer, Second Lieutenant Robert L. Immel stated there were no facilities at NAS Iwakuni for firing the CO_2 bottles carried by the para-rafts. His method of checking the bottles was to weigh them at the post office every three months. He stated that Taylor's bottle was last checked a week prior to the accident. Immel also noted the toggle to release the CO_2 sometimes had to be pulled twice in order to fill the raft properly. Taylor, when asked about this, said he only pulled the toggle once and was unaware he had to pull it twice. To test this claim, accident investigators picked one raft at random and tried to inflate it. They did so but did have to pull the toggle twice. As for the emergency radio, Immel said the radios were checked every three months by Marine Aircraft Repair Squadron 17 and that Taylor's radio was checked to be operating properly eight days before the accident. Again, investigators picked a radio at random. It was found to be working as it should.

While Zoch was being grilled by the investigation team, he told them it was his opinion that Iwakuni Tower was not monitoring the guard channel as he was unable to contact them. When confronted with this information, the base operations officer claimed there was a power outage at Iwakuni Tower and they could not respond to Zoch's Mayday, but that they did receive Zoch's and Plante's radio messages and initiated rescue operations. An examination of the tower tape recording confirmed the officer's statement.

Plante told investigators he was 15 miles south of Iwakuni when he heard Zoch transmit a Mayday at 1402. He relayed the message to Iwakuni Tower. Like Zoch, he received no reply. He went to a different channel and the tower immediately came up on that frequency. A minute later, an unidentified Air Force plane relayed Plante's message to an unknown tower.[49] Plante then proceeded to the scene of the accident and orbited at 6,000 feet.

Kibbe confirmed he made the pass on the aircraft and was turning away when he noticed the smoke coming from Taylor's engine. Kibbe's radio was weak, and he could not relay the Mayday message. He circled the crash area at 5,000 feet in case he could be of any assistance.

The squadron's engineering officer, Chief Warrant Officer Samuel R. Clapsadl, told investigators that, based on the pilot's description and his own experience, it may have been a failure of a part or parts that caused the engine explosion. An examination of the history of the engine revealed nothing; it had just 32 operational hours prior to the accident.

What the conclusions and recommendations of the Aircraft Accident Board were are unknown since the section in the official report was redacted.[50]

The special weapons unit[51] continued its work at Atsugi. Because of the nature of its training in the use of tactical nuclear weapons, the work was classified as secret. Ralph Sabroe, a squadron Marine assigned to the unit, recalled "on at least one occasion we provided security while a R4Q [the Navy/Marine designation for the Fairchild C-119 transport aircraft] loaded or unloaded what we believed were nuclear weapons on our base. We were required to look outbound of the progress, so we never saw what was occurring." In another incident, Sabroe remembers a sentry discovering "a Japanese National (a woman) on our flight line one night. We believed she had an accomplice outside the fence who was to set explosives on our aircraft. This was unsubstantiated by our officials."[52]

First Lieutenant Jay E. Velie was attached to the unit at Atsugi shortly after joining the squadron on 21 April.[53] He only had 80 hours of flight time in the Skyraider. On 27 July, he was scheduled to take a familiarization flight. Apparently, it was required by the squadron for newly arrived pilots. Velie recounted his accident:

> Before coming to Japan, I had been flying F2H-4 Banshees and the FJ-2 Fury [both jets] at Cherry Point, North Carolina. As was the procedure, when a new officer arrived from the states, he was given an indoctrination and a couple of fam hops.
>
> On this day, a new aviator and I took off to tour the area and our bombing site, which was north of Tokyo about a hundred miles, on the east coast. As we were leisurely tooling along, at 3000 feet, viewing the sights, my wingman advised me that I was leaking oil. Hey, what a surprise, this is an AD. He said no, I mean really leaking, like a fire hose. By this time, my wind screen was well covered with oil and then suddenly the nose of the plane burst into flames. Again, my observant wingman told me about this happening. He was very informative. I sat there for a while in a state of almost total panic. I froze. I was never so

frightened in all my life, before or since. Finally, after what seemed like 10 minutes, although my wingman later told me it was about 10 seconds, I decided that no one was going to get me out of this mess but me. Then, as corny as it may sound, the training kicked in. I slowed the aircraft some, trimmed for level flight, opened the canopy, unbuckled my seat harness, and checked to see that my chute was secure. I pulled down my goggles, which were the rubber frame and plastic lens type that were about as effective as a pair of two bit sunglasses. We did have hard hats, but no fancy pull-down visors. We had no ejection seat or extraction device in this model of the AD-6. I partially stood up and placed my feet in the seat, while crouching, and turned to the right side (at least I think it was to the right). Then I dove over the side.

That is how it was supposed to go, but as the top half of my svelte body moved into the air stream, I was forced back against the canopy. I was hung up, half in and half out, being slightly broiled by the flames. I don't remember the airspeed, but it was probably around 150 knots. No doubt I should have taken more time to slow down, but I was rather anxious to depart. I was flailing madly about and must have kicked the stick, which, according to my wingman caused the plane to roll up to about a 90 degree bank. This well executed, planned maneuver, flung me away from the poor old able dog [AD]. Now for the first time in my 24 year old life I was free as a bird and flying like a rock. I found the D-ring and pulled hard. Nothing happened, or at least I thought nothing happened. Then the chute opened and about jerked my head off. Now I was floating down toward the farmland below, and I was happy to see no populated area.

As I was taught, I decided I would be more comfortable sitting in the sling than hanging by my crotch. The instructions were to slip your thumbs into the sling, bend your knees up and slide back into the sling. Ha! I tried but it didn't work, I just hung there, not too comfy but feeling pretty good anyway. Then I looked down and saw that I was drifting directly toward some power lines. What to do? Calling again on my rigid training, I pulled on the chute cords in the direction away from the power lines. This theoretically would spill air from the chute and float me away from danger. I might as well have been pulling on Hoover Dam. No spilled air, no chute movement, just floating merrily along toward the power lines. As I had calculated the wind changed and I was carried well clear of the lines. When I was about to touch down, gliding backwards, I braced for the landing. Fortunately, the landing site was a freshly plowed field and so I suffered no broken bones or sprained ankles as I hit. Now back to my training. To prevent being dragged by the chute, I pulled on the bottom cords to collapse it. Again, I couldn't budge the damn thing, but, because there was no wind, the chute collapsed of its own accord. I knew that would happen.

I'm now standing in the middle of nowhere when all of a sudden about 90 local farmers come running from every direction. Now, they had surrendered only eleven years before, and I wasn't too sure what they had in mind. As it turned out they were more excited than I was. They were laughing and hollering and jumping around. Since we couldn't communicate, I hand signed a telephone and spoke a few of my limited Japanese words, "Mushi, mushi, ah no nay" which is similar to the greeting they used instead of "hello" on the telephone. This was supposed to indicate to them that I wanted to be taken to a phone. So, my greeters loaded me into one of those little three-wheeled motorized pick up things they drove and hauled me away. I could see my wingman circling and assumed he had called for a chopper. The farmers took me to the home of an American Catholic priest who was a missionary in the area. I don't think he had been around anybody that spoke English in a long while. He was concerned about my health, but except for some burns on my forearms and chin, I was

> in good shape. It did give him a reason to break out the brandy, and naturally, I couldn't offend his hospitality, so we popped a couple. Then I convinced him I needed to get back near the crash site so the rescue helicopter could find me. He was enjoying a rare visitor so much he didn't want me to leave. I also was sort of enjoying being such a big frog, in this small pond, but they finally took me back to the deep hole that used to be my craft. It went straight in and deep.
>
> The AF chopper picked me up and took me to Johnson AFB [Air Force Base] where I spent a couple of days in their hospital. The Red Cross gave me a cute little shaving kit which I thought was nice, until I checked out to go back to Atsugi. I had a bill from the generous Red Cross for about three bucks for the "donated" shaving kit. That was the last money they ever got from me.
>
> The accident investigation deduced that an oil line had ruptured and fed directly on to the big engine, which ignited.

Velie eventually returned his parachute to his rigger, Corporal John Harris. As a reward for saving his life he gave Harris a bottle of Jack Daniel's Black Label, the corporal's preferred drink.[54]

On 3 September First Lieutenants Daniel I. Carroll and Joseph W. Hazen were set to depart NAS Atsugi to return to NAS Iwakuni. Both were cleared to taxi north to Runway 19. Hazen (in an AD-6, BuNo 134573) followed Carroll. Near the end of the east taxiway, construction had been started to repair a crack on the right side of the taxiway. Both pilots had arrived the previous day from Iwakuni and had noticed a construction crew working on the taxiway. The construction crew was protected by a sawhorse and two flare pots. It was necessary to taxi around them as the planes proceeded to the special weapons unit hardstand area.

Hazen was taxiing north to the Runway 19 warm-up area on the east taxiway when his right main landing gear dropped into a construction ditch between the old and new concrete. The ditch was 12 inches deep, 29 inches wide and 8.5 feet long in the shape of an elongated triangle. Only two unlit flare pots marked the area, the sawhorse had been removed.

The aircraft, traveling at nearly ten knots, continued on as the right main gear wedged into the hole. The landing gear sheared off and caused the aircraft to fall on the collapsed gear. The Skyraider skidded on the left main gear, tailwheel, propeller, the right main wheel well doors, the two right outboard rocket rails, the outer tip of the right aileron, and the trailing edge of the right wingtip, finally coming to a rest about forty-two feet past the construction ditch.

The engine continued to idle after the propeller blades were bent when contact was made with the ground. Hazen shut the aircraft down and exited it without further incident. Crash crews arrived on the scene in less than five minutes and quickly rigged the aircraft for removal from the taxiway when permitted to do so by the investigators.

The aircraft suffered significant damage but was repairable. The responsibility of repairs fell to H&MS-11 at Atsugi.

Just what the conclusions and recommendations were as to the cause of the accident are unclear. These items were redacted in the aircraft accident report received from the NHHC. Whether the construction crew was at fault, or authorities at the base, or the pilot, or a combination of all three, remains unanswered. Fortunately, Hazen was unhurt, and the aircraft was eventually repaired only to meet its end two months later.[55]

The loss of First Lieutenant William R. Rifino and the AD-6 (BuNo 134573) hit Ralph Sabroe hard. He was assigned to the aircraft and recalls Rifino as "a competent pilot and a fine Marine."[56] Rifino was scheduled to fly two different missions on 23 November. His first was to fly as an instrument chase for another pilot. For reasons unknown, the aircraft assigned to fly the instrument mission was out of commission and the mission scrubbed. The second mission was a night familiarization, usually flown once or twice a week by pilots in the unit. Night flying was not stressed by the unit, deemed not necessary when training in tactical nuclear weapon delivery. Consequently, night flying was limited to familiarization and navigation exercises. Hence, Rifino had less than 10 hours in night flying hours in the AD-6. He checked out with Marine Air Control Squadron (MACS) 1 at 1605 and took off from Atsugi 10 minutes later. No transmissions were received by anyone from Rifino prior to his take-off.

At around 1730, several witnesses noticed an aircraft on fire, in level flight, north of Atsugi. Two reported an aircraft on fire slamming into the ground about seven miles north-northeast of the Camp Zama Field Tower.[57] The AD-6 hit the ground at an 85-degree nose-down angle and at a high rate of speed. The right wing hit the ground first, followed by the propeller which ended up downhill of the impact. External fuel tanks came to rest uphill of the wreck. The fuselage was flattened like an accordion with the left and right wings to the left and right of the destroyed fuselage which remained in the impact crater. The crater was 17 feet deep and 35 feet wide.

Shortly after 1800, squadron personnel instructed NAS Atsugi and MACS-1 to contact Rifino. All attempts failed. Other squadron pilots in the air at the time and monitoring the squadron tactical frequency heard no transmissions from Rifino. Two ground control intercept stations in the area also reported no distress signals. An examination of recordings from the tower at NAS Atsugi revealed nothing was received from the aircraft.

With all attempts to contact Rifino failing, the special weapons unit dispatched a member of its permanent accident board by helicopter to the scene of the reported accident at 1845; he arrived 45 minutes later. By the time the helicopter arrived, military police and Japanese authorities had sealed off the area to keep curious civilians and souvenir hunters away from the scene while the crash and fire crew attacked the burning wreckage. Burning magnesium and minor explosions hampered the crash crew's effort to fully extinguish the fire. It would take them three days to do so.

When the board member arrived at the scene at 1930, fires still burned nearby, and the crater area was smoldering. The board member went to the crater and was able to identify the aircraft as the one flown by Rifino. He could not be immediately located, and search teams combed the area late into the night to locate him. The search was halted and resumed the next morning. The search teams finally found Rifino's body in the wreckage. He was still strapped into his seat.

Photographs were taken of the wreck and, over the course of several days, the remains of the aircraft were recovered—the largest part being the engine. They were taken to NAS Atsugi and, after a thorough inspection of the debris by the accident board members in their attempt to find a cause, turned over to the salvage unit at the air station.

The investigation was thorough, but the cause is unknown. The conclusions and recommendations of the accident board were redacted in the report received from the NHHC through a Freedom of Information Act request. The examination of the wreckage revealed no clues as to the cause of the fire. The squadron's accident board examined the maintenance history of the aircraft and noticed two items of concern. Maintenance records revealed the aircraft had a fuel contamination problem six flights prior to Rifino's crash which necessitated an engine change. The problem was corrected, and no other incidents were noted in a test flight and four other flights prior to the deadly crash.

It was also noted the aircraft used an inflammable hydraulic fluid in the hydraulic system, and that several AD-type Skyraiders within MAG-12 had had faulty hydraulic lines installed. It was also discovered that 11 squadron aircraft within the special weapons unit also had faulty hydraulic lines installed. However, Rifino's aircraft was not listed as one of those aircraft.

Whatever sparked the fire and engulfed the aircraft, it must have happened quickly. The fact that Rifino was found in his seat indicates he may not have had time to bail out or was incapacitated as the Skyraider plunged to the ground. He was instructed in bail-out procedures for the AD-6 and had successfully performed them in a drill prior to his first flight in one.[58] One has to wonder if Rifino's aircraft may have also suffered a severe oil leak spilling onto the hot engine, much like Velie's.

The squadron had two more incidents in February 1957, one of which resulted in the loss of another Skyraider. Sometime in February, the squadron sent a detachment to Naha Air Base, Okinawa, to provide close air support for a Marine landing exercise on Kia Beach about a mile from the town of Kin-ne. At 0800 on 18 February, the squadron launched four AD-6s from the base to support the 9th Infantry Regiment, 3rd Marine Division, landing on the beach. The flight—call sign *Clothesbrush*—consisted of Captain Frank D. Topley, flight leader; Second Lieutenant Robert D. Kehs, wingman; First Lieutenant Ronald B. Luther, section leader; and Second Lieutenant Henry D. Mullins, wingman.

Within 10 minutes, the aircraft were over the beach area and began simulated attack runs. When the landing force was within 500 yards of the beach landing area, Topley called off the attack and ordered his flight to begin making individual simulated strafing runs. Each aircraft made four successful runs over the beach. On the fifth run, Kehs—his speed at 240 knots (276 miles per hour)—did not maintain sufficient altitude to avoid hitting a tree which was approximately thirty feet tall. The Skyraider (BuNo 135299) hit the trunk of the tree—which was about six inches in diameter—about ten feet from the top with the propeller and right wing at the fuselage. In addition, a branch from the tree tore into the right center wing section near the landing gear wheel well; the right horizontal stabilizer was also damaged. Kehs immediately lost much of his forward momentum, killing any chance of continuing his flight. He maintained control of the Skyraider, steered toward open water and ditched about a half-mile offshore of the invasion area. Kehs hit the water at about one hundred five knots, causing more damage. The plane did not swerve or turn and continued across the water for about three hundred feet before coming to rest. Kehs, uninjured, exited the cockpit and abandoned his mount. It sank within 20 seconds. His fellow pilots circled overhead while Kehs struggled to pull himself into his life raft. Within five minutes, a nearby tank landing ship—USS *Sumner County*—arrived and retrieved Kehs from the water. Despite passing an exam by the ship's doctor, he was taken by an Air Force rescue helicopter of the 33rd Air Rescue Squadron to a nearby hospital for observation. When the plane was recovered, the engine and propeller could not be located.[59]

Nine days later, First Lieutenant Robert N. Link was scheduled to fly a test hop in an AD-6 (BuNo 134568) from NAS Iwakuni. In the late morning hours of 27 February, following a routine pre-flight inspection and run up, he taxied to the runway for take-off. With his Skyraider at full power, Link began his run and soon became airborne. Not long after, Link noticed his engine running rough. He pulled back on the throttle and the roughness ceased.

Link felt he needed to test the aircraft thoroughly, so he opted to continue the flight. He added full power, the roughness returned but this time the engine soon quit. With the Skyraider under 200 feet, and to the right of the runway, Link decided he would be unable to land on the runway so elected to land straight ahead as he had been trained.

He attempted to restart the engine to no avail. The Skyraider hit the ground slightly nose high. Immediately after contact, the left wing dropped, tearing off the left flap as it hit the ground. The prop made five rotations before quitting. After skidding nearly three hundred feet in sandy soil, the Skyraider came to a halt. Link was uninjured and, noticing no fire, secured the cockpit and left the aircraft before the crash crew arrived on the scene. The aircraft suffered heavy damage but was repairable.

Investigators ran a thorough check of the Skyraider once it was rebuilt in the configuration at the time of the accident. The aircraft appeared to operate normally but they did notice the spark plugs would break down when pressure of 95 to 145 psi was applied. In viewing past maintenance records, two similar occurrences of a rough-running engine were found.[60]

It is not known if there was any fault or cause attributed to the accident. As in most of the aircraft accident reports received through the Freedom of Information Act, that information was redacted.

The squadron received word in October 1956 that it would finally be leaving the Far East. Per a Commandant of the Marine Corps letter dated 4 October, the squadron's new duty station was to be Marine Corps Air Station (MCAS) Miami, Florida.[61] By March 1957, squadron activities slowed down as VMA-251 began preparations to deploy back to the United States. After nearly four years in the Far East, the squadron was going home. That occurred in April 1957. Leaving its Skyraiders behind, the squadron deployed to its new duty station and on 20 April established itself at MCAS Miami, reporting to MAG-31. A new chapter was about to begin.

CHAPTER 5

The Jet Age Begins

There was a large changeover of personnel once the squadron established itself at Marine Corps Air Station (MCAS) Miami. In addition, the squadron was assigned a new aircraft: the jet-powered FJ-3 Fury. With the acquisition of the new fighter, the squadron was redesignated as VMF-251 on 20 April 1957 per Chief of Naval Operations message 261314Z dated December 1956.[1] In addition, the squadron tail code was changed from AL to DW.

With a change in the designation the black patch was shelved and a new one designed. Captain Richard E. Carey is credited with designing the insignia. It consisted of a blue background with a red shield and a white cross on top. A thunderbolt (originally silver and later orange) lay diagonally across the cross and shield. This gave the squadron its new moniker, the "Thunderbolts." Along the top was a banner with the words "Custos Caelorum," meaning "Guardians of the Sky." At the bottom of the patch was another banner with the new designation VMF-251.[2]

Delivery of the new jets began in May; 21 aircraft were on hand by August 1957. The squadron spent the next eight months transitioning and training with the Fury.

The FJ-3 Fury can trace its design lineage to the Navy's FJ-1 Fury, a straight-wing carrier jet fighter. North American Aviation began development of the FJ-1 in the latter stages of World War II. At the same time, North American was developing the XP-86 swept-wing fighter for the Army (this later became the F-86 for the United States Air Force), but the Navy turned down the design when offered it. In 1948, the FJ-1 entered service and began its short naval career. While teaching many lessons in carrier jet operations, the FJ-1 did not perform as well as the XP-86. North American subsequently developed a version of the F-86 for the Navy—the FJ-2 Fury—which had folding wings and arresting and catapult hooks. The Navy accepted the design in early 1951 and, after a few design changes, carrier trials began in December 1952 and revealed many problems. The Navy passed on the FJ-2 and only six Marine squadrons used the type from 1954 to 1956.

A new version of the FJ-2—the FJ-3—began development in early 1952 and by 1954 began entering service with the Navy and Marine Corps. A modified version of the FJ-3—the FJ-3M—had several modifications made: wing stations were added, as well as aerial-refueling capability and the ability to fire Sidewinder missiles. The FJ-3 remained in active service until late 1962.[3] There was an additional version of the Fury—the FJ-4. However, it appears VMF-251 did not have this aircraft officially assigned to it. "OPNAV 03110" is a Navy publication which lists aircraft allowances by type, and locations of every unit and station. From the months of April 1957 to March 1958, the FJ-3 is the only aircraft listed in VMF-251's inventory. The exception was the F-8 Crusader which began to appear in December 1957. None were carried by the squadron; but future projections showed that by September 1958 it was to have 20 of the supersonic Crusaders.

Intensive ground training in the flight characteristics and flight systems of the Fury was conducted for all pilots as the aircraft began to arrive. The training included lectures by technical personnel and squadron pilots; special meetings were held by the squadron's operations department. In addition, pilots were required to read and initial all publications pertinent to aviation safety, the FJ-3 and jet aircraft.[4] Maintenance personnel underwent similar training.

Training with the Fury took its toll. Through the 11 months the squadron used the type, seven aircraft were involved in accidents; four of them were destroyed. Fortunately, no pilots lost their lives though several were injured.

Captain Paul S. French and First Lieutenant Basil L. McCallister took off for a scheduled section tactics hop late in the morning of 20 August. As they became airborne, French's door, which enclosed the air turbine generator, had come open and could not be closed. French decided to return to base while McCallister—after getting permission from French, the section lead—continued with the mission. Both aircraft were about five miles northeast of MCAS Miami at 6,000 feet. French climbed and leveled off at 8,000 feet, dumped his drop tank fuel and returned to base.

McCallister continued to climb until he reached 40,000 feet. After transferring fuel from his external drop tank, he began to practice aerobatic maneuvers. He completed a few wingovers and barrel rolls and was performing a loop when he felt a mild explosion which jerked his control stick. Since he was on the backside of the loop, he decided to continue to pull through rather than roll out. When his Fury approached the horizon at a 20-degree nose-down attitude, he felt another explosion and the compressor section fire warning light flickered on and off a few times, then remained on.

With the Fury at a nose-down angle at approximately ten thousand feet, and at a speed of nearly four hundred fifty knots (518 miles per hour), McCallister ejected safely from the smoking aircraft. As he floated down, he watched his Fury slam into the water and sink about sixteen miles southeast of Miami Beach.

McCallister hit the water, inflated his life vest, and deployed his para-raft. He secured his parachute to the raft and hoped for a quick rescue. As the hours passed, he tried to signal several ships and aircraft that were observed nearby but was unsuccessful in getting their attention: his day flares and night flares did not ignite, instructions to assemble the raft's radar reflector were destroyed when the raft deployed, and his signal mirror had broken apart. The next morning, he spotted a small coastal freighter—*Privateer*—and began flashing with fragments from his signal mirror. The ship saw the flashes, changed course, and picked him up shortly before 1000 on 21 August.

Two days later, after McCallister had a chance to recover from the incident, he was questioned by the squadron's Aircraft Accident Board, representatives from North American Aviation, and representatives from the engine manufacturer, Wright Aeronautical Corporation. The detailed interrogation revealed no concrete cause of the accident.[5]

Two weeks later, the squadron lost another Fury. Shortly after 1300 on 4 September, Captain Richard J. Kern and his wingman First Lieutenant David C. Myers took off on a navigation exercise that would take them to Naval Air Station (NAS) Jacksonville, Florida, approximately three hundred fifty miles to the north on the east coast.

No problems were encountered on take-off. They climbed to 20,000 feet to level off briefly as they stayed under a cloud layer, then resumed their climb to 40,000 feet. Thirty minutes later, the two pilots entered what they thought was a thin layer of cirrus clouds. It turned out to be dangerous thunderstorm.

Within minutes the two aircraft became separated due to heavy turbulence. Kern nosed down and began a 180-degree turn to port. Myers radioed Kern and advised he could no longer see him. Kern ordered Myers to turn to starboard to avoid a collision. Myers began a descent to 20,000 feet. The turbulence made handling the aircraft difficult; Myers was fighting to recover from his nose-down attitude. At 10,000 feet, the aircraft was approaching Mach 1 and still diving. Myers, having made the decision he could not recover his aircraft, ejected. He dislocated his left shoulder in the process and received several cuts to his face as rain and hail pelted him.

Myers finally broke through the cloud layer at 200 feet, landing about a mile southwest of Flagler Beach, Florida. His Fury, on a southerly heading, crashed in heavy rain, with its left wing down, in a 30-degree dive about four miles southwest of Flagler Beach on the Old Dixie Highway. The aircraft exploded on impact. Power lines brought down by the aircraft knocked out electricity in the area.

When Myers landed, the strong winds from the storm dragged him through a swampy area. He spilled the air from his parachute by wrapping the lines around his legs. Coming to a halt, he extricated himself from the lines and began to walk in search of a phone.

He came to a farmhouse and asked a woman who lived there if he could use her telephone. She agreed, and Myers called NAS Jacksonville. When he asked the woman for her address, she appeared not to know it. Myers, still on the phone, informed authorities at Jacksonville that he would call back when he could determine his location. Myers thanked her and resumed his walk in search of a telephone.

He found a restaurant off nearby highway A1A and called Jacksonville once again. With an address at hand, a helicopter was dispatched and picked him up. He was transported to the air station and admitted to the United States Naval Hospital in Jacksonville.

An inspection of the crash site revealed the engine was turning when the Fury impacted, the control cables were broken by the crash, and a check of hydraulic valves and lines revealed fluid in the system. During Myers's interrogation in the hospital, he told investigators he could not see outside his cockpit and was experiencing heavy turbulence. He tried to level off at 20,000 feet. Myers felt he was stalling and momentarily neutralized his controls. He found his stick pressure to be normal and tried to regain control. Despite the attempt, he remained in a nose-down attitude and his wings were fluctuating rapidly. His rate of descent was 6,000 feet a minute, and his altimeter was unwinding rapidly. With his aircraft at 10,000 feet and still in a nose-down position, Myers made the decision to eject. He also told investigators that he felt he did not have vertigo.

If any cause or blame was assigned for the accident, it is not known; the conclusions and recommendations in the report were redacted.[6]

A week later, the squadron lost another Fury while on an exercise. Major Ernest I. Melin led a four-plane division consisting of First Lieutenant Billy M. Hansen, Second Lieutenant Michael J. Barkovich and First Lieutenant Richard M. Irgens. The aircraft took off at 1242 for a scheduled division

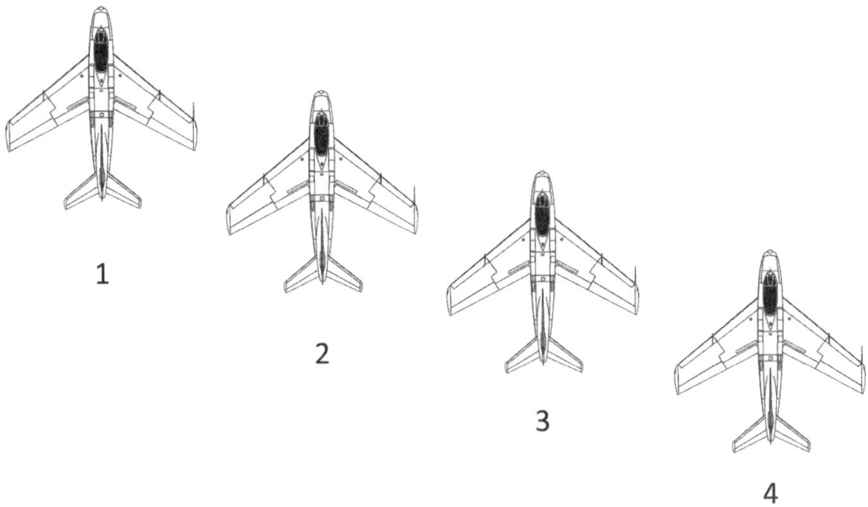

Echelon right formation showing positions prior to accident 11 September 1957 From left to right: 1. Division Leader Melin; 2. Melin's wingman Barkovich; 3. Section Leader Irgens; 4. Irgens' wingman Hansen.

tactics flight. All went well during the exercise until the approach back to MCAS Miami.

During the approach, Melin's wingman, Hansen, requested he fly the number four spot. Permission was granted and Hansen put himself at the rear of the formation, moving Barkovich to number two and Irgens to number three. When the division was approximately ten miles from the air station and at an altitude of 2,000 feet, Irgens noticed an engine rumble and roughness in his aircraft. He slightly increased the power to his engine, lessening the noise. He requested permission from Melin to further increase his power but received no acknowledgment. He repeated his request, again nothing from Melin. As the division approached the field boundary, they switched to the tower frequency. Irgens asked again to increase his power, this time receiving permission from Melin to do so. As he added power, Irgens's Fury immediately decelerated.

Irgens believed he had flamed out and decided to eject. Pulling into a left climbing turn, he steered his aircraft toward an open field. When the aircraft was at the top of its climb, the engine began to stall. Wasting no time, Irgens ejected.

He drifted west, landing in a man-made lake approximately a half mile west-northwest of the approach end of the station's Runway 9. Uninjured, he inflated his life vest and was quickly plucked from the lake by an air station helicopter.

Once Irgens had ejected, the Fury quickly nosed over into a steep dive from 2,500 feet. The aircraft exploded on impact, with parts of it being blown nearly a thousand feet ahead of the impact point. Pieces of the engine and airframe were recovered in the impact crater; everything else was obliterated. It was determined the engine was nearly seized upon impact and not producing enough thrust to keep the plane in the air. An examination of the turbine blades and turbine wheel revealed the engine was running at low RPMs prior to the crash.[7] What exactly caused the engine to seize is unknown.

As noted earlier, the squadron was already set to receive the F-8 Crusader. In January 1958, it was informed of a pending move to MCAS El Toro, California, to be executed in April.[8] Until then, training continued with an emphasis on missions to be flown in an upcoming exercise in Puerto Rico.

On 9 January, the squadron sent an advance party of one officer and 11 enlisted men to Port Everglades where they embarked aboard USS *Fort Mandan* (LSD-21).[9] The ship departed and made way for NAS Roosevelt Roads, Puerto Rico. It arrived on 16 January and the advance party spent the next several weeks preparing for the squadron's arrival later in the month.[10]

On the last day of January, the squadron sent six officers, 49 enlisted men, one naval officer and three civilian technical representatives to NAS Roosevelt Roads by R4Q transport aircraft to participate in *Traex* (Training Exercise) *1–58*[11] in conjunction with the 2nd Marine Regiment.[12] The exercise was scheduled to last through the month of February. Soon after the R4Q took off, the squadron flew 19 of its 22 FJ-3s to Puerto Rico. A rear party of eight officers and 21 enlisted men stayed behind at MCAS Miami.[13]

It was during the training exercise that the squadron suffered the loss of another Fury. At approximately 1430, Second Lieutenant John M. Burbank and First Lieutenant Archie B. Neuwirth took off on an assigned gunnery exercise. With them were two other aircraft, one piloted by Lieutenant Colonel Wiley A. Green, the designated flight leader and commanding officer of the squadron. Burbank was the tow aircraft, trailing a gunnery sleeve. Neuwirth was assigned as escort for Burbank. Their course took them to a designated target area about forty miles southwest of the air station.

They leveled off near the target area when Burbank felt a muffled explosion in his aircraft. As his aircraft began to vibrate engine RPM began to drop off. The explosions continued and smoke began to trail from his tailpipe. Neuwirth contacted Burbank to inform him of the smoke. Burbank notified Green he was dropping his tow and heading back to Roosevelt Roads. As Burbank turned towards the air station; the explosions increased. He shifted to manual fuel control and activated his pop-out turbine generator. When exhaust gas temperature reached 1,000°C, Burbank shut down his engine. Neuwirth observed flames emanating from what appeared to be the left compressor compartment air vent just forward and above the left speed brake. Neuwirth tried contacting Burbank on several frequencies and channels, but he never received the transmissions. Neuwirth joined up on Burbank's aircraft and used hand signals to get his attention. Burbank, preoccupied, did not see the hand signals. He saw no indication of a fire on his instruments nor smoke in the cockpit.

Burbank had activated his alternate flight control manual override handle which allowed the pop-up turbine generator to power the flight controls. The controls froze. Unable to save his aircraft, Burbank ejected at approximately nine thousand feet. As he drifted towards the water, he and Neuwirth watched the Fury, trailing fire, until it hit the water. The aircraft sank under the waves in water between 400 to 600 fathoms deep. Burbank landed in the water about six miles from Roosevelt Roads. Once he freed himself from his parachute, he inflated his raft and pulled himself in. Within 30 minutes, a rescue helicopter from the base plucked him from the water. Burbank suffered a few scratches but was otherwise uninjured.

Since the aircraft sank in water too deep to be recovered, determining a cause of the engine failure was impossible. However, a review of maintenance records for the aircraft revealed previous faults.

The Fury had been one of three that stayed behind at MCAS Miami when the main echelon left for Roosevelt Roads. It was scheduled for a cone and duct replacement. When the new duct and cone assembly was received, it was discovered the latter was warped and unfit for installation. When the replacement assembly arrived, it and the duct were installed in the aircraft. It then went on a check flight on 2 February and found to have a communication problem with its TACAN (Tactical Air Navigation) system. It was flown nine more times, including a flight to Roosevelt Roads, without any engine problems. During these flights, there were several communication problems noted along with, in one instance, slow fuel transfer.

Previous engine problems noted prior to the accident revealed a cracked exhaust duct, tail pipe brackets, and tail pipe blanket. These were repaired. The aircraft's engine had been overhauled once and checked several times with no problems recorded.

While the problems noted were significant, apparently no direct evidence of a fault could be determined. What the investigators concluded is not known.[14]

The training exercise concluded at the end of February. Personnel from the squadron, as well as its aircraft, shuttled back to MCAS Miami. Upon arrival, many of the men were transferred out of the squadron as it prepared to move to MCAS El Toro. The aircraft were to stay at Miami. The cadre of personnel who remained with the squadron boarded an R4Q transport and departed for El Toro on 28 April.[15] The next day, the squadron reported to MAG-33 of the 3rd MAW and began operations.[16]

CHAPTER 6

The Crusader Years

Once again in the span of a year, VMF-251 found itself rebuilding and familiarizing its personnel with a new aircraft—the F-8 Crusader built by Vought, a now independent part of the company responsible for the unit's old Corsairs. The company needed a winner, since its previous two designs for the Navy did not fare well: the XF6U Pirate never made it to active service while the F7U Cutlass made it to the fleet but did not live up to its potential.[1] It scored a win with the Crusader. The type served well into the 1990s before being retired from active service.

The squadron now had in its hands a fighter capable of exceeding the speed of sound. Ironically, despite the growing use of air-to-air missiles, the early models carried four 20mm cannons in the nose area as its main weapon, along with an internal rocket pack. Early models did not have an aerial-refueling probe; this was added later during production or as a field modification.[2]

The ability to use AIM-9 Sidewinder missiles was also added later. It appears the initial batch of the F8U-1 was not capable of firing the Sidewinder. Racks aft of the cockpit on each side of the fuselage were added later during the F8U-1's life cycle. Each rack could carry one Sidewinder.[3] In the case of VMF-251, racks for the Crusader were added as a field modification. By December 1958, the squadron made a plea for more racks. Only 27 had been received and, with 19 aircraft then assigned, it needed 11 more. Eleven of the aircraft had two racks (one on each side) installed and five had only the left rack installed.[4]

VMF-251 ended up using three different models of the Crusader: the F8U-1 (F-8A) 1958–59, 1961–62; the F8U-1E (F-8B), 1960; and the F8U-2 (F-8C), 1962–64.[5] Unique to all models was the high-mounted variable-incidence wing, capable of rising seven degrees. This allowed for the angle of attack that needed to be maintained during approach for landings while providing better visibility for the pilot.[6]

The F8U-1E was nearly indistinguishable from the F8U-1 except for the nose. The radome was made larger to make use of the full area of the nose rather than just the tip. The F8U-2 saw the addition of "ventral fins and afterburner cooling scoops to the rear fuselage."[7] The Sidewinder launch racks were also modified to carry four missiles, two on each side of the fuselage.[8] During the course of its production run, a little over 1,200 Crusaders of all models were built.

It took time for the squadron to acquire its Crusaders. According to "The Almanac and Location of Navy Aircraft" for 1958, it was not until the end of June that the squadron had in its possession five Crusaders, far short of its allotted number (20). With the unit needing to train its incoming pilots and maintenance personnel, it needed aircraft. To do that, aircraft from Marine Air Group (MAG) 33 and VMF-334 were used. Whether MAG-33's Crusaders were assigned or loaned to the squadron is unclear. This led to an unusual occurrence: for a short time, the squadron flew with the wrong tail code.

The DW designation for the squadron had been applied the previous year and was used by its Furies while flying from Marine Corps Air Station (MCAS) Miami. It was part of a Navy-wide change to its tail-code system which began in 1957. For a short while, the squadron flew from MCAS El Toro with the VL tail code. This may have caused some confusion since VMA-331 was allocated the VL tail code in 1957. The exact circumstances for this occurrence are not known but Steven Albright, who has written extensively on Marine Air, suspects it was a series of errors. It was "an interesting point in 251's history," wrote Albright. They "used the last known tail code, 'AL' (First Marine Air Wing's tail code from the Skyraider era). By that time, all Marine tail codes beginning with the letter 'A' were switched to 'V,' so they applied 'VL' to their Crusaders instead of 'DW.' I do not know how long they used the erroneous tail code, but it is an interesting point."[9] By July 1958, the squadron was flying with the correct tail code.

It is not clear when the first familiarization flights began. They were flying by July and with most of the new pilots arriving having next to no experience on the Crusader, accidents were bound to happen during this transition period. The first Crusader lost by the squadron occurred on 10 July. It was an aircraft that belonged to VMF-334.[10] Harry Black, then a young second lieutenant who had joined VMF-251 when it arrived at El Toro in late April, learned he was picked to pilot the ill-fated aircraft (BuNo 143765):

> … myself and three other second lieutenants were transferred to VMF-251 from VMA-311 at MCAS El Toro. I do not remember all the names. One was John Kretsinger who subsequently became a Blue Angel. We were only fresh out of the training command and there was some discussion as to whether or not very young pilots should be allowed to fly the Marine Corps' prize supersonic aircraft, the Crusader. For no particular reason, I was the first young 2ndLt. to fam in the aircraft.[11]

In the weeks leading up to his first flight in the Crusader, Black spent a week at the Vought factory school in Dallas, Texas, another week at the Naval Air Mobile Trainer at El Toro, and yet another going through the training syllabus as required by VMF-334. On the day of the flight, Black felt he was ready for the training mission set for that afternoon.

As the hour approached for his flight, Black took the required pre-familiarization-1 hop oral test on safety procedures given by the safety officer and listened to a lecture by the Vought test pilot. Lastly, he was briefed on the actual flight.

When the time arrived, Black, accompanied by his chase pilot from VMF-334, made a slow and methodical pre-flight check of his assigned Crusader. Each pilot then climbed into their cockpits and secured themselves. During the start-up checks, the chase pilot informed Black there had been some difficulty in replacing the canopy on his aircraft the previous day in order to change an oxygen converter. There was a problem in re-centering the cams of the pins which hinge the rear of the canopy to the airframe. Concerned, Black activated the canopy at least once while on the line, and again while taxiing to the runway; in each case the hooks of the canopy felt to be engaged, with the lock handle going full forward and the canopy indicator showing "down and locked." The handle, however, was full forward but not stowed—the telescopic extension of the handle was not pushed in. His chase pilot did a visual check of Black's canopy prior to take-off. The canopy lock appeared to be flush with the side of the aircraft.

Shortly around 1600, Black started his take-off run. Four seconds later, his chase pilot started his run. Following a normal take off without afterburner, gear retraction and wing transition, Black turned on his cabin pressurization, fuel transfer, and left the leading-edge wing slats droop out. As the two aircraft climbed, a port climbing turn was performed without incident. When the two aircraft rose above 15,000 feet at nearly four hundred knots (460 miles per hour), the chase pilot radioed Black to go into afterburner. With the afterburner kicked in, Black pulled away from his chase pilot. Black was contacted again and advised to throttle back to about 92%. By doing so, the chase pilot was able to catch up. Once both planes joined up, they executed a combat climb at .93 Mach on a heading due north.

As the flight passed 21,000 feet, the chase pilot saw Black's canopy separate from his Crusader. Shortly after, Black and the seat also left the plane. Black, partially blinded and in a state of semi-consciousness by the extreme force of the wind blast that struck him when the canopy was lost, attempted to pull his face curtain but did not think he had. His last recollection was after his parachute had opened. In fact, it was seconds after he left the aircraft that the parachute deployed. The pilotless Crusader yawed and rolled slightly, then began a nose-down starboard turn with afterburner still operating. The aircraft was obliterated when it crashed into the westside of a hill about sixteen miles southeast of MCAS El Toro. The resulting explosion gouged a hole in the hillside that was 38 feet long, 31 feet wide and 12 feet in depth.

The chase pilot circled Black as he slowly descended to the ground. He contacted El Toro Tower to alert rescue units in the area. The pilot of a HUS-1 helicopter (also designated as a UH-34 Seahorse) from Marine Helicopter Transport Squadron (HMR) 362 contacted the chase pilot and reported his position over San Juan Capistrano. The chase pilot directed the helicopter to Black's location. When it arrived, the helicopter hovered over Black, allowing the co-pilot to lower himself at which point he jumped approximately fifteen feet to the ground to reach Black's position. He freed Black from his parachute, which was entangled in the trees on the side of the steep slope. The pilot of the helicopter then contacted the chase pilot and informed him Black was fine. Satisfied, the chase aircraft made its way back to El Toro.

As the helicopter lingered above the hillside, it lost power and began a descent towards Black and the co-pilot. The co-pilot, realizing the helicopter was going to crash, knocked Black to the ground and then threw himself to the ground. The rotor blades of the helicopter chopped through the trees, ripping the remains of Black's parachute to shreds and gouged holes in the ground on both sides of the two Marines. Debris struck Black's left hand, breaking a finger. His rescuer and the pilot of the wrecked HUS-1 were uninjured. The three Marines pulled themselves together and walked to a nearby highway. A patrol car soon picked them up and returned them to El Toro.

As the chase aircraft called for landing instructions at El Toro, the tower requested the position of the helicopter. It had not been heard from since the surviving Crusader left the scene of Black's accident. The chase pilot returned to the area where he last saw the helicopter and tried contacting it. Unable to make contact, he made several passes over the area. He noticed that Black's parachute was no longer visible. With no luck in finding the helicopter, the chase aircraft returned to El Toro.

What remained of Black's Crusader was eventually recovered by the Salvage Section from MCAS El Toro. If any cause or blame was assigned to the unintended ejection, it was not available in the aircraft accident report.

The loss of Black's Crusader was the first in a series of accidents the squadron suffered prior to its departure to Japan in October 1959. The majority of the accidents occurred at El Toro; the others were at El Centro and Yuma.

Indicative of the problems the squadron would encounter with the Crusader in the future was the mishap involving Second Lieutenant Glenn H. Downing early in the morning of 20 August 1958. Shortly after 0700, he and his chase pilot were airborne. It was Downing's first familiarization flight in the Crusader (BuNo 145365). About an hour later, he entered the landing pattern for Runway 8L at NAAS El Centro.

After executing two wave offs, Downing made his first touch-and-go landing. Immediately after touchdown the starboard landing gear came off the aircraft. He made an immediate take-off and proceeded to climb to 3,000 feet. After the chase pilot surveyed the damage to Downing's Crusader, he was instructed to make a normal approach and landing.

Downing came in with his remaining landing gear. Upon touchdown, he kept the Crusader up on its nose wheel and the left main gear for nearly three thousand two hundred feet. At that point, he lowered his right wing to the runway. The aircraft veered to the right on to Runway 12L. The Crusader skidded for nearly a thousand feet and made a 190° turn before coming to a stop on the runway. Downing was not injured in the incident.

His Crusader suffered extensive damage. Upon initial impact, the starboard tension strut locknut was fractured, the starboard shock strut was torn from the head nut, the lower end of the shock strut was torn from the starboard tension strut, the starboard actuating strut was torn from the fitting assembly and its attaching pin was broken, the brake assembly hydraulic and pneumatic lines were broken, the leading edge of the starboard horizontal tail was split open possibly by the disintegrating strut, the undersurface buckled, the air intake duct was cracked in the right wheel well, and the forward bulkhead of the wheel well was slightly dented.

When Downing let his aircraft down after touchdown, the Crusader received further damage. The starboard wing outer panel, the starboard outer panel droop assembly, the starboard lower main gear door assembly, and the starboard door assembly were all torn from the aircraft. The right aileron was also damaged as was the underside of the fuselage. The aircraft was not written off, but it was out of service for quite some time.[12] Landing gear problems would plague the squadron for the next few years.

Downing's mishap was the last for several months. Pilots and maintenance men finally settled into a schedule to get the squadron ready for operations. Things went smoothly until November when another incident occurred involving the landing gear.

In the early afternoon of 25 November Second Lieutenant Richard L. Chappelear took off from El Centro for his third air-to-air gunnery flight. He had joined the squadron in May 1958 and had slightly over 63 hours in the Crusader.

The exercise went smoothly and Chappelear returned to El Centro. After he completed his landing roll, Chappelear took his Crusader to a de-arming area at the end of the airfield's Runway 21. After an uneventful de-arming, he continued to taxi down Runway 21 to the squadron's designated area on the flight line.

At approximately two thousand five hundred feet down the runway, the aircraft started drifting to the left. Chappelear kept the steering button depressed and applied right rudder in an attempt to correct the problem. When right rudder was engaged, the Crusader began a violent swerve to the right. Chappelear applied left rudder and finally brakes in his attempt to bring the Crusader to a halt.

He was unable to stop; the aircraft went into a hard right turn, skidding on the left main wheel and nose wheel. It continued its skid, turning nearly one hundred sixty-five degrees to the right, and was skidding sideways toward the edge of the runway. Just before it reached the edge, the Crusader keeled over on the left wing and nose duct, then settled back on the landing gear. The left main gear then tore through the edge of the runway. The left wingtip gouged a hole into the dirt. When the nose duct scraped the ground, debris was sucked up into the engine. The aircraft had finally come to a halt. Chappelear, unharmed, shut down the engine and evacuated the Crusader.

The aircraft suffered a laundry list of damage, especially to the nose gear, left wing, and engine. An examination of the nose gear for a possible malfunction revealed nothing except for a slightly bent shaft. However, the bent shaft was deemed to be insufficient to cause a malfunction. As in other Aircraft Accident Reports obtained through the Freedom of Information Act, the determination of the cause of the accident was redacted.[13]

The new year was highlighted by the squadron's notification of its return to the Far East in October 1959. Operations accelerated; this could be the reason for the numerous accidents that occurred prior to its departure (see Appendix

7). There was one fatality in 1959, claiming the life of a respected pilot in the squadron—Captain Joseph F. Mayfield, Jr. Mayfield had arrived soon after the squadron arrived at El Toro. By the time he joined the "Thunderbolts," he had accumulated over 150 hours in the Fury and had earned another 180 hours in the Crusader with the squadron by the time of his accident.

In the late afternoon of 26 May, Mayfield and two other VMF-251 pilots departed El Toro on an Advanced Instrument training flight. Their destination was Nellis Air Force Base (AFB) in Nevada. They arrived at the base at approximately 1934 local time. No problems were encountered on the first leg of their training flight.

However, due to refueling problems at Nellis, the three Crusaders were delayed on their return leg. It wasn't until 2315 that they took off from Nellis. They were cleared to George AFB, California. Upon reaching George, Mayfield requested clearance to El Toro Approach Control, which was given.

It was during his approach for landing that Mayfield crashed. After a series of maneuvers as he lined up for landing at El Toro, his aircraft slammed into the ground, soon after midnight, at a 70-degree nose-down angle about nine miles from the base. Radar contact was lost and an explosion was witnessed by El Toro Tower personnel. The Crusader was destroyed, killing Mayfield. Nothing was left of the aircraft; the engine and aft section being the only parts not completely destroyed. Debris was scattered around the aircraft, thrown clear by the impact explosion. What may have caused the crash, as well as contributing factors, was redacted from the aircraft accident report.[14]

Training operations slowed as the squadron began preparation for its deployment overseas as an operational squadron. Deployments to Yuma and El Centro followed, as well as a brief cruise on board USS *Oriskany* (CVA-34) for carrier qualifications.

In early October, the squadron's Crusaders, as well as an advance party, arrived at Naval Air Station (NAS) North Island. There, the Crusaders were prepped for overseas shipping and loaded on board USS *Core* (T-AKV-41), a Bogue-class escort carrier from World War II now serving as an aircraft transport. The rest of the squadron followed closely behind the advance party.[15]

With crew assigned to their quarters, and the aircraft stowed away, USS *Core* departed San Diego for NAS Atsugi on 19 October, arriving at Yokohama, Japan, on 1 November 1959 following a brief stopover in Hawaii.

Once at Yokohama, the planes were offloaded and made ready for flight. From there, the Crusaders were flown to NAS Atsugi where the squadron made its home at the East Camp of the station. Operations soon picked up.[16]

In December, the squadron deployed for a short cruise on USS *Midway* (CVA-41). Then, from January to June 1960, the unit flew operations from NAS Cubi Point in the Philippines. While at Cubi Point, the Marines participated in Operation *Blue Star*, providing air cover for a joint amphibious exercise with military forces of Taiwan.[17] During the operation, the squadron flew from the southern town of Ping Tung. It returned to Atsugi in June 1960 and, in the following month, operated from the aircraft carriers USS *Oriskany* and USS *Ranger* (CVA-61).

It was then back to Atsugi for a few months, at which point the squadron sent a detachment to Naha, Okinawa, in October. It was at Okinawa that the squadron suffered its only fatal accident during the deployment.

On 18 November, Captain Robert L. Leathers and his wingman departed Atsugi for an authorized instrument flight plan to Naha. Soon after becoming airborne, Leathers lost external lights on his Crusader (BuNo 145436) with the exception of the starboard wing light. As the flight approached Okinawa, the gyro in the wingman's Crusader became erratic. He lost sight of Leathers's aircraft, so he joined the same holding pattern as Leathers.

When they finally joined up, both aircraft were cleared for the ground control approach (GCA) frequency. Naha GCA obtained radar contact when the two Crusaders were about four miles out at 9,000 feet altitude. Once the flight was identified, they were cleared to descend to 1,300 feet. Soon after, the wingman noticed reflected light on the bottom of Leathers's Crusader (BuNo 145436). The wingman quickly saw the water and immediately pulled up while transmitting "pull up, pull up!" After the wingman pulled up, he saw the speed brake of Leathers's Crusader dragging in the water. Soon after, the aircraft hit the water with a large splash and quickly disappeared.

The location of the accident (approximately sixteen miles south and west of Naha) was determined by the GCA controller and search-and-rescue units were dispatched. Upon arriving on the scene, surface ships and aircraft searched the area. Some debris from the Crusader was recovered but Leathers was not found. Salvage operations to recover the aircraft were not conducted due to the extreme depth.[18] Along with the loss of Leathers, three other aircraft suffered damage due to various causes during 1960.

The squadron concluded its remaining time in the Far East at Atsugi. In December 1960, leaving its Crusaders behind for VMF-312, VMF-251 personnel departed for the United States and a new duty station, MCAS Beaufort, South Carolina. On 1 January 1961, the squadron took over VMF-312's Crusaders, consisting of a mix of F8U-1s (F-8A) and F8U-1Es (F-8B).[19]

At Beaufort, the squadron began to rebuild with an influx of new pilots and enlisted men. By the time the squadron concluded its deployments to Guantanamo Bay, Cuba, in August and September 1961, and to Jamaica during the time between the Pay of Pigs Invasion and the Cuban Missile Crisis,[20] it had completed its reforming. On 1 October, the squadron was notified it would deploy to the Mediterranean, courtesy of USS *Shangri-La* (CVA-38), assigned to the Sixth Fleet.

During the period prior to its departure in February 1962, VMF-251 lost one aircraft and four were damaged. The loss of the aircraft occurred on 6 July 1961. Captain O. H. McClelland took off at 0915 in his F-8B (BuNo 145540) to perform a fly-by. McClelland was flying lead in a four-plane division. While awaiting clearance for the fly-by, a fuel leak developed near the starboard main landing gear door. McClelland, accompanied by his wingman, immediately proceeded to the airfield and broke for landing. As he rolled into his approach for landing, the fuel ignited. McClelland secured the engine and a normal Morest[21] arrestment was made using the airfield's emergency equipment. The Crusader, the tail section engulfed in flames, came to a quick stop. McClelland exited his aircraft without injuries and, with crash crews already on the scene, the fire was quickly extinguished. The fire nearly destroyed the tail section; it was severe enough that the aircraft would not fly again.[22]

Following notification of the deployment to the Mediterranean, extensive planning began. At least a dozen Crusaders assigned to the squadron would be embarked.[23] Day carrier qualifications were planned with USS *Franklin D. Roosevelt* (CVA-42) and began as scheduled on 30 October.

Qualifications went smoothly for a few days; they were soon halted when the carrier developed major problems with its arresting gear system. The carrier qualifications were rescheduled for the week of 10–16 December on board USS *Shangri-La*. Until they resumed, day and night flights, ordnance training, air refueling, and instrument training became the daily syllabus.

Day and night carrier qualifications began aboard *Shangri-La* as planned. Despite lousy weather, they were completed on 16 December. During the period, two Crusaders were damaged. One of the damaged aircraft ended up at Cecil Field and the other, flown by First Lieutenant Myrl Allinder, had its nose gear collapse into the wheel well upon touching down on the carrier. Damage was substantial and the jet was sent off for overhaul and repair. Allinder was not injured in the incident.[24] Upon completion, the squadron became the first day- and night-qualified Crusader squadron in the Marine Corps.

During the months of November and December, the planes had their landing gear re-worked, struts were packed, and corrosion control applied as well as normal maintenance. All this was performed around the clock, getting the aircraft ready for their long periods at sea, offering no let up for maintenance personnel.

The squadron embarked aboard USS *Shangri-La* in mid-January 1962 to participate in *Lantflex 62* (Atlantic Fleet Exercise 62). Little flying was involved, but the Marines gained valuable experience in shipboard procedures as well as establishing a working relationship with the CAG (Commander, Air Group).

With 21 officers and 165 enlisted men, the squadron re-embarked aboard *Shangri-La* on 4 and 5 February at Mayport, Florida.[25] The ship shoved off on the 7th and set course for the Mediterranean Sea.

As the carrier crossed the Atlantic, two squadron Crusaders were placed out of commission when their starboard main gear struts collapsed when the hollow axle broke upon landing. Replacement parts were ordered and eventually arrived. The aircraft were placed back on operational status after repairs were performed.

The ship passed through the Strait of Gibraltar on 17 February. Two days later, it anchored at Mallorca and relieved USS *Intrepid* (CVA-11). Operations in the Mediterranean were conducted from 19 February through 18 August 1962, cruising in all parts of the eastern, central, and western areas of the sea. Liberty ports were visited in mainland France, Italy, Greece, and Turkey, and the islands of Malta, Sicily, and Rhodes.

The squadron lost one aircraft and pilot, as well as three aircraft damaged, while operating in the Mediterranean. On 3 May, after landing, and while taxiing forward, Captain Harry H. Grunwald, Jr. skidded over the side in an area where no flight deck combing was installed. Allinder, flight leader for the flight, recalled the accident:

> Captain Grunwald boltered his first pass: the plane was lighter than "usual," tended to accelerate and get "flat," causing the hook to skip over the wire, and a bolter. On his "go around" the LSO advised of the need to pull the power back for lower fuel weights, even though it was "uncomfortable." Captain Grunwald was the last plane to trap; all others were aboard. As he pulled out of the wires, the *Shangri-La* commenced an immediate turn to port, causing the ship to heel to starboard. CVA-38 had a WWII wooden deck, greased by JP (aviation fuel), hydraulic fluid, etc. As Captain Grunwald folded the wings, pulled forward into the pack and swung the F8 nose forward, the aircraft began to slide sideways toward the starboard wooden deck edge. The starboard main landing gear dropped over the deck edge, Captain Grunwald released his shoulder harness fasteners, and began opening the canopy to exit the cockpit when the F-8 dropped completely off the starboard deck edge, to the water 60 feet below. The F-8 floated for a minute or so with Captain Grunwald still strapped to the seat pan. The Angel (rescue helicopter) dropped the rescue swimmer after

> the plane passed clear of the carrier. The F-8 sank, and Captain Grunwald went down still strapped to the seat pan. Years later a Greek fisherman's trawler snagged "something" on the bottom in the area Captain Grunwald had gone down. And indeed, it was the lost F-8 and its pilot.[26]

The discovery of Grunwald and his Crusader occurred on 9 May 1969, just over seven years later.[27] Grunwald is buried at Arlington National Cemetery.

In addition to the loss of Grunwald, three other aircraft suffered collapsed struts upon landing. The aircraft were repaired and returned to service in a short amount of time. These three accidents occurred in March, June, and July (see Appendix 7).

June saw the squadron set a new record by a Sixth Fleet-based Crusader unit by flying in excess of 600 hours for the month.[28] Operations continued until 18 August when flying was halted, and the next day USS *Shangri-La* was relieved by the nuclear-powered USS *Enterprise* (CVAN-65). Immediately after being relieved, *Shangri-La* set course for the United States. All aircraft were flown off on 28 August and the ship docked at the Naval Station at Mayport later in the day. Personnel and equipment disembarked and were transported to MCAS Beaufort via truck and bus. Upon arrival, a majority of squadron personnel departed immediately on leave, officially bringing an end to the cruise.[29]

Once leave ended, the Marines returned to Beaufort and began the routine of daily operations and the occasional deployment. From late 1962 to 1965, the squadron participated in many competitive exercises, making deployments to MCAS Yuma;[30] NAS Roosevelt Roads, Puerto Rico; Key West, Florida; and Guantanamo Bay, Cuba.

Because of its excellent performance during exercises at Roosevelt Roads, in April 1963, VMF-251 earned the 2nd MAW commanding general's award for achievement in July 1963. The squadron placed first in air-to-air gunnery, Sidewinder missiles, and individual top guns.

Carrier qualifications were apparently made in June 1963, with USS *Lexington* (CVS-16) serving as the training ship.[31]

The operational pace picked up in 1964, as the squadron made three deployments in slightly over a month. During this period, and for a few months afterward, the squadron familiarized over two dozen pilots for other Marine F-8 squadrons; conducted carrier qualifications aboard USS *Saratoga* (CVA-60); and also participated in an exercise, providing close air support and Short Field for Tactical Support (SATS)[32] demonstrations for NATO members and the 2nd MAW commanding general.[33]

During the torrid pace of operations from 1962 to 1965, the squadron lost three Crusaders, and over a dozen aircraft were damaged in various air and ground incidents. Fortunately, no pilots were lost.

The first accident occurred during the morning of 24 January 1963. Following a mission briefing at 0800, Major K. C. Palmer and First Lieutenant Thomson took off at 0900 from MCAS Beaufort for an advanced tactical exercise.

About an hour into the flight, things began to unravel when the two aircraft became separated. Palmer tried to raise Thomson on his radio but got no response. Concerned, he changed course to head back to Beaufort to locate his wingman. Thomson, with radio failure, also turned back for Beaufort.

Palmer, unable to locate Thomson, asked the air station's tower to try to raise him. At this time, Palmer's low fuel warning light came on, indicating he had about a thousand pounds of fuel remaining. A quick check of his fuel gauge confirmed the low fuel.

As he was making his approach to line up for touchdown, he spotted an F-8B Crusader inbound to the station. He thought it might be Thomson and notified the tower he was going to join up with the aircraft. Nearing the rendezvous point, Palmer brought his throttle to the idle position to reduce his airspeed to match that of Thomson's Crusader: 300 knots (345 miles per hour) at 3,000 feet.

Once he slowed, Palmer moved his throttle forward to add power but got no response from the engine—it remained at idle. A quick look at his instruments indicated that, regardless of throttle position, the engine remained at idle. Palmer notified the tower and switched to emergency fuel control. The emergency fuel control light came on, indicating Palmer was now manually controlling fuel to the engine. Advancing the throttle again did no good, the engine remained at idle. Even with the throttle moved to the afterburner position, it remained at idle. He heard a power change when going to afterburner and his RPM began to drop. He tried to restart the engine, but there was no improvement. As the RPMs decreased, the generator went offline. Palmer decided to leave the aircraft.

He turned to avoid Marine Corps Recruit Depot Parris Island and, after crossing the Beaufort River, ejected at approximately a thousand feet and at an air speed of 170 knots. The parachute deployed normally; Palmer landed near the edge of St Helena Island. Upon landing, he injured his left shoulder, making it difficult to release himself from the parachute.

Thomson, who had seen Palmer as his Crusader passed behind his, landed safely at MCAS Beaufort. The runway duty officer had Palmer's aircraft under observation until the aircraft dipped below tree level. He alerted the tower, and a helicopter was dispatched to the scene.

Palmer's aircraft (BuNo 145480) struck the upper branches of a tree 70 feet high at approximately a twenty-degree glide path. The aircraft continued its descent for another 210 feet before it hit the ground with its right wing down. Thirty feet later, the nose hit the ground at which time the Crusader disintegrated. Wreckage was scattered along the line of impact with the engine coming to rest 630 feet from the initial point of impact. The aircraft was completely destroyed.

The injured Palmer was able to retrieve his flares from his survival kit, but not until the helicopter was already in the area. With the helicopter apparently heading his way, Palmer lit one of his flares. The helicopter turned away and flew to the Parris Island Boat Docks where observers gave directions to Palmer's location. When the helicopter returned, Palmer lit another flare. The helicopter spotted Palmer, picked him up, and returned him to the naval hospital at Beaufort.

The second aircraft was lost while the squadron was deployed to Roosevelt Roads, Puerto Rico. On 26 November 1963, First Lieutenant William A. James was scheduled for a radar calibration flight with the assistance of the Royal Navy destroyer HMS *Devonshire.* Following a briefing with the squadron's Operations Section, James began a preflight inspection of his assigned Crusader. All appeared normal except that he noticed the safety pin had not been installed in his seat. James had the assigned plane captain install the face curtain pin prior to entering the cockpit. Just before he started his aircraft, James was shown all seven safety pins which were then stowed in a cloth container on the left side of his ejection seat.

The startup for flight went without a hitch. At 0907, James took off and climbed to 11,000 feet. Upon reaching his altitude, he leveled off and contacted *Devonshire.* No problems were encountered. However, at about 0915, still at 11,000 feet with an indicated airspeed of 375, James heard a loud explosion aft of the cockpit. His Crusader began a violent yaw and roll to the left.

James attempted to recover to normal flight, but his efforts failed, so he decided to eject. He positioned himself in the seat and pulled the face curtain. There was no ejection and the canopy remained closed. He pulled the face curtain at least twice with no results. He then pulled the canopy interrupter handle in preparation of ejecting through the canopy. As he was preparing to do so, James noticed the aircraft seemed to stabilize itself, except it was inverted. He attempted to recover the aircraft (BuNo 145461), but the

Crusader again resumed its violent maneuvers. If that wasn't enough to deal with, James noticed a fire while looking at his starboard mirror.

He pulled the face curtain again, this time with success. He ejected through the canopy at around 8,000 feet with the Crusader slightly nose down and inverted. During the ejection, James injured his back.

As he descended towards the water, James saw that his Crusader was streaming a bright orange flame, originating high on the starboard side between the cockpit and the leading edge of the wing. The Crusader hit the water approximately seventeen nautical miles from Roosevelt Roads. With the depth at 1,000 feet, the aircraft could not be recovered. James did not observe it hit the water; he was busy prepping himself and his gear for his own impact. Once in the water, he inflated his life raft. With his injured back, it was a struggle to enter it.

The search for James started at 1030 hours. After slightly more than an hour, he was picked up by helicopter and returned to Roosevelt Roads.

The last Crusader lost (BuNo 145461) occurred on 13 January 1965 while the squadron was transitioning to the Phantom II. Second Lieutenant Danny R. Slayden was assigned to fly as wingman to section leader First Lieutenant Gibson for a local ground control intercept mission. Take-off from MCAS Beaufort was at 1615. Slayden, approximately two miles behind Gibson and climbing, was passing 20,000 feet when he felt or heard a "thump" aft of the cockpit area.

His Crusader yawed to the left, but Slayden noticed his cockpit instruments were normal. About a minute later, the aircraft again yawed to the left and the yaw stab light illuminated. Concurrent with the yaw, the PC 2[34] pressure was reading zero. Slayden contacted Gibson, who instructed him to remain at a heading of 20 degrees for a rendezvous.

Immediately after contacting Gibson, Slayden saw that his tachometer was reading zero, the engine fuel pump light was on, there was no fuel flow, and the utility hydraulic pressure was dropping below 2,000 PSI. He contacted his section leader again. Gibson ordered him to turn for MCAS Beaufort. It was then that Slayden's engine flamed out.

Gibson had the ailing Crusader in sight and noticed a bright, yellow fireball near the left main wheel well. Slayden's aircraft had entered violent uncontrolled flight, yawing 45 degrees left to right, and pitched nose down. The young pilot extended his emergency power package and turned off the main generator while trying to regain control. The nose rose above the horizon and then pitched down again. With the aircraft at 8,000 feet, Slayden ejected. Upon touching down, he sprained his ankle. Within half an hour, a search-and-rescue helicopter from MCAS Beaufort picked up Slayden and returned him to Beaufort.[35]

During 1964, the squadron finished its task of retraining its enlisted maintenance personnel as it prepared to receive the McDonnell Douglas F-4B Phantom II.[36] With the transition to the new aircraft, the squadron was redesignated as VMFA-251 (Marine Fighter Attack Squadron) on 31 October 1964. The patch was modified to reflect the name change. On a side note, the squadron let go of its last Crusader in 1965 (the type soldiered on in U.S. service until the mid-1980s). So, for a time, the squadron was briefly maintaining two different aircraft types.

CHAPTER 7

The Phantom Years

It was affectionately called the "Flying Brick," "Lead Sled," and "Iron Pig" by some pilots who flew it. For maintenance crews who kept the aircraft flying, there were other names. No matter what it was called, the McDonnell Douglas F-4 Phantom II became one of the most successful fighters of the Cold War era.

The Phantom II had its start as a private endeavor by McDonnell in the early 1950s. Following several design changes based on the needs of the U.S. Navy, the aircraft made its maiden flight on 27 May 1958. From that day until its retirement from U.S. service, the F4H Phantom II set numerous aviation records.

The key to the Phantom's success was its two General Electric J79 engines and unique variable ramp inlets, which regulated airflow into the engine intakes. The engines could provide speeds of Mach 2 on some models, depending on armament configuration. Two other features which characterized the Phantom were its upward extending wing tips, providing a unique look to its angled main wings, and its downward extending horizontal stabilizers.

The U.S. Navy took delivery of its first Phantom II (the initial F4H designation becoming the F-4A and F-4B during initial production runs) in December 1960. In June 1962, the Marine Corps took delivery of its first F-4B. The U.S. Air Force, noting the type's excellent performance after a competition with an F-106 Delta Dart, quickly followed suit and adopted the F-4 as part of the Tri-Service Aircraft Designation System (the USAF originally had the F-4 designated as the F-110). The Phantom thus became the first modern "joint strike fighter," in today's parlance, to see flying duty in all three air services. The U.S. Air Force eventually became the largest user of the F-4 Phantom. VMFA-251 used three versions: F-4B, F-4J, and F-4S.

More than 5,000 Phantom IIs of all variants were built. The aircraft stayed in U.S. service until 1996. It saw combat in Vietnam and Operation

Desert Storm. It also flew with 12 foreign nations: Australia, Egypt, Germany, Great Britain, Greece, Iran, Israel, Japan, South Korea, Spain, and Turkey.

As of mid-2021 four countries continue to fly the Phantom: Iran, South Korea, Greece, and Turkey. Japan retired its aircraft in March 2021; chosen to replace the venerable aircraft was the F-35 Lightning II.[1]

Thus began another long period of training and familiarizing personnel with a new aircraft. Pilots received further training on the F-4B at Marine Corps Air Station (MCAS) Cherry Point, North Carolina, and Naval Air Station (NAS) Oceana in Virginia Beach, Virginia. Radar Intercept Officers (RIO) also received specialized training. The RIO occupied the rear cockpit and had various duties including handling aircraft communications and radar equipment, as well as operating weapons and defensive systems. Some of the enlisted men also went to MCAS Cherry Point for specialized schooling on the aircraft. In December 1964, the squadron's commanding officer, Lieutenant Colonel Arthur Schmagel took VMFA-251's first delivered Phantom II into the air for a one-hour check flight.[2]

Training continued into 1965 and by the summer of that year the squadron was declared operational. The next deployment took place in September when, on the 19th, it transferred to Roosevelt Roads, Puerto Rico, where it remained until 1 December.[3]

The squadron lost an aircraft in an odd incident while at Roosevelt Roads. An errant drone crashed into the squadron's flight line, destroying one of its F-4B Phantoms, BuNo 149417. Apparently, no other aircraft were damaged nor was anyone injured. The incident occurred on 22 September and no official report of it could be located. The late Jerry Dorneker recalled the incident:

> … a "remote controlled" drone (an F-9 piloted from a trainer) crashed into our flight line. It was during lunch break, otherwise it would have killed a bunch of our guys (no one even injured). They informed us when a drone was to be landed so there were no aircraft anywhere on the taxiways etc. Since we knew when they were coming in, I watched the whole thing from on top of a trailer (one of our guys thought he was going to save our lives and pushed me off the top, the fall could have killed me and him both) and darn near was involved in what could have been a terrible tragedy.[4]

Dan Shinabery, a plane captain with 251, was working the flight line that day and had a unique perspective of what he calls "the Navy's failed attempt to eliminate 251":

> I remember the drone incident very well. We lost one bird, the "hanger [*sic*] queen" from Beaufort, No. 17. It had just arrived a week late after several attempts to make the trip.
>
> The Navy had two QF9 drones used for air-to-air practice. The sequence was for a T28 to take the F9 away from the area and hand it off to a special F8 that controlled the drone.

> On that late afternoon, the reverse handoff to the T28 went bad and they lost control of the drone as it was on final approach to runway 25 in a southwest direction.
>
> Most of the squadron was in the chow tent about 100 feet from the impact point.
>
> The QF9 drone at about 100 ft. altitude, stalled, rolled to its right, impacting wing down behind the right wing of hanger queen DW 17. The Queen lost her right outer wing, and main landing gear along with the external fuel tank.
>
> The two junior lowest ranking plane captains were fueling the birds and towing from the fuel pit area and parking them on the line. I was one of them and Dan Mueller the other. I rode brakes on 17 and it was then my turn to tow the next bird. I was headed back to the fuel pits when I heard a jet engine at idle and it was above me just as it stalled and rolled over.
>
> A large bang and lots of fire. The crash crew must have been waiting because they were there right away. It could have been a lot worse. The real tragedy was that the "Queen" was to be our parts source for the deployment and the Navy impounded it right away.
>
> I could have had a better view, but it was safer where I was located 100 feet away. We stopped all flight ops for two days and everyone "FOD walked" the flight line. I think we were still finding QF9 bits and pieces the rest of the deployment.[5]

In 1966, the squadron was a given a new responsibility: training aircrews for the ongoing war in Vietnam. This was in addition to its other duties pertaining to NATO commitments. Crews were trained within seven to eight months and then reassigned to squadrons in South Vietnam or squadrons destined to be stationed there. Training of these crews involved a mix of air-to-air combat tactics and training in close air support (CAS) for ground units. Late in the first half of the year, the squadron deployed to MCAS Yuma to practice air-to-ground attacks. Operations were cancelled briefly when a sandstorm struck the base in May.[6]

During the second half of the year, the squadron was on the move once again. It deployed to MCAS Yuma on 6 September to hone its skills in air-to-ground ordnance delivery before returning to Beaufort on the 19th. The last deployment of the year occurred on 26 November. The squadron made another trip to Roosevelt Roads and stayed there until 16 December. It immediately began work on three tasks assigned to it. The first was Project *Sparrow Shoot* in which the squadron test fired the Sparrow air-to-air missile. Next came the squadron's participation in *Lantflex 66* (4–9 December), the largest U.S. Atlantic fleet exercise held that year. It performed as both friendly and aggressor air assets during a variety of missions. It also provided air support for a planned amphibious landing and subsequent operations inland. During the *Lantflex* exercise, the squadron was assigned to Provisional Marine Aircraft Group 20. The remainder of its time was spent conducting normal training exercises.

In between the two deployments, the squadron saw its first Royal Air Force pilot assigned as part of an exchange program. Flight Lieutenant Christopher

Carr-White arrived on 9 October and was assigned as the Assistant Operations Officer and squadron pilot.[7]

No aircraft were lost during the year and only four were damaged in separate incidents.

Training of pilots and maintenance personnel destined for Vietnam continued into 1967. Some combat veterans from Vietnam found themselves assigned to VMFA-251 and no doubt bore the burden of training pilots destined for the war. In addition to stressing training for combat operations, standard operational flights continued for the squadron.

February was somewhat busy for the squadron. The first day of the month began early for the Marines due to their participation in *AAWEX 1–67* (Anti-Air Warfare Exercise). Starting at 0345, VMFA-251 maintained two manned Phantoms in a five-minute scramble status. Three scrambles were flown. Five days later, Major L. R. Hawkins, completed the 10,000th accident-free hour for the squadron. On the 18th of the month, a detachment of aircraft was sent to Dyess Air Force Base (AFB) near Abilene, Texas. The objective of the deployment was to test different types of tactical air landing surfaces to determine which type was the most acceptable for Navy and Marine Corps usage.

In April, the squadron deployed once again to MCAS Yuma. From 9 to 30 April, crews flew training missions in air-to-ground ordnance delivery.[8]

The squadron's stellar performance began to reap awards. On 5 July, it received the 1967 Fleet Marine Force, Atlantic, Annual Aviation Safety Award for 6,083 accident-free hours during the fiscal year 1967. Two months later, on 27 September, the deputy commander of FMF Atlantic, Major General G. S. Bowman, presented the squadron with the CNO Annual Aviation Safety Award during a formal ceremony at MCAS Beaufort. At the time of the Chief of Naval Operations award, VMFA-251 had racked up 29 accident-free months and compiled a total of 12,720 hours.

During August, it was back to MCAS Yuma for training in ordnance delivery. The squadron spent slightly over two weeks at the air station, having departed on 9 August and returning on the 24th.

On 28 September, squadron aircrews and aircraft participated in *Testex 15*, providing the Commander, Second Fleet with requested air cover.

The following month the squadron continued its record number of accident-free hours. This was accomplished with aircrew flying with Marine Air Group (MAG) 32 skipper G. J. Collins and occurred on 25 October.

From 12 November to 7 December, the "Thunderbolts," along with VMFA-312, deployed to NAS Roosevelt Roads. The Atlantic Fleet Weapons

Range was kept busy by the "Thunderbolts" while they flew a wide range of air-to-air missions, including the firing of Sparrow III and Sidewinder missiles, as well as dropping tons of conventional ordnance on nearby targets.

It was an accident-free year for the squadron, with no aircraft lost. However, the squadron did suffer several incidents that resulted in little or no damage to five Phantoms.[9]

Training of aircrews and enlisted men destined for WestPac (Western Pacific) deployments continued as the squadron entered 1968. Nine pilots and 11 RIOs, as well as 71 enlisted men, were transferred to WestPac by the end of June. During the same period, VMFA-251 had 16 Phantoms assigned to it, but only 13 on hand. The accident-free record continued to pile up with nearly nineteen thousand hours achieved.

On 29 January, VMFA-251 was ordered to deploy six of its Phantoms to NAS Key West by the next day to assume the air defense commitment under Commander, Fleet Air Key West (COMFAIRKEYWEST). Six other aircraft arrived by 2 February. During its three-week stint at Key West, the squadron maintained a round-the-clock hot-pad posture which resulted in 26 practice scramble sorties and eight actual scramble sorties.

In early April, the "Thunderbolts" were once again deployed to MCAS Yuma for three weeks of training in air-to-ground ordnance delivery.

The Marines participated in exercises with Naval Forces Atlantic from 8 to 24 May. During the period, six sorties were launched to aid in the evaluation of the fleet's detection capabilities.

For the period 18–21 June, the squadron conducted a missile shoot in an area known as W-122. This designation referred to a warning area off the coast of North Carolina for use during missile firing exercises. The area fell under the Cherry Point Operational Area and was managed by MCAS Cherry Point.[10] The squadron flew 18 sorties and launched six Sparrow missiles at various targets.[11]

In August, the squadron completed its 20,000th accident-free hour. At the time, it was the only F-4B Phantom II unit to reach that mark. The safety record was confirmed by the Naval Safety Center[12] in Norfolk, Virginia. Later in the year, the squadron was awarded the Outstanding Achievement Trophy and the Commanding General's Trophy for its excellent performance. The commanding officer of the 2nd Marine Aircraft Wing (MAW), Major General Marion E. Carl, presented the latter trophy to the unit's commander. In addition, McDonnell Douglas Aircraft Corporation presented a trophy to the squadron for its accomplishments in the Phantom II.

The following month, on the 14th, a small detachment deployed to Key West. Following completion of the deployment, the detachment returned to MCAS Beaufort on 14 October.

The RAF exchange officer assigned to the squadron, Carr-White, completed his tour of duty with the squadron on 10 October and was replaced by Flight Lieutenant William A. N. Lane. Eleven days later, the squadron was assigned the task of providing air superiority and fighter combat air patrol (CAP) for attack aircraft in an exercise which simulated a strike on enemy forces located about two hundred fifty miles north of MCAS Beaufort. All personnel were called in at midnight and were ready for operations four hours later. Four aircraft were placed on a five-minute alert pad with six others ready if needed. The exercise was a success with the MAG-32 commander extending a "well done" to the squadron.

Another exercise was completed on 13 November with the squadron participating in "Apache Brave," an air defense operation held in conjunction with the USAF's 32nd Air Division. The air division, with headquarters at Gunter AFB in Alabama, was responsible for air defense of the southeast area of the United States. VMFA-251 was presented with an award by the air division for its excellent support during the exercise.

During the last six months of 1968, a further 20 pilots, eight Naval Flight Officers (NFO), and 58 enlisted men were transferred to WestPac. At the end of the year, the squadron had 32 officers, 384 enlisted men, and 19 assigned Phantoms on hand.[13]

The first half of 1969 was relatively quiet. The squadron participated in two live-fire exercises involving the Sparrow III air-to-air missile and one exercise involving the AIM-7 Sidewinder heat-seeking air-to-air missile. The three 3-day exercises were conducted from 13–16 January, 23–25 April, and 19–21 May respectively. In between the first two missile shoots, from 14 March to 14 April, the squadron deployed to NAS Key West to stand hot-pad duty for COMFAIRKEYWEST.

The squadron's impressive accident-free record continued. For fiscal year 1969, ending in June, it flew nearly four thousand five hundred ninety accident-free hours. The "Thunderbolts" were nearing 24,000 hours without an accident in the Phantom. In addition, aircrew training resulted in five pilots, seven Naval Flight Officers and 10 temporarily assigned officers designated as combat ready and transferred to WestPac. In addition, at the end of May, Captain John D. Cummings was recognized by McDonnell Douglas for being the first Marine pilot to surpass the 2,000-hour mark in the F-4 Phantom II.[14]

A new fiscal year—1970—began on 1 July 1969. Normal flight operations were the norm until 17 August when the squadron once again deployed to MCAS Yuma. It flew 353 air-to-ground sorties, dropping different types of ordnance in the Chocolate Mountain area. They were aided in their missions by HML-276 OV-10 Broncos[15] acting as forward air controllers and observers for the bomb runs.

Upon the squadron's return to MCAS Beaufort on 6 September, the "Thunderbolts" became the first unit of any U.S. military branch to complete 25,000 accident-free hours in the Phantom II. James Walker, representing McDonnell Douglas, presented then squadron commander Lieutenant Colonel Rodney O. Lawrence with a plaque commending the squadron for its incredible safety record.

Between 14 and 16 October, a missile-firing exercise utilizing both Sparrow and Sidewinder missiles was conducted. The exercise qualified 15 replacement aircrews in the firing of the missiles. Another exercise followed on 3 November, ending on the 7th. MAG-31 controlled the exercise which saw the squadron fly 29 sorties for 51 hours and fire nine missiles.

In between the two missile shoots, the squadron participated in another air defense exercise, dubbed *Snowtime 70–2-E*. The one-day exercise, conducted on 29 October, was led by the 33rd Air Division which was based out of Fort Lee Air Force Station in Virginia.

Training of aircrew destined for WestPac continued during the period. The squadron flew another 2,617 accident-free hours in the last six months of 1969. By the end of December, 24 aircrewmen were designated combat ready and transferred to WestPac.[16]

The command chronology for January through June 1970 could not be located. However, according to documents obtained from the Naval Safety Center, no incidents or accidents occurred during this six-month period. The squadron's safety record remained intact going into July 1970.

As the demand for training aircrews for WestPac decreased, in July 1970 the squadron began an intensive program to qualify its aircrews in aerial combat maneuvering (ACM). Aided by four officers from the Marine Aviation Weapons and Tactics Battalion (MAWTB), MCAS Cherry Point, North Carolina, aircrews were made ready for an upcoming deployment which would hone their skills in air-to-air missile firing.

The deployment occurred on 23 July 1970 when the squadron began its move to NAS Roosevelt Roads, Puerto Rico, via Homestead AFB in Florida. It was also on this date that the unit's stellar safety record came to a deadly end.

First Lieutenants James R. Vance (pilot) and Denis K. Hagaman (RIO) were one of four aircrews destined for Roosevelt Roads, Puerto Rico. The flight plan was to meet up with a tanker for air-to-air refueling before proceeding to Roosevelt Roads. Hence the aircraft did not go to the fuel pits or carry external fuel tanks. Prior to taxiing, the flight was informed the tanker would not be at the designated rendezvous point due to bad weather. Instead, they were to head for Homestead AFB to refuel. It was also during this time that Vance called the flight leader informing him of a trim problem with his aircraft. Within a few minutes, he called again, reporting his aircraft was good to go.

The four Phantoms were in the air shortly after 1300. The flight en route was without incident. Prior to the initial approach to Homestead, the leader informed all aircraft to dump fuel to obtain a comfortable landing weight. Vance and Hagaman—in DW 07 (BuNo 151437)—had no issues venting their fuel.

The aircraft received their landing instructions. At approximately two-second intervals, each aircraft began its break for approach and landing. DW 07 was seen to make a normal entry into break but continued to roll and quickly slammed into the ground. Prior to impact, the RIO, Hagaman, ejected while Vance remained in the aircraft. Both men did not survive. The accident report seemed to indicate the servo pool plungers of the left and right aileron control cylinders recovered from the wreckage may have been a contributing factor in the crash. While no evidence of binding was noted during tests, "the physical application of a torque of only 1.5 ounces per inch to the plunger in the same rotational direction as noted during tests resulted in severe binding of the control lever." Because of this possibility, the investigators of the accident recommended that action be initiated "to redesign the servo valve to eliminate any possibility of binding," citing several similar incidents that had been previously reported.[17]

Once the "Thunderbolts" arrived at Roosevelt Roads, training operations began on 27 July and included two weeks of air-to-air missile firing and one week of air-to-ground weapons delivery. During the missile-firing exercises, use of the maneuverable BM-34 drone target, as well as patterning the training after that utilized by the U.S. Navy's Fighter Weapons School at NAS Miramar (TOPGUN), provided a realistic "combat" environment. Preparations made prior to the deployment paid off. Ten aircrews were qualified as they scored direct hits on three of the drones, along with six other "killing" hits. During a competition led by MAWTB, the squadron earned 27 "E" awards for excellence in air-to-air employment. A total of 28 missiles were fired during the two-week missile-training period. During its week of air-to-ground training, the "Thunderbolts" provided CAS for Aviation Ordnance School, 2nd Marine Division, and the 2nd ANGLICO Air Naval Gunfire Liaison Company, as well as simultaneous operations with VMO-1, an observation squadron flying the OV-10 Bronco.

The squadron performed well during the deployment, but several issues were noted that affected operations: it rained every day, the heavy downpours covering the runways with water. The summer rains also forced the cancellation of operations for one day. The rainfall, coupled with high humidity and high temperatures, hampered maintenance and operations every day; the TACAN (Tactical Air Navigation) Station died on 5 August and remained out of service for the remainder of the deployment. With the lack of local IFR (Instrument Flight Rules) procedures, coupled with the daily rain, and lack of protection for the aircraft, the original exercise schedule had to be shortened. Several other factors were noted leading the squadron commander at that time—LtCol. Rodney Lawrence—to recommend that deployments to Roosevelt Roads be limited to air-to-air exercises only and that air-to-ground operations be conducted at MCAS Yuma.

Returning to Beaufort on 17 August, the squadron continued to conduct intercept, air-to-ground, and ACM training. It was during ACM training on 30 September that the squadron suffered its second deadly accident for the period.

Following an early morning briefing, Major Vincent P. Nolan (pilot from MAWTB, MCAS Cherry Point) and First Lieutenant Michael K. Kilpatrick (RIO) climbed into the cockpit of their F-4B Phantom II (BuNo 153048). At 0930, the F-4B took off from MCAS Beaufort and proceeded to the designated area for the ACM, located about fifty miles southeast of Beaufort. Another Phantom II and a TA-4 Skyhawk were also participating in the exercise.

The aircraft met up and began the exercise. Vance was performing an Immelmann maneuver during a second engagement when, at 20,000 feet and closing to within 2,500 feet of the TA-4 acting as the enemy, pieces of the aircraft began ripping away from the Phantom. The aircraft was seen to spiral downward with the right wing down. In addition, fuel was streaming out at a rapid rate. Pieces of the aircraft continued to break off as it plunged into the ocean at 40 degrees nose down. No ejections were observed but two emergency tones were picked up. One parachute was seen to land in the water.

Search efforts began immediately. An HH-52A Seaguard helicopter was launched from the Coast Guard Air Station at Savannah, Georgia. Upon reaching the crash site, the rescue crew spotted a floating life raft with Kilpatrick's body approximately six to eight feet underneath it and still attached to his parachute. There were no visible signs of life from the RIO. During the recovery attempt, the body and equipment sank, Only the life raft was recovered. The search continued for the pilot, but Nolan was not found.[18]

The two accidents hit the squadron hard. Ken Hanson, who joined the squadron as a RIO on 3 July 1970, credits the squadron commanding officer and executive officer—Lieutenant Colonels Lawrence and Robert "Rocky" Plant—with handling "the two crashes and four deaths with proper respect, a few toasts, and put the squadron right back to work."[19] Separate memorial services at the MCAS Beaufort chapel were held for the lost Marine aviators. Services for Vance and Hagaman were held on 27 July at Roosevelt Roads and on 19 August when the squadron returned to MCAS Beaufort. Services for Kilpatrick and Nolan were held on 7 October. Kilpatrick received a special send off in the form of a poem:

> For 14 months he served right here,
> Adding humor and lots of cheer.
> When on the scope and in the air,
> He was a lion in search of a bear.
> Then, one day out over the sea,
> Mike moved on to his destiny.
> We're sorry, Killer, to see you go,
> But you'll always live on as a real
> T-Bolt.[20]

To close out the year, the squadron received three awards for its performance through June 1970. On 2 October, Major General G. C. Axtell, Commanding General of the 2nd MAW, presented the squadron with the Fleet Marine Force, Atlantic, Safety Award in recognition of over 29,000 accident-free flight hours. On 20 November, the squadron learned it had been selected to receive the Robert M. Hanson award as the best Marine fighter squadron for 1969. Axtell also presented the squadron with the Hanson Trophy as well as the CNO (Chief of Naval Operations) Safety Award on 8 December.[21] The Hanson Award was named in honor of Captain Robert M. Hanson, a fighter ace with 25 confirmed kills during World War II. He was posthumously awarded the Medal of Honor.[22] Hanson was lost on 3 February 1944 in the vicinity of Cape St. George, New Ireland. His body was never recovered.

The squadron began 1971 at MCAS Beaufort. However, it was not long before it was on the move once again. From 10 February to 1 March, the "Thunderbolts" returned to Roosevelt Roads for another round of air-to-air and air-to-ground training. For three days of the deployment—15, 16, and 17 February—the squadron participated in a joint air-to-ground operation with the 2nd Marine Division. Dubbed *Firex 71*, VMFA-251 was a component of Provisional Marine Air Group 20 and conducted 56 sorties in support of the division. All ordnance drops were under the control of a ground or airborne forward air controller on the Vieques Air Impact Area located 18 miles east of Roosevelt Roads. For its role in *Firex 71*, the "Thunderbolts" received a favorable mention in a communication from the Commanding General, 2nd Marine Division.

The remainder of the deployment was devoted to air-to-air missile firing. Aircrews were required to intercept and identify, and then fire at, a maneuvering jet-powered drone—a Ryan Firebee. Twenty-four missiles with deactivated warheads were fired, one of which scored a direct hit on the drone, destroying it. For the feat, First Lieutenants D. Snook and R. B. Fyke were each awarded a Firebee kill plaque. Hanson also scored a direct hit on a target with a Sparrow. "I was properly rewarded with a control wire from the missile by the ordnance crew. I still have it today," recalled Hanson.[23] Telemetry devices in the area revealed the remaining missiles passed near enough to a target drone to result in a kill.

On 7 April, the squadron hosted an air-to-ground weapons competition with the "Bumblebees" of VMA-331 and their A-4 Skyhawks. The exercise was conducted at the Putnam target area 170 miles south of Beaufort. Although the pilots of VMA-331 obtained better accuracy in their weapons deliveries, the fighter pilots of 251 flew a total of 40 sorties on that day, providing experience for the aircrews.

From 14 April to 14 May, five squadron aircraft were detached to NAS Key West, Florida, for operational alert duty. While only two aircraft were required to meet the alert commitment, the other three were used for advanced intercept training. Those on alert duty were flown at least once daily in accordance with the Joint Air Reconnaissance Control Center's "scramble" procedures. "A beautiful place to fly," recalls Hanson. "Cuba never launched a MiG, much to the disappointment of 1stLt. Bill Schaekel and myself." Hanson's disappointment was no doubt short-lived since he met his future wife during the deployment.[24] During their stay at Key West, the aircraft flew 154 sorties.

At some point during the period, the squadron began its transition from the F-4B to the F-4J. The F-4J came with a new radar, the AWG-10. To prepare for the new equipment, 44 aircrew completed the AWG-10 Weapons Systems Naval Aviation Maintenance Orientation course, while 14 enlisted radar technicians completed a three-month AWG-10 organization course, and an additional 15 enlisted technicians completed an AWG-10 familiarization course.

The squadron held a second missile-firing exercise from 1 through 3 June. A total of 29 sorties were flown with 27 AIM-9B Sidewinders successfully fired. The heat-seeking missiles were fired at airdropped flares and the intercepts were accomplished while under the control of Marine Air Control Squadron 9.

The day following the end of the missile exercise, the squadron suffered its only mishap for the six-month period. First Lieutenant Richard E. McLane, piloting an F-4B (BuNo 148398), was flying a training mission when the aircraft suffered utility hydraulic failure followed by a port engine fire warning light, and an engine bay fire or explosion. McLane was able to bring his aircraft home, performing an arrested landing. The jet suffered extensive damage and was recommended to be written off due to limited remaining service life. McLane and his RIO, First Lieutenant Ronald E. Woernle, were not injured in the incident.[25]

The squadron continued to transfer personnel to WestPac during the period, sending four Naval Aviators, five NFOs, and nine enlisted men in support of operations in the Far East.[26]

Starting on 1 September 1971, the "Thunderbolts" participated in a MAG-31 exercise, *Night Hawk*, an annual training operation testing the mission readiness of aircrews and aircraft in air-to-ground and air-to-air operations. Lasting a week, the exercise provided sought-after training for the aircrews, particularly in night/all-weather conditions.

From 14 September through 14 October, five aircraft were sent to NAS Key West and took over alert duty under control of the Commander, Key West Forces. As was the case during their April–May detachment, two of the five aircraft were committed to alert status and were scrambled at least once a day. Daily air operations provided advanced interceptor training for the "Thunderbolt" pilots. The aircraft ended up tallying 137 sorties for the month-long duty.

The five Phantoms returned to Beaufort as the rest of the squadron was preparing for another deployment to NAS Roosevelt Roads. On 22 October, the "Thunderbolts" departed for the air station in Puerto Rico. While at Roosevelt Roads, the squadron participated in a Phase II missile shoot, which was designed to evaluate aircrew training and the reliability of the Phantom's weapons system. Each of the squadron Phantoms was required to intercept the target drone—once again the Ryan Firebee—and fire a Sparrow missile (radar guided) at it in the forward quarter. Then the crew had to visually identify the target, approach from the rear quarter of the drone and fire a Sidewinder (a heat seeker). Telemetry devices tracked the flight path of the missiles to determine if they scored a kill on the drone. To make hitting the drone more difficult, it began evasive maneuvers as the opposing Phantoms were about eight miles from the target. When the exercise ended, 18 Sparrows and 19 Sidewinders were considered "on target." The "Thunderbolts" became the first Marine fighter squadron to complete the missile exercise. They returned to MCAS Beaufort on 8 November.

Ten days later, VMFA-251 was selected to represent the USMC in the USAF's Air Defense Command "College Dart" program. The squadron immediately began preparing for the exercise, which was to be held in January 1972. The Air Force program provided dissimilar air combat training (DACT), using F-106 Delta Darts as enemy aircraft.

A month later, the squadron was ordered to provide aircraft for a classified detachment, testing its readiness posture and response capability. This occurred on 18 December. Within 48 hours, four fully response-capable aircraft were loaded and ready to go with four other Phantoms as back-ups. The back-up aircraft were also fully loaded and ready. The aircraft were still on alert status at the end of the year.

In addition to the alert status, on 27 December 1971, VMFA-251 participated as aggressor aircraft in an air/ground exercise with other units of the 2nd MAW and 2nd Marine Division, codenamed *Blue Ax*. The exercise emphasized CAS during amphibious operations. The squadron was still participating in the exercise as the year ended.[27]

Once *Blue Ax* ended on 7 January 1972, training shifted to concentrate on the first round of the upcoming *College Dart* exercise with the USAF. Following the completion of the training, the squadron deployed six Phantoms, six aircrews, and maintenance personnel, to Tyndall AFB in Florida from 17 to 22 January. There, they engaged F-106 Delta Darts from the 318th Fighter Interceptor Squadron in two-vs-two, two-vs-four, and fighter escort missions. The exercises provided the "Thunderbolt" aircrews with simulated combat experience that could not currently be provided by the 2nd MAW.

Following the return from Tyndall, the squadron sent six Phantoms, while rotating aircrews, to NAS Key West for hot-pad duty. Arriving on 25 January, the squadron flew 144 sorties for nearly two hundred forty-nine hours before its aircraft and personnel returned to Beaufort on 14 February. During the deployment, one jet (BuNo 155821) was damaged in an unknown incident.

From the time it arrived back at MCAS Beaufort until it flew back to NAS Key West a month later, the squadron concentrated on training its aircrews in air-to-air and ACM tactics. During the training, another aircraft was damaged in an unspecified incident (BuNo 153776).

On 14 March, VMFA-251 returned to NAS Key West to assume hot-pad duty, arriving on 14 March with 10 aircraft. Five of the Phantoms were assigned alert duties while the other five were used for aircrew training. ACM had a high priority with two-vs-one and two-vs-two sorties flown against A-4M Skyhawks of VMA-324. Air-to-ground delivery of ordnance also occupied the squadron, flying numerous missions to the Avon Park Target Complex, a USAF bombing range east of Avon Park, Florida. During the month-long deployment, the squadron flew 320 sorties for 450 hours.

Soon after the detachment returned to MCAS Beaufort from Key West in mid-April, MAG-31 ordered a rapid recall exercise. Within two hours of the order, the squadron reported all Marines on hand and within five hours had launched eight aircraft. After the brief exercise, the squadron resumed its operational routine of training flight crews until the end of the month. During this period, another Phantom II was damaged in an unknown incident (BuNo 155836).

The first day of May saw eight aircrews assigned to a missile-shooting exercise at the Cherry Point Missile Range (North Carolina). By the time the exercise was completed four days later, five Sparrows and eight Sidewinders had been fired at MQM-74 Chukar target drones. Five of the participating aircrews were qualified during the shoot.

Three days later, the squadron hosted aircrews from Marine Air Weapons Training Unit, Atlantic (MAWTULANT) out of MCAS Cherry Point, North Carolina, for an air combat tactics instruction course. The evaluation included knowledge of tactical manual procedures, briefing, debriefing, and airborne instruction. Following completion of the course, four aircrews were designated air combat tactics instructors.

Operational training continued for the squadron for the rest of May and most of June. On 25 June, four Phantoms and five aircrews, as well as selected maintenance personnel, were deployed back to Tyndall AFB for the second round of the *College Dart* program. Upon completion of the exercise, the small contingent of "Thunderbolts" returned to MCAS Beaufort on 30 June.[28]

Deployments slowed down as July rolled around. During the second half of 1972, the squadron remained at Beaufort for the majority of the period. In late July, its Phantoms participated in another missile shoot at the Cherry Point Missile Range. As the shoot concluded on 27 July, the squadron conducted simulated raids against the amphibious assault ship USS *Guam* (LPH-9). The next day, four Phantoms were committed for CAP and radar missions as ordered by the 2nd MAW.

Air-to-air gunnery and air-to-ground ordnance delivery dominated training during the month of August. When September rolled in, the squadron participated in air intercept training with the guided-missile cruiser USS *Albany* (CG-10). At the conclusion of that exercise, the unit sent nine aircraft, crews, and maintenance personnel to NAS Key West for operational missions and training flights. By the time the deployment ended on 14 October, the crews had racked up nearly four hundred hours.

During November, squadron Phantoms conducted ACM exercises during the day and radar intercept missions during the night. In addition, they also participated in SATS operations out of Bogue Field, North Carolina. Soon after, the squadron participated in the 20th North American Air Defense Command (NORAD) exercise dubbed *Snowtime*. November operations also included dropping live ordnance during close-combat training missions. As the month ended, the "Thunderbolts" began preparations to participate in another *College Dart* dissimilar air combat maneuvering (DACM) exercise at Tyndall AFB in Florida.

The *College Dart* program was conducted over the period 11–15 December. The squadron deployed five F-4J Phantom IIs, eight combat-qualified aircrews, and maintenance personnel. The Phantoms again flew against Air Force F-106 Delta Darts, flying a total of 26 sorties during the exercise.[29] The remaining Phantoms at Beaufort continued their normal operations.

These continued into January 1973. At the end of the month, a detachment of squadron Phantoms and relevant personnel were sent to NAS Key West to assume hot pad duty. During their month-long stay, the detachment flew day and night practice missions before returning to MCAS Beaufort on 1 March. The remainder of the squadron at Beaufort continued with their training flights, with an emphasis on intercept missions. These continued through March since the squadron had received orders to prepare for a missile-shoot at NAS Roosevelt Roads, Puerto Rico.

Before its deployment to Roosevelt Roads, the squadron participated in Exercise *Exotic Dancer VI* from 29 March to 7 April. The Phantoms flew 126 sorties which consisted of beach strafes, CAP, CAS missions and one SATS demonstration. Two successful data link sorties were flown under the control of MACS-6 (Marine Air Control Squadron). The first few sorties of the exercise were flown from Beaufort, but on 1 April the squadron deployed 12 Phantoms to MCALF (Marine Corps Auxiliary Landing Field) Bogue Field, North Carolina, and conducted the remainder of its missions from there. All aircraft returned to MCAS Beaufort on 8 April.

The highlight for May was the deployment to Roosevelt Roads on the 4th and 5th. The aircraft that departed on 4 May hooked up with aerial-refueling tankers from VMGR-252. With their tanks topped off, the Phantoms proceeded to Puerto Rico. The next day, the KC-130 Hercules from VMGR-252 was down for mechanical reasons, so the remaining Phantoms flew to NAS Key West to refuel before proceeding to NAS Roosevelt Roads.

Operations began on 7 May and, for the next four days, air-to-air missile exercises on the Atlantic Fleet Weapons Range were conducted. Squadron pilots fired 12 Sparrows and 12 Sidewinders at BQM-34 target drones.

Upon completion of the missile shoot, the squadron shifted to ground support. From 12 May to the 19th, the "Thunderbolts" conduced air-to-ground and live ordnance training at the Culebra and Vieques Target Complexes near Roosevelt Roads. Crews flew 96 day and 20 night sorties. During the air-to-ground missions, a detachment from VMO-1 provided airborne tactical air control support. Upon completion of the deployment, the squadron returned to MCAS Beaufort on 23 May.

Aircrew training emphasized air intercepts and air-to-ground training during the month of June. During the evening of 20 June, three Phantoms participated in Exercise *Amalgam Arrow*. They were used as friendly force interceptors under the control of 21st NORAD.[30] The squadron racked up slightly over 207 hours for the month, and no aircraft were reported lost for the first six months of the year.[31]

The air intercept and air-to-ground training missions continued into July. By August, training shifted to concentrate on CAS missions as well as air-defense missions in preparation of the squadron's deployment to Cigli Air Base in Turkey in support of the NATO exercise *Deep Furrow*—a large amphibious training exercise to be held in northwest Turkey. During the first week of

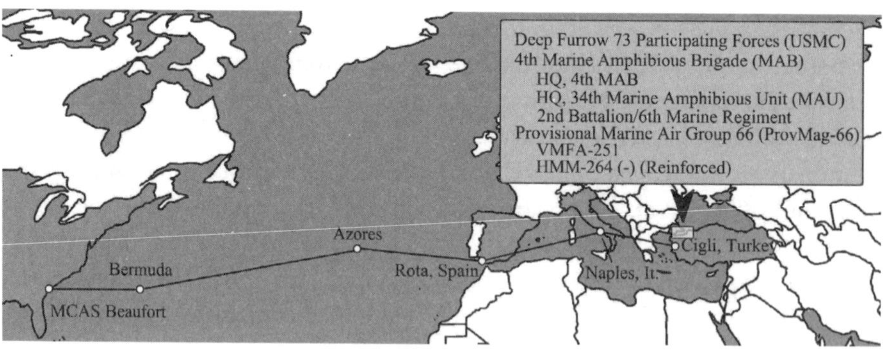

Deep Furrow 73 Participating USMC Forces

September, a series of lectures were held to brief personnel on the purpose of the exercise, as well as navigation briefs for aircrews. On 13 and 14 September, the squadron stood down to allow two days of training to prepare ground personnel for *Deep Furrow*.

All of the squadron's Phantom IIs were assigned for the deployment. Three Phantoms came from VMFA-333. "We took 3 birds from 333 because we had three down for maintenance and didn't have enough operational birds for the Turkey deployment," recalled 251 veteran John Bryson.[32] Thus, when the squadron departed for Cigli on 17 September, it had nine of its own Phantoms and the three from VMFA-333. The flight took them to Bermuda, then the Azores and from there a stop at Rota, Spain, then off to Napoli, Italy.[33] The 12 aircraft arrived at Cigli on 22 September and immediately began operations providing support to participating ground units. By the time *Deep Furrow* ended on 26 September, the squadron had flown 40 CAS missions as well as eight air-defense missions.

Unlike the uneventful flight over the Atlantic to Cigli, the return trip to Beaufort—which occurred from 27 September through 7 October—was marred by two accidents. One of the accidents claimed the lives of two squadron aviators: First Lieutenants William C. Rogers (pilot) and Robert W. Jacobs (RIO).[34] Rogers and Jacobs were lost in a landing accident at Naval Air Facility (NAF) Naples on 27 September.

Rain from weak thunderstorms had soaked the runway as three of 251's Phantoms approached the naval airfield from Cigli, Turkey. Each of the aircraft in the flight were loaned to 251 from VMFA-333 prior to leaving MCAS Beaufort (BuNos 155520, 153772 and 153886). Rogers was piloting 153886.

As the flight approached Naples on an IFR flight plan, it was informed that it was raining, and visibility was about ten kilometers (six miles). The Phantoms were cleared to descend to 10,000 feet and to contact approach control. Unable to contact approach control, the flight was given another frequency. As frequencies were being changed, Rogers lost radio contact with the other two aircraft. No contact was made with approach control on the second frequency. The flight leader decided to have the three aircraft drop to 2,500 feet since he was under visual meteorological conditions. Contact with the tower was finally made at 2,500 feet, so the flight was sent back to approach control.

The flight navigation gear was not operating at 100%; Rogers's aircraft had no TACAN, radar or navigation computer. The landing field was located using information relayed by the lead number two aircraft. The field was visually sighted about six kilometers (almost four miles) out, far below the 10 kilometers given to them.

At approximately mid-field, the flight broke at 1,500 feet mean sea level. As the lead completed his 180-degree turn, he acknowledged that the arresting gear was not rigged and advised the first 100 meters of the runway was not usable. Arresting gear was available but the lead did not request it be hooked up. As he was coming in for his landing, he briefly lost sight of the runway, but it became visible at about three-quarters of a mile. He landed normally, having no problems with the wet runway. He reported to the tower that braking action was not severe.

The number two Phantom had the same conditions on his approach, but he decided to wave off at 600 feet. He began to climb and paralleled the runway for a heading. At 2,000 feet, he saw the ground and began his turn for another approach.

While number two repositioned for another attempt, Rogers made his descent to the runway; he was observed to be above the proper glidepath. According to witnesses, he had a good attitude but was coming down too fast. At the point where the lead had picked up the runway, the nose of his aircraft was seen to go down, perhaps in an attempt to touch down closer to the end of the runway. As Rogers's Phantom II reached the point of no return, his nose began to rise. Witnesses at the scene thought his aircraft stalled in a very nose-high attitude as it hit the runway hard on its main left landing gear about a thousand feet from the approach end of the runway. Rogers appeared to correct to his right. The correction, with the high sink rate, caused the right main landing gear to collapse on impact. The strut punctured the wing fuel cell, spilling fuel as well as severing linkages and control cables to the right wing control surfaces.

Rogers deployed his drag 'chute, but the F-4J veered to the right. The right wing dragged the runway, causing sparks to ignite the streaming fuel. Rogers kicked in his afterburners in an attempt to get airborne. The aircraft skidded into the grass and crossed a taxiway when the nose dropped hard. The nose gear collapsed causing severe damage to the front cockpit floor and striking the bottom of Rogers's ejection seat; he was fatally injured. At the same time, the radome separated from the Phantom. The nose dug into the ground, demolishing the radar. The tail rose and the aircraft began to roll to its left. As this was happening, Jacobs attempted to eject but suffered fatal injuries. As the wrecked aircraft skidded on its back, the fuselage fuel tanks were torn open, spilling fuel and causing a ground fire. The aircraft tumbled upright which tore off the outboard portion of the right wing. As the Phantom

World War II pilot LtCol. Herb Peters during the Korean War before he accidentally landed behind enemy lines and was captured by the North Koreans. Peters served with VMO-251 during World War II. (Author's collection)

K-6 flight line, winter of 1953/4. (Burrel Sumner, used with permission)

A VMA-251 Skyraider with a load of bombs, K-6, South Korea, 1953/4. (Burrel Sumner, used with permission)

K-6 flight line. Trying to keep the engines from freezing by pumping in warm air. (Burrel Sumner, used with permission)

K-6 Base, Pyoengtaek, South Korea, 1953/4. (Burrel Sumner, used with permission)

2ndLt. Burrel Sumner in the cockpit of a Skyraider, K-6 Base, South Korea, 1953/4. (Burrel Sumner, used with permission)

Douglass R. Annand during flight training. Annand was severely injured in an accident on 10 April 1952 which left him without the use of his legs. (Photo courtesy of the Annand Family)

VMA-251 Douglas AD-4 Skyraider "Marie" AL-9 being worked on after a wheels-up landing at K-6 in South Korea, 1953. (USN, Tailhook Society, used with permission)

North American FJ-3 BuNo 135935 VMF-251 DW-611, circa late 1950s. (Aldrich collection, Tailhook Society, used with permission)

Maintenance personnel work on an F-8 Crusader, probably 1957/8. Note the incorrect tail code on the Crusader in the background. (USMC Photo)

Marine Attack Squadron VMA-251, Atsugi, Japan, 5 December 1956. (Courtesy of CPL. Ralph J. Sabroe)

Main building at NAS Roosevelt Roads, Puerto Rico, November 1963. (William James, used with permission)

1stLt. William James in the cockpit of a VMF-251 F-8 Crusader, MCAS Beaufort, SC, 1963. James was forced to eject from a Crusader on 26 November 1963. (William James, used with permission)

Squadron building at NAS Roosevelt Roads, November 1963. (William James, used with permission)

1stLt. William James grabbing a quick nap on the squadron flight line, MCAS Beaufort, SC. Date unknown. (William James, used with permission)

VMF-251 carrier qualifications on USS *Saratoga*, April 1964. (William James, used with permission)

Roosevelt Roads, December 1965. Plane captain giving the pilot the "spread wings" signal. Captain D. Bassitt is the pilot. (Dan Shinabery, used with permission)

MCAS Yuma, Arizona, May 1966. Aircraft on the way to the Chocolate Mountain aerial gunnery range. DW 8 (BuNo 148402) and other Phantom photographed from the rear cockpit of DW 10; 2ndLt. Gary Sloman was in the front seat of DW 10. (Dan Shinabery, used with permission)

1967 deployment to Roosevelt Roads. The nose of DW-1 as it gets the finish rinse at the desalting spray area used by the Navy. (Dan Shinabery, used with permission)

Roosevelt Roads, November 1967 deployment. Saturday morning crew of plane captains assembled in front of the dirty bird to be washed: DW-1, BuNo 152230. (Dan Shinabery, used with permission)

Roosevelt Roads, November 1967 joint deployment with VMFA-312. This picture is of four aircraft. Left to right is DW-10, BuNo 149458. Next is DR-1, BuNo 152236, VMFA-312. Then DW-1, BuNo 152230, and DR-7, BuNo 149470, the unlucky bird that lost its nose gear on take-off and landed in a shower of sparks as the radome and nose were ground away. Notice the unusual angle of the aircraft as its nose, or what's left of it, rests on a flatbed trailer. (Dan Shinabery, used with permission)

F-4B over Puerto Rico, February 1971. This is a fine study of the squadron's markings at the time. (Ken Hanson Collection)

Capt. Robert Dwyer's Phantom II following the belly landing at Charleston AFB on 29 May 1974. (Robert Dwyer, used with permission)

Remains of right main landing gear of BuNo 153770 after its crash landing at Reese AFB, Texas, in April 1975. (Jay Cluelow, used with permission)

Aerial view of the remains of Hynes and Cluelow's Phantom (BuNo 153770) following their crash at Reese AFB, Texas, on 27 April 1975. (Jay Cluelow, used with permission)

Aft canopy from BuNo 153770, Cluelow having ejected prior to the crash. (Jay Cluelow, used with permission)

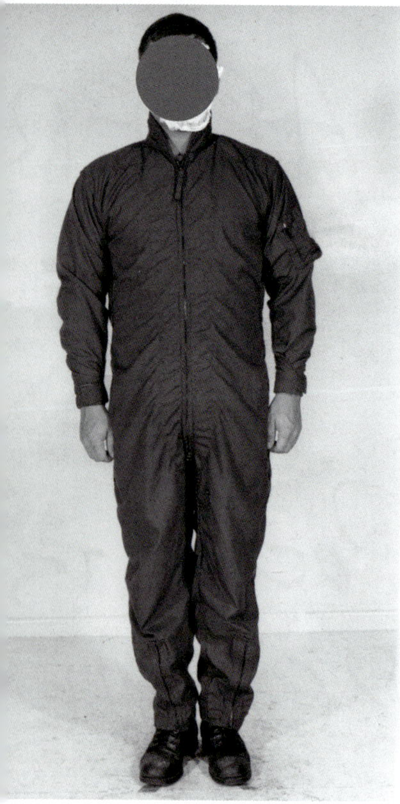

Flight suit developed by VMFA-251 personnel, based on those used by NASCAR drivers at the time, that afforded better fire protection for aircrew. It was not adopted. (LtCol. Josephus Mavretic, USMC, Ret., used with permission)

LtCol. Josephus Mavretic was VMFA-251's squadron commander from December 1973 to January 1975. (LtCol. Josephus Mavretic, USMC, Ret., used with permission)

LtCol. G. E. Walsh (left) assumes command of the "Thunderbolts" from LtCol. Mavretic on the last day of January 1975. (LtCol. Josephus Mavretic, USMC, Ret, used with permission)

Following Mavretic's change of command ceremony, squadron personnel enjoyed a cookout, 31 January 1975. (LtCol. Josephus Mavretic, USMC, Ret, used with permission)

The Northrop Aviation YF-17 technology demonstrator aircraft in flight during a 1976 flight research program at NASA's Dryden Flight Research Center, Edwards, California. The YF-17 was developed into the F-18 with the help of McDonnell Douglas. (NASA)

251 Commanding Officer LtCol. Wuertz, MCAS Beaufort, January 1977. (T. H. "Mac" McAllister)

VMFA-251 on the flight line at Cubi Point, Subic Bay, Philippine Islands, October 1977. The aircraft carrier in the background is USS *Midway*, now a museum ship moored in San Diego. (Author's collection)

Electrician Stephen Robb looks on as radar technician P. J. Whitehall works his magic on a Phantom's AWG-10 radar. (Author's collection)

Cranking up for a flight, Cubi Point, October 1977. (Author's collection)

Aerial shot of Ground Zero, where the rivers meet, Hiroshima, Japan, 1978. (T. H. "Mac" McAllister)

Marines at the top of Kintai: Neil Cummings, Jack Shaffer, Steve Dixon, "Buster " Parker, "Gramps" Denson, and T. H. McAllister. (T. H. "Mac" McAllister)

Tech talk, September 1977. Buster Parker (left) and T. H. McAllister. (T. H. "Mac" McAllister)

Taking over from the "Red Devils," July 1977, Japan. (T. H. "Mac" McAllister)

Left to right: Kyle Leonard (Elec. Shop), Joe Sullivan (Elec. Shop), Steve Dixon (Elec. Shop) and Lee Foster (Ordnance) on a chow break, Exercise *Team Spirit*, 1978. (Author's collection)

Interior of the squadron hangar while deployed to MCAS Yuma, early 1979. (Author's collection)

Charlie Pitarys next to an armed Phantom II at MCAS Yuma, 1981. (Charlie Pitarys, VMFA-251, 78–81 (SFC USA, Retired), used with permission)

Armed F-4J ready for action at NAS Key West during the Mariel Boat Lift, 1980. (Charlie Pitarys, VMFA-251, 78–81 (SFC USA, Retired), used with permission)

"Thunderbolt" Phantoms at rest in the Azores between transit flights during Exercise *Teamwork 1980*. (Charlie Pitarys, VMFA-251, 78–81 (SFC USA, Retired), used with permission)

Chase crew maintenance personnel work on a squadron F-4J in the Azores during Exercise *Teamwork 1980*. (Charlie Pitarys, VMFA-251, 78–81 (SFC USA, Retired), used with permission)

A VMFA-251 F-4J Phantom II (BuNo 155833) intercepts a Soviet Topolev Tu-95 *Bear D* off Iceland in April 1982. The pilot was squadron commander LtCol. Norman G. G. Kerr and the RIO was Major John E. Daubert. The latter was killed in an accident a few months later. (Bill Houser Collection, used with permission)

Living quarters while on deployment in Norway, 1982. (Bill Houser collection, used with permission)

VMFA-251 F-18 Hornet at Twentynine Palms in California, 1988 or 1989. (Bill Lipcsey)

Squadron insignia from top left to bottom right. The bomb-carrying duck was used in the late 1940s into the 1950s. The Black Patch (VMA-251) was used in the 1950s. The VMF patch was used in the late 1950s and the early 1960s when it acquired the Fury and Crusader. When VMFA-251 acquired the F-4 Phantom II, the patch on the bottom right was used. It remained the squadron's patch until the squadron was deactivated in April 2020.

AD-1 Skyraider, VMFA-251, early 1950s. While the unit replaced its Skyraiders with the FJ Fury jet, the Skyraider outlived its replacement in U.S. military service. While the Fury was retired in the late 1960s, the Skyraider soldiered on with the Americans until 1973, having been heavily used by the USN and USAF during the Vietnam War. (Created by SSGT David Roof, USMC, Ret., used with permission)

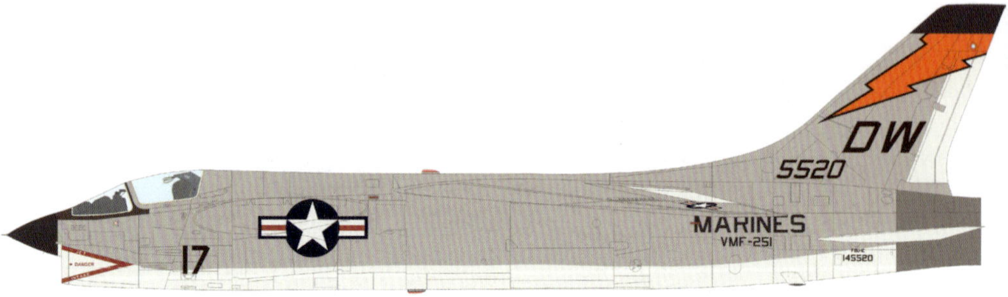

F8U-1E Crusader, VMF-251, early 1960s. The Crusader, referred to as "The Last Gunfighter" because it was designed with four cannons as its principal weapons. With the continuing development of air-to-air missile technology, the type was adapted to carry up to four Sidewinders. Indeed, during the Vietnam War, most of the Crusader's "kills" were achieved by firing missiles. The French Navy finally retired its Crusaders in late 1999. (Created by SSGT David Roof, USMC, Ret., used with permission)

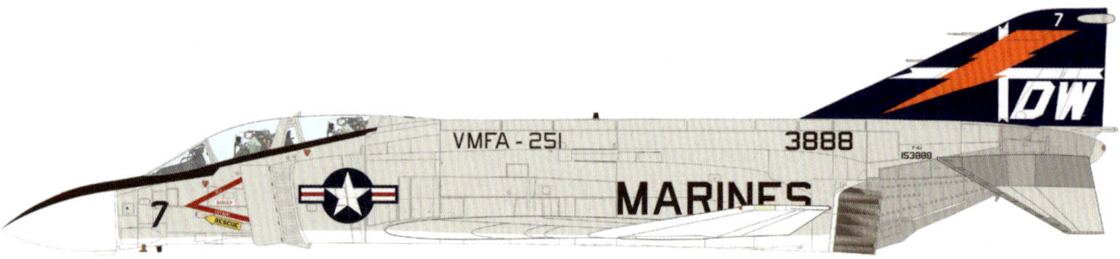

F-4J Phantom II, VMFA-251 early 1970s to mid-1977. Probably the most recognisable of the American Cold War-era fighters, the Phantom equipped units in the USN, USAF and USMC and proved just as popular with air arms around the world. (Created by SSGT David Roof, USMC, Ret., used with permission)

F/A-18C Hornet, VMFA-251, late 1980s. The C-model replaced the A-model and remained in service with the squadron until its deactivation in April 2020. Hornets are still in service with the U.S. military, including the USMC, but they are the larger and substantially more capable Super Hornet variants. The advanced F-35C Lightning II, a fifth-generation jet, is scheduled to bring in the unit's next iteration in 2025. (Created by SSGT David Roof, USMC, Ret., used with permission)

continued to roll, the left wing broke away. The wrecked aircraft came to a stop approximately three thousand feet from the point where it had touched down on the runway. Once crash crews extinguished the fires, the crew's remains were retrieved.

The number two aircraft was still circling the airfield when Rogers and Jacobs met their fate. It was diverted to another airfield and made a safe landing.

Several factors contributed to the crash. First, the flight leader failed to brief the flight on possible alternate landing fields if they had to divert. Second, ground control approach—operational at the time—was not utilized. Third, as noted previously, arresting gear was available but no request was made to have it hooked up.

The men Rogers flew with considered him a good pilot. Despite being a careful pilot and pursuing his job as Safety Officer with gusto, the accident board discovered several incidents which suggested he seemed to have become overconfident in his abilities. A recent take-off was reported to the commanding officer as being dangerous. He also made several hard landings that were not reported to his CO.

The accident, according to the accident board, may have been avoided if Rogers had elected to go around for a better approach. The board also stated better leadership by the flight leader, or by those who did not report the previous hard landings, may have prevented the accident.[35]

The second incident that resulted in the loss of another "Thunderbolt" aircraft (BuNo 153774) occurred on 2 October. Five Phantoms, which included one flown by First Lieutenants William T. "Woody" Ayers and Richard O. Lamers (RIO), took off from Lajes AFB in the Azores for NAS Bermuda. The flight was to rendezvous with four KC-130F tankers, orbiting over 500 miles from Lajes, to refuel their aircraft. No problems were encountered at take-off and the rendezvous of the five Phantoms went as planned. As they closed with the tankers, Ayers's aircraft experienced an internal wing fuel transfer failure. Lamers then "took the info and worked out the best altitude and airspeed. I told the other aircraft our situation and they in turn did their own calculations. They called back and all were in agreement with me. We immediately changed to that altitude and airspeed for max efficiency."[36] Ayers diverted his aircraft to head back to Lajes. Ninety-five nautical miles out, Ayers put his Phantom into an idle descent. He had coaxed the aircraft as close as he was going to get to Lajes. At about four miles short of the runway, the engines flamed out. Ayers and Lamers successfully ejected and were picked up with no injuries sustained. The aircraft continued its descent and crashed a mile from the approach end of the runway.[37] Lamers was not happy with the final disposition of the accident. "The findings were that we should have made those decisions faster and gone to a higher altitude, thereby 'possibly' landing the aircraft. Because of that fitness report, Woody and I were both out of the Marine Corps," wrote Lamers.[38]

In addition to the two losses, one other aircraft was damaged (BuNo 153776) on 23 November. Whether this was a ground or air mishap is not known.

Following the squadron's return to Beaufort on 7 October, the squadron commenced its normal training operations, which included a missile exercise at Cherry Point on 6 and 7 November. About a month later, the squadron sent a detachment to NAS Key West to assume hot-pad duty. The detachment was still in Key West at the end of the year.[39]

For a variety of unknown reasons, morale in the squadron was at a low ebb. Its performance was not up to standards. In addition to the recent aircraft losses, the days of Colonel W. C. Service III's tour as commanding officer were numbered. Tom Hens, who served with the squadron until November 1973, wrote that "Colonel Service was a good and honorable man, but 72 and 73 were not good years for 251."[40]

Colonel William L. Shanks, Jr., commanding officer of MAG-31, and Lieutenant Colonel Josephus L. Mavretic arrived at the squadron hangar on 12 December. It was not a typical change of command ceremony: no parade formation, no speeches, no band, no hand off of the squadron colors. Mavretic recalled:

> The group commander and I went over to the squadrons' spaces. It was in a building with two squadrons in it. Each squadron had first and second floors. We went up to the second floor into the CO's office. He was relieved of command. I was made the commander—appointed, ordered. And he (Colonel Service) went across the building on the top floor down the back stairs and went away. The group commander and I went down the front stairs into the radio room where the officers will assemble. And on the way the group commander said to me "fix it." And we went into the ready room, and he introduced me as the new commander and left, and there I was. That was my change of command.[41]

Mavretic grew up in Havelock, North Carolina, close to Marine bases in the area. He knew he wanted to be a Marine and his goal was to command a Marine aviation squadron. His dream came true but certainly not in the way he thought it would happen.[42] Mavretic had a tough job ahead of him to straighten out the "Thunderbolts." By the end of 1973, the squadron was rated as marginally combat ready.[43] The year 1974 would be a rebuilding period.

By mid-January 1974, the detachment in Key West had returned to MCAS Beaufort. The hours flown by the detachment accounted for nearly half of the

272 hours flown during the month. Upon their return on the 14th, a two-day safety stand-down was ordered. Following the stand-down, personnel and their wives met their new commanding officer and his wife at the station theater. Mavretic informed all in attendance of the squadron's future operations as well as which of the air station's facilities and services were available to all. This meeting was dubbed "Family Fam."

The squadron also enacted a comprehensive conservation program stressing personal awareness of the energy crisis, as well as cutting back on the lighting and heating within the squadron area.[44]

To improve the squadron's performance, goals were set, and a method established to meet them. Guiding the changes was the fact that Mavretic believed Marine squadrons were combat squadrons, not garrison squadrons, and should be combat ready. The changes made reflected that belief. Most of the changes were embraced by squadron personnel; some were not and took time for them to get on board with the idea. The plans to reach the goals also took time to implement (the last being the use of the squadron videotape cassette system) but, by the second half of 1974, the unit was well on the way to improving itself.

The goal: "improve its probability of success in battle through the production of full systems aircraft to be flown by full systems capable aircrew."[45] A full-systems aircraft was defined as an aircraft where all sub-systems required to complete a mission in a single sortie were fully functional. A full-systems capable aircrew was defined as an aircrew that could operate all sub-systems in any combination required to accomplish a mission on a single sortie.[46] With goals established, plans were laid out to provide a map to reach the established goal. This involved developing new plans or tweaking existing plans. Mavretic recalled:

> What I wanted to do was to make sure that squadrons in garrison (like 251), especially acted like a squadron that was either in combat or combat ready. So, we did a couple of things. We got rid of all the garrison furniture, turned it back into [the] station. And we started living out of our embarkation gear, the boxes, the cartons, that kind of stuff. Very different, very difficult to get everybody to buy into this, but they understood combat ready.[47]

When it came to the wellbeing of squadron personnel, Mavretic wanted to make sure they were "healthy and happy."[48] He ordered "every staff NCO in the squadron to take at least two consecutive weeks of leave a year and not concentrate on backing or banking it when they retired."[49] Many did not take that well. However, over time, the program worked. "A few months after that one of the staff NCOs came in and said 'Skipper, I've never taken two days, two weeks leave in my life. And it's the best thing I ever did for me, and my family and I appreciate you making me do it and I'll continue to do it the rest of my career'," recalled Mavretic.[50]

A family day was also held in which every Marine's loved one visited the squadron area and spent a couple of hours learning what their Marine did. After that, a large picnic was held for everyone. "I think those things kind of turned the squadron around—that everybody was important down to enlisted, and everybody had a family, everybody had a task, and we were doing something significant," said Mavretic.[51]

Changes were also made in how information was circulated through the squadron and how pilots earned their hours. The monthly maintenance plan reports were modified to include all squadron activities. The modified report became the single-source document detailing all squadron functions and was renamed as the Squadron Planning Document. The reports were used to ensure each Marine in the squadron knew what was expected of him as well as informing everyone of all activities for the coming month. With the document, each department could forecast what it could actually accomplish for the month.

Mavretic reorganized the squadron on a trial basis to make it more efficient. It was a temporary measure to get things back on track. At the time, a Marine fighter attack squadron was composed of several sections: headquarters, administration, safety, medical (flight surgeon), logistics/supply, and maintenance. The administrative department was further broken down into four sections: S-1 (personnel/manpower), S-2 (intelligence), S-3 (operations), and S-4 (logistics). The maintenance department had its own administrative section as well as a maintenance control section. Maintenance control coordinated aircraft maintenance with the following maintenance sections: Line/GSE (Ground Support Equipment), Airframes, Flight Equipment, Ordnance, and Avionics. Mavretic's plan reduced the squadron's number of departments to six by combining departments to improve efficiency, curb redundancy, and improve communication. As an example, since the maintenance department employed the majority of squadron personnel, Mavretic had the head of the S-1 section assigned to it. The change in organization was defined as a "Functional Nucleus" and became the norm for Mavretic's tour as commander (see diagram). "I brought the staff NCOs in and explained to them my concept of how a squadron worked in combat and said that they no longer had an officer to turn things over to who were responsible, and that they were responsible to the sergeant major," he said.[52] Officers would answer to the executive officer (XO) and

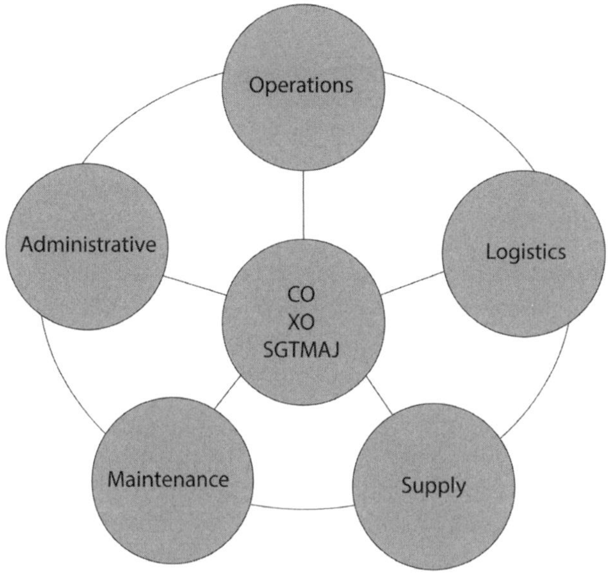

VMFA-251 Functional Nucleus Organization

Mavretic would handle issues that could not be legally handled by the XO and the sergeant major.

To help get the aircrew rated as fully systems capable, a "251 Playbook" was created. Mavretic borrowed the idea from the Washington Redskins (now the Washington Commanders). Since they were the only professional football team near where Mavretic grew up in North Carolina, he wrote to them asking if he could use their playbook idea and adapt it for use in his squadron. The playbook was a three-ring binder issued to each pilot and RIO. Its use was intended as a personal notebook where each officer could keep personalized notes during training lectures and all officer meetings. Additionally, the operations department produced handouts for insertion in the playbook. These inserts were items that had a professional significance to the aircrewman. To ensure the playbooks were up to date with the latest information, Mavretic or the XO would inspect them from time to time.[53]

In addition, the squadron's videotape cassette system, alluded to earlier, was used to provide training briefings for both aircrew and ground personnel, and to inform all "Thunderbolts" of squadron policy and other information deemed necessary. Mavretic got the idea from when he was aboard the dock landing ship USS *Pensacola* (LSD-38) and was able to witness first-hand the use of the ship's closed-circuit TV system.[54] The squadron acquired the video gear needed in February 1974:

> The project that we developed for the officers was to make a video of the briefing of every flight that was on the flight syllabus ... So we happen to have a guy from the University of North Carolina, from which I graduated, who was a radio and television major, he was a RIO, his name was Capt. William Moore ... so I tasked him to do this. The leader for the flight would brief the departure and on return. But the meat of the mission would be in the cassette. And you push the cassette in, and you watched the briefing for the mission. And the reason for this was that it could involve every aircrew member in a squadron so they were kind of caught up in this project.[55]

It took time to get the program rolling since briefings and safety videos (such as proper pre-flight checks) had to be taped and edited. Others involved in the startup of the program were Major Graham Kerr, squadron Aviation Safety Officer Flight Lieutenant Jack Haines (RAF exchange RIO), and Lieutenant Donn Ramey.[56]

In the midst of all the ongoing changes, flight training continued but at a slower pace than the previous month. There were several reasons for this, and they would be a constant problem during Mavretic's tenure as commanding officer of the squadron: an energy crisis that led to fuel cutbacks, lack of manpower, lack of money, supply issues, lack of aircraft availability, and commitments to periodic exercises. All of these led to cutbacks in flight training hours for the pilots and RIOs. "We told it exactly like it was. We didn't try to sugarcoat it at all, because we really didn't do well from a training point of view," said Mavretic.[57]

The squadron compiled slightly over 181 hours during February 1974, which included acting as friendly forces on 27 and 28 February in the 20th NORAD exercise *Amalgam Mute*. During this short exercise, night intercept training was accomplished.

Flight operations continued into March. Five aircrewmen were designated air combat tactics instructors after successfully completing a week-long training period provided by instructors from MAWTULANT out of MCAS Cherry Point. Towards the end of the month, a representative from MAWTULANT briefed aircrews in preparation for an upcoming missile shoot in May. At the end of the month, the squadron had completed nearly one hundred eighty-four flight hours.

Aerial-refueling exercises, flight training, and other missions to prep aircrews for the upcoming missile shoot continued through the month of April. In addition, Captains N. G. G. Kerr and William W. Moore visited VF-124 at NAS Miramar, California, and the American Airlines Flight Academy in Dallas, Texas. While visiting VF-124, Grumman Aerospace and Navy training personnel guided the two "Thunderbolt" officers in their training techniques. At Dallas, American Airlines personnel showed Kerr and Moore their approach to training aircrews. In addition, ideas were gained in the use of video equipment for aircrew education purposes.

The missile firing exercise began on 13 May and ended on the 17th. The missile firings occurred off the North Carolina coast and were controlled by MACS-6. Twenty-five sorties were flown, and six AIM-7 missiles were fired. Soon after the four-day exercise, the squadron committed four Phantoms, crews, and maintenance personnel to MCALF Bogue Field in support of Exercise SOLID SHIELD, a two-week amphibious operation at Onslow, North Carolina. The "Thunderbolts" flew 19 fighter-support missions before the detachment returned to MCAS Beaufort on 6 June. It was during this exercise that one aircrew dodged a fatal bullet. Then Captain Robert G. Dwyer recalls the 29 May incident:

> In the spring of 1974, Dave Van Esselstyne and I were the new guys in VMFA-251, an F-4J squadron at MCAS Beaufort, SC. We'd hit it off pretty well and were looking forward to flying together. One day we walked into the scheduler's office and made some lame remark about flying together so we could wreck one of his airplanes. "Okay (expletive deleted), you clowns have the 3am brief with the Skipper for air support at Camp Lejeune." Lesson learned; never volunteer especially with a wisecrack.
>
> The next morning, we were about halfway to our tanker rendezvous near Cherry Point, NC when I saw the MASTER CAUTION and CHECK HYD GUAGES lights illuminate. Sure enough, the utility hydraulic pressure was zero. I told the Skipper what our problem was and, after determining that everything else was okay and that we had plenty of fuel, he detached us to return to Beaufort for an arrested landing while he went on to complete the morning's mission.
>
> En route to Beaufort I noted that the pneumatic pressure was slowly dropping (the air compressor was powered by the utility hydraulic system and was now inoperative). I told Dave that once the pressure hit the lower limit of the normal pressure range, 2,680psi, I'd blow the gear down just to be certain of sufficient pressure. When that occurred, we went through the checklist; airspeed less than 250KCAS, gear handle down, gear circuit breaker pull, gear handle pull aft and hold. At that point, the pneumatic pressure went to 1,500, then to zero, and the gear remained up and locked. I said, "Dave, the gear didn't come down." He answered, "The gear didn't WHAT?" "The gear didn't come down and I don't think it's gonna." There was still air in the emergency flap bottles so we successfully blew the flaps. In the Naval Phantoms, you got leading edge flaps, ½ trailing edge flaps, but no 16-degree aileron droop when using the emergency lowering system.
>
> We got to Beaufort and talked our problem over with Captain Ev Stenman who was the squadron ops duty officer that morning. Since the gear was up, that ruled out a short field arrestment; so, we requested a foamed runway. At that point we were informed that the Beaufort foam truck was broken—remember what I said about not volunteering? About this time Ev suggested we see whether Charleston AFB (70 miles away) could foam a runway for us. They said, "Sure! Y'all come on up." (Marine aviation is always SO entertaining!). We had 8,500 pounds of fuel remaining at this time and headed north. In Naval Aviation we utilize the assistance of a Landing Signal Officer for abnormal field landings so Captain

> Scott Dudley, VMFA-333/MAG-31 LSO jumped in the station helo (helicopter) and headed north to give us a hand.
>
> En route, Dave and I discussed our landing configuration. We had an empty 600-gallon centerline tank and LAU-17/A pylons on the inboard wing stations. I chose to retain the tank reasoning that if we got rid of it, in our touchdown attitude the nose would slam down, and we'd tear up the bottom of the aircraft not to mention possible compression injuries to our backs. I gambled that we'd have enough PC-1 and 2 hydraulic pressure following engine shutdown to keep the wings level until the tank ground down and put us on the pylons. I told Dave to make sure he still had "command eject" selected and that if we hooked a wing and headed off the runway, to punch us both out.
>
> The Crash Crew at Charleston laid a strip of foam 24 feet wide and 4,000 feet long. We burned down to 1,500 pounds of fuel and, since the angle of attack reads low with the nose gear retracted, manually computed our landing speed to be 150K CAS. With some helpful words from the LSO, we touched down smoothly (not all Naval Aviation landings are controlled crashes!) about 400 feet into the foam. I placed the throttles to idle, deployed the drag chute, and shut the engines down. I had no difficulty keeping the wings level until the tank finally collapsed and we ground to a halt 10 feet from the end of the foam, still on centerline. We quickly ground egressed and, since there was no evidence of fire, I was able to stop the crash crew from foaming the intakes and cockpits.
>
> The damage was limited to the destruction of the centerline fuel tank, minor abrasion to the inboard trailing edge of the flaps, minor damage to the pylons and a broken static drain fairing under the radome. The aircraft was shored up, the gear lowered, and taken for a thorough wash down. The broken hydraulic and pneumatic lines were replaced, and the aircraft flown back to Beaufort where it was declared mission capable and was back on the schedule the next day. Sadly, ten months later it was destroyed in a near fatal crosswind landing accident at Reese AFB, TX. Dave and I got our wish and wound up flying over 100 missions together. He was one of the best RIOs I ever flew with and a good friend to boot.[58]

Soon after the squadron detachment returned from Bogue Field, a detachment consisting of three aircraft was sent to NAS Key West to assume alert duty. Departing MCAS Beaufort on 14 June, the detachment stayed in Florida for 30 days. Squadron pilots flew day and night intercept exercises, as well as practicing navigation techniques for overwater flying. Back at Beaufort, squadron planning continued in preparation for exercise *Deep Furrow 74*. It is unclear when the squadron received word it would be heading back to Turkey.[59]

The Key West detachment returned on 14 July. The next day, a safety stand-down was ordered and lasted through to the 16th. The stand-down included a visit from the commanding general of the 2nd MAW, Major General Ralph H. Spanjer. He addressed squadron personnel on the importance of safety. On the same day, Mavretic spoke with all squadron dependents. During his talk he informed them of the squadron's upcoming deployments and local operations. A Dependent Deployment Folder prepared by the squadron was given to all dependents to guide them on what to do before and after the squadron deployed.

Inspections were held towards the end of July, as was the quarterly physical fitness test for all squadron personnel. The squadron passed with an overall score of 93, garnering MAG-31's Quarterly PFT Award.

Planning continued for *Deep Furrow 74*. Kerr and Major H. F. Sharp attended the Air Operations/Logistics Conference for the exercises at Norfolk, Virginia. Apparently, this was the last meeting the squadron participated in concerning *Deep Furrow 74*. Soon after, word was received it would not participate in the exercise. By the end of July, the squadron compiled slightly over 172 hours. The Key West detachment accounted for nearly fifty-three hours of that total.

During August, the squadron received numerous visitors. The first were representatives from McDonnell Douglas. They were seeking input from aircrew for their new design of a single-seat lightweight fighter for the U.S. Navy.[60] Next came visits from the Assistant Wing Commander of the 2nd MAW, BGen. A. O'Donnell; Col. J. V. Cox from Headquarters, Marine Corps; and BGen. E. R. Miller, Jr., Assistant Commander, Fleet Marine Force, Atlantic (FMFLANT). All received briefings on various aspects of squadron operations.

The changes made by the squadron began to pay dividends. It received the MCAS Beaufort Ground Safety Award after coming second for the previous three months. First Lieutenant Jay Cluelow was the Ground Safety Officer and he and his ground safety committee worked hard to earn the award.

Sometime between 20 July and 20 August the squadron received a huge boost in morale—at least for the enlisted men. The unit finally moved into its newly renovated barracks. Despite missing drapes, rugs, and bed lamps, the barracks were in good condition and no doubt a welcome sight to the Marines after sharing parts of two barracks with two other squadrons.

With no exercises or deployments for the month, the squadron was able to increase its flight time, amassing nearly three hundred forty hours.[61]

The highlight for the month of September was another deployment to NAS Key West to assume alert duty as Detachment 14. The detachment began operations on 14 September and continued until 14 October.

As a follow up to the McDonnell Douglas visit the previous month, Kerr and Captain H. L. Logan, visited with company representatives in St. Louis to evaluate the experimental fighter's estimated performance against current threat aircraft in a simulator. Logan recalled:

> I flew several sorties in a theoretical VFAX (Fixed Wing Fighter Attack Experimental) fighter configuration in a domed/360° simulator against some pretty capable McDonnell Douglas program managers (one was a retired USAF F-106 pilot, for example) in an adjacent dome. I don't remember what aircraft he was supposed to be flying, but the VFAX configuration

> I was in was clearly dominant with exceptional turn and energy addition and subtraction rates. I didn't fly against it in any of my fights (only in it against others), so I don't know what it looked like. So, I'm not sure if it was intended to be an early iteration of the F-18 or not. I later flew F-18s a lot and as good as the F-18 was, it was not as good as the VFAX simulator was! I guess I foolishly dreamed it would be.[62]

The squadron put in plenty of flight training during the month, flying 256 sorties while accumulating 436 hours of flight time.

October was not as busy for the squadron. The 2nd MAW performed a safety survey at the squadron. All areas inspected received either satisfactory or outstanding marks. On top of that, the squadron earned another Ground Safety Award. Flying its standard mix of training missions, pilots flew cross-country navigation exercises, air-intercept missions, radar missions, simulated CAS missions, and simulated missile-firing missions, to name a few, flying 217 sorties for slightly over 330 hours during the month. The squadron had exceeded its flight hour goal by 2%.[63]

The slow operational pace continued during November. The "Thunderbolts" did participate in two exercises though. On the 13th, the squadron flew three early morning intercept sorties for the NORAD exercise *Showtime*. On the same day, and continuing into the 14th, the "Thunderbolts" flew four sorties in support of *Bascolex 7-74* at Camp Lejeune, North Carolina. The highlight of the month was a visit by the Commandant of the Marine Corps, General Robert E. Cushman, Jr. Mavretic briefed the general on several projects taken on by the "Thunderbolts": the functional nucleus organization of the squadron, the systems approach to aircrew training, and aircrew flight equipment.

A flight suit had been developed over the previous several months. It was born out of Mavretic's experience in Vietnam. He had "seen a couple of guys get burned pretty badly in Vietnam. And it was my thought that the people who knew more about fires in machinery were NASCAR drivers. So, I went to Charlotte and talked to the folks at NASCAR and said, you know, what do you wear when you're driving, and they showed me the stuff."[64] Mavretic returned with underwear, socks, gloves, and headgear. He tasked several officers to come up with a better suit than what they were currently wearing—lighter and better fire protection—using off the shelf items. According to Logan:

> Bill "Whiskey" Moore, one of our senior RIOs was quite involved. He was a particularly capable and professional RIO and put in a lot of effort on LtCol. Mavretic's flight gear program. Most of it was centered on making best use of commercially designed and available Nomex race driver gear as I recall. I think some of the guys wore part or all of that gear for an extended period of in-flight testing, but I was not one of them. If I remember correctly, much of it was from Simpson Racing Products and it was heavier duty and with more extensive full body coverage than our "issue" gear. My recollection was that it was very good

> equipment but better suited to colder weather than we normally had in Beaufort. That it would have been useful and very safe flight equipment, particularly in harsher temperatures, seemed obvious to me.[65]

Mavretic remembered removing the pockets except for one on the left sleeve to hold cigarettes. The suit also fit quite well underneath the equipment they were using at the time.

The flight gear was sent to the Naval Safety Center for evaluation. "And they said, thank you very much. We appreciate that. Now, I don't think it ever went much further than that," said Mavretic.[66] Logan believed "the greater problem would have been that it wasn't invented by Naval Air Systems Command (NAVAIR), so the 'not invented here' syndrome would have come into play."[67]

Once again, the "Thunderbolts" exceeded their planned flight hour goal, flying 227 sorties while accumulating slightly over 370 hours.

In early December, the squadron was visited by famed aviation writer Jeff Ethell,[68] then with *Air International*. He was on assignment with the magazine, writing a feature on Marine Corps aviation. He spent three days with the unit, participating in all phases of squadron flying and social activities.

On 7 December, the squadron sent four aircraft, aircrew and 28 enlisted personnel to Nellis AFB northeast of Las Vegas, Nevada. For the next week, the "Thunderbolts" flew 44 ACM sorties against USAF T-38 Talons of the 64th Fighter Weapons Aggressor Squadron. Following the return of the detachment, two crews received Air Combat Tactics Instructor training through MAWTULANT. By the end of the month, the "Thunderbolts" again exceeded their projected flight hour goal by 3.3%: 237 sorties for 345 hours. For the last six months of the year, the squadron flew nearly two thousand hours.

The end of the year saw VMFA-251 on the road to recovery. Awards were being earned, morale was good, and most important, there were no accidents for the last six months of the year.[69]

Early in January 1975, the squadron conducted a two-day safety stand-down. The theme for the stand-down was "Strength through Knowledge." The squadron's videotape system was heavily utilized since many safety procedures involving the Phantom II had been videotaped during the previous months. The taped segments were used to augment the lectures provided by safety representatives from the 2nd MAW and the Naval Safety Center. Ordnance safety was stressed during the stand-down since the squadron was committed to several exercises or deployments in the coming months. The day after the conclusion of the safety stand-down—8 January—the commanding officer of MAG-31 recommended to the commanding general of the 2nd MAW that VMFA-25 be awarded the Commanding General's Safety Award for 1974.

Beginning on 21 January, and lasting until the end of the month, the squadron participated in an Operational Readiness Inspection and was assigned as the contingency squadron for Provisional Marine Air Group (PROVMAG) 20. In addition, the unit provided aircrew, manpower, aircraft, and equipment in support of PROVMAG-20, and a VMFA-451 tactical test.

On the last day of the month, Lieutenant Colonel G. E. Walsh assumed command of the "Thunderbolts" from Mavretic. All hands were present, and the squadron colors were passed over to the new CO in sharp contrast to the way Mavretic took command in December 1973. During the ceremony, the 2nd MAW commanding officer, Major General Spanjer, acknowledged Mavretic's role in getting the squadron back on course. "Of particular note was your unique organizational structure and innovative training techniques that may well have a lasting effect on Marine aviation. These and other achievements of 251 during your tenure serve to mark the high degree of professionalism that has been placed on you and your squadron," he said.[70]

Walsh inherited a squadron well on its way on becoming a top-notch Marine fighting unit. He recognized the contributions of Mavretic and squadron personnel to make VMFA-251 the best fighter squadron in Marine aviation. To that end, Walsh continued the programs and added a few of his own. The videotape program was expanded to include briefings of foreign countries to be visited by the squadron during Operation *Agile Condor*, scheduled for May 1975. In addition, an in-house magazine was produced labeled *Fox Two*. Guided by the operations officer, the magazine served as a forum for concepts, developments, and news geared towards Marine fighter aviation. The squadron also put up a "MiG Board" next to the Beaufort air station refueling pits. As aircrews refueled, they could peruse scale pictures of enemy aircraft at various ranges and altitudes. Lastly, new aircrews to the squadron were utilized during safety stand-downs and pre-exercise briefings to prepare and present briefings.

Towards the end of February, the squadron provided fighter support for the Basic School Landing exercise held at Camp Lejeune, North Carolina. By the end of the month, the Marines had flown 230 sorties for 336 hours.

The squadron was on standby for two exercises in early March. It assumed duty as the contingency squadron for PROVMAG-80 in support of the 38th Marine Amphibious Unit (MAU) on 1 March. A week later, it was once again serving as the contingency squadron in support of the 34th MAU with PROVMAG-40.

In April, 12 Phantoms and all squadron personnel deployed to MCAS Yuma for air-to-air and air-to-ground weapons training, strike escort missions for Marine A-4 Skyhawks and F-8 Crusaders, as well as Navy A-7 Corsair II aircraft, and penetration missions. In an unusual exercise during the Yuma deployment, the squadron was ordered by the 2nd MAW commanding general to engage in DACM with AV-8A Harriers. The purpose was to document the vectored thrust concept used by the Harrier and its role in ACM. Five sorties were flown, and all were videotaped.

The Yuma deployment concluded on 27 April. All squadron aircraft were launched to make their way back to Beaufort. One Phantom (BuNo 153770) flown by Major Michael W. Hynes, with Captain Jay M. Cluelow serving as RIO, did not make it back.

Hynes and Cluelow performed the customary preflight check of the aircraft. Hynes preferred not to use command eject so, if the RIO ejected, only he would punch out. Hynes would have to initiate his own ejection.[71] During start up, the aircraft suffered a hydraulic malfunction which was quickly repaired by replacing the PC-1 pump. The aircraft was then reassigned as the fifth aircraft in the third division for takeoff.[72] Cluelow said:

> As I recall, we had three tanks and the flight lead, Skip Sharp, decided we were going to try to one-leg it from Yuma to Beaufort, going west to east with the jet stream.[73] The airplane we had had a couple of old gripes. One of them was a light burner light—which is no big deal. Better than no burner light. It was ok. Taxiing out to take the active (runway), all my charts were sitting on the canopy rail. The guy in front of us really goosed it and all my charts flew out. No big deal because the NAV (navigation) officer had given both pilot and me up-to-date-navigation charts.[74]

Hynes and Cluelow took off with no issues. As the aircraft climbed to its designated altitude, Cluelow asked for Hynes's navigation charts which were promptly handed over. However, as they gained altitude, they kept falling back from the rest of the division. Hynes applied more power and caught up. Soon afterwards, the Phantom fell back again. Realizing they would not be able to make the cross-country flight back to Beaufort, they contacted their flight leader, letting him know they would have to land, refuel, and then catch up. The flight leader gave his permission to allow Hynes and Cluelow to detach from the formation, but no escort was provided. "Usually if you are going to detach somebody, you send somebody with them," said Cluelow.[75]

Problems continued. Alone at 30,000 feet, they lost their radio. There was a line of thunderstorms on Cluelow's radar they would not be able to penetrate. The decision was made to land—anywhere. Fortuitously, the radio began working again. "Finally, whoever I talked to, Albuquerque Center, someone said 'Ok, your closest military airport is Reese AFB, Lubbock, Texas'," recalled Cluelow. At about a hundred miles from Lubbock, the controller came back reporting the airfield was closed due to severe crosswinds. Since they could see the airfield, and with the troubles they were having, Hynes and Cluelow decided to land at Reese.[76]

"We discussed using the drag chute for the crosswind. One thing led to another; they gave us a GCA (Ground Control Approach). We were crabbed into the wind at about 40 degrees because I'm looking out the side of my canopy—I'm looking at the runway. Talking about taking the crab out right as you land," said Cluelow.

The aircraft hit the runway hard. Cluelow continued, "Well, unbeknownst to me, things happened so fast. As we came down the airplane started rolling. We had touched down on the left main and the left wing tip and we got about 30 or 40 feet and the airplane was probably 70 degrees wing down at that point."[77] Cluelow asked Hynes repeatedly if he had the aircraft under control. Hynes said no. Cluelow ejected.

A wave-off had been initiated and Hynes tried to recover but it was too late. The aircraft became airborne crossing the Visual Approach Slope Indicator System (VASIS) at a very low altitude in a severe nose-high attitude. Thrust from the engines (in afterburner) buckled and separated the VASIS unit from its foundation, destroying it. The aircraft traveled over 1,300 feet between the point of runway contact and impact point. Just prior to impact, with the aircraft in a nose-high attitude with the right wing down between 70 to 80 degrees, Hynes ejected.[78]

The doomed Phantom hit the ground at an estimated speed of 140 knots. It burst into flames, destroying the starboard wingtip and starboard engine intake. The aircraft broke in half, scattering the engines and chunks of the aircraft in all directions as it tumbled.[79]

Cluelow had ejected safely but was unconscious for some time before being awakened by rescue personnel. "The next thing I know they're kind of waking me up. I was dragged, they think, about a quarter of a mile until a barbed wire fence caught my chute. Luckily, my oxygen mask disconnected so I could still breath. I probably would have suffocated if it hadn't. The seat was destroyed," said Cluelow. His left leg was broken. It took Cluelow nine months to recover and return to the squadron. Hynes also survived his ejection, breaking both ankles in the incident.[80]

Hynes was determined to be at fault for the loss. According to Cluelow's flight logbook, per "NAVSAFECEN MSG 101232Z Oct 75 failure to recognize and correct left drift at landing touchdown point." The entry was signed by the commanding officer of the squadron, LtCol. G. E. Walsh.[81]

Activities for May included two exercises. During the early part of the month, the squadron participated in a missile-firing exercise near MCAS

Cherry Point in an area designated as W-122 and supervised by MATULANT. Controlling the aircraft in the designated airspace was MACS-6. By the time the four-day exercise ended, "Thunderbolt" Phantoms qualified 10 crews while expending seven AIM-7E Sparrows and eight AIM-9G Sidewinders.

Three days after the exercise concluded, the "Thunderbolts" found themselves tasked with a Training and Readiness exercise conducted by a 2nd MAW Inspection Team. During the three-day inspection, the squadron flew a variety of missions including fighter weapons, fighter escort, air defense, CAS and large-scale strike missions. At the conclusion of the exercise, the squadron's efforts resulted in a satisfactory rating.

Exercise *Solid Shield 1975* kept the squadron busy during the first week of June. CAS and CAP missions were flown in the Camp Lejeune area while supporting participating Marine ground forces.

Beginning on 7 June and lasting until the 11th, the squadron conducted instruction, and briefings were held, to prepare all hands for the upcoming deployment to Rota, Spain, to participate in Exercise *Agile Condor*. Special use was made of the videotape playback system with videos produced by the Naval Human Resources Management Center out of Norfolk, Virginia, providing background on the foreign counties the squadron would visit during the deployment. Following conclusions of the briefings, the aircraft took off on 12 June for the long trek to Rota via NAS Bermuda and NAF Azores.

Five days later, the "Thunderbolts" arrived in Rota and immediately commenced operations. They flew a variety of missions during the short exercise and arrived back at Beaufort by 24 June. Once the last aircraft was recovered, all flying ceased for the squadron to perform mandatory inspections of the stabilator horn assembly in all of its Phantoms.[82]

July was a quiet month for the squadron. Typical operational training missions were flown throughout but at a reduced rate due to modifications and technical directives that forced all or some of the aircraft to be grounded. This lasted until the end of the year. In between the flying, the squadron took time to host Major General Spanjer once again. During his visit, he spoke with squadron officers and staff NCOs on the subject of attaining a high readiness and training posture. At the end of the month, four of the squadron's Phantoms flew a demonstration flight for officer candidates and their guests at MCAS Quantico, Virginia.

Inspections and safety stand-downs were the focus of activities during August. Near the end of the month, four officers and two enlisted men were sent as representatives to NAS Roosevelt Roads for a pre-deployment conference. Despite the stand-downs, as well as an "open house" event, the squadron flew 199 sorties for slightly over 275 flight hours.

From 7 September to the 19th, two aircraft were deployed, on a daily basis, to NAS Oceana, Virginia, for DACM with F-14 Tomcats of VF-143. The squadron flew 54 sorties against the Tomcats. It was during this exercise that another aircraft (BuNo 153888) was lost, again flown by Dwyer (who had made the foam landing at Charleston in mid-1974). The incident occurred on 16 September.

Dwyer and his RIO, Captain Richard A. Cote, had an uneventful, start up, taxi, and take-off. The Phantom was vectored in by ground control intercept and engaged the F-14 off the northern coast of North Carolina. A mock dogfight ensued, and at 30,000 feet, during a maneuver, Dwyer's Phantom suffered compressor stalls and both engines flamed out. The RAT[83] also malfunctioned and did not open. Unable to restart the engines, Dwyer and Cote ejected from their doomed aircraft. The F-14 had a visual as they descended into the water and radioed location information to rescue units. Other F-14s had converged on the area and guided the Coast Guard rescue helicopter—an HH-52A—towards the men. After they had spent half an hour in the water, the helicopter pulled them out. They were flown to Elizabeth City, North Carolina, where they were given a cursory exam by a flight surgeon while they walked to an awaiting NAS Oceana search-and-rescue (SAR) helicopter. Once at Oceana, they were transported to the station hospital and given a thorough examination. Both were quickly returned to duty following the exam. As for their Phantom, it was destroyed upon impact with the water. It sank to the bottom at a depth of 100 feet. The aircraft was deemed unrecoverable.[84]

Within days of their return to the squadron, Dwyer and Cote departed MCAS Beaufort for the Navy Fighter Weapons School (TOPGUN) and NAS Miramar, California. The month-long TOPGUN program began in 1969 and taught fighter and strike tactics to selected officers who then returned to their squadrons as certified instructors to teach their fellow pilots on what they learned.

Another deployment to Roosevelt Roads highlighted the month of October. Nine of the squadron's F-4J Phantoms departed MCAS Beaufort on 18 October. Inflight refueling was planned, but the rendezvous was cancelled so the nine aircraft refueled at NAS Key West before completing their move to Puerto Rico.

Three days later, the squadron began its missile-firing exercises, expending six AIM-7B Sparrows and 10 AIM-9G Sidewinders at TDU-22A targets being towed by BQM-34 Firebee drones. After the missile-firing exercises, two crews were awarded an "E" for excellence during the Sparrow portion of the exercise, while nine crews earned the award for the AIM-9G portion of the test. Following the exercise, the squadron spent the next two weeks flying day and night sorties to hone its air-to-ground skills. Both live and practice ordnance was dropped on CAS targets on nearby Vieques Island.

The Roosevelt Roads deployment ended on 7 November at which time the squadron returned to MCAS Beaufort. All aircraft eventually made it back safely, but Lieutenant Eddie Daniels's aircraft encountered a fuel transfer problem 400 miles from Key West which forced him to declare an emergency and divert to Homestead AFB, thus delaying his return by a day. As he approached Homestead, his utility pressure began to drop, soon reaching zero. Daniels used his pneumatic air to blow the landing gear down. He made a safe landing with very little fuel to spare as evidenced from a maintenance check made the next day. Within two minutes of engine start up, the engines flamed out due to fuel starvation.[85]

A week later, the squadron deployed two of its aircraft to Nellis AFB, Nevada, to support the 64th Aggressor Squadron. The participating "Thunderbolt" aircrews gained much needed exposure to Soviet tactics and MiG-21 flight characteristics as demonstrated by the opposing T-38 Talons.

No exercises or deployments were planned for December. Standard operational training continued throughout the month, interrupted by a four-day safety stand-down ordered by MAG-31. At the end of the month, the squadron flew 244 sorties, earning 331 flight hours.[86]

January 1976 saw planning begin for another deployment to MCAS Yuma. Two F-4Js and crews were sent to the air station for a pre-deployment conference. The squadron also welcomed a new commanding officer, Lieutenant Colonel Joseph B. Wuertz taking over from Walsh. In addition to its normal training routine, two Phantoms participated in a Basic School Exercise at Quantico, Virginia.

The deployment to MCAS Yuma began on 6 February. Original plans called for the deployment to last two days. However, two days before the scheduled deployment date, USAF Military Airlift Command (MAC) support for personnel was cancelled, as were aerial-refueling plans for the squadron's Phantoms. New plans had to be quickly drawn up, spreading the deployment to Yuma over six days.

Half of the Phantoms departed as scheduled on the 6th, stopping at Carswell AFB (northwest of Fort Worth, Texas) to refuel. On 8 February, they departed Carswell for MCAS Yuma. The remainder of the Phantoms left Beaufort on

7 February, also stopping at Carswell to stay overnight. They took off the following day for Yuma.

Getting personnel and gear to Yuma took longer. USAF C-141s and a C-5A were originally scheduled to be used but, with the cancellation, other aircraft had to be acquired. After much scrambling, the 2nd MAW provided C-130s to move the gear. Used on an "as available" basis, two C-130s departed on 6 February, one on the 7th, one on the 9th, two on the 10th, one on the 11th, and two on the 12th. To get the squadron's 226 Marines to Yuma, five Marine C-9 transport aircraft were used.[87]

With the squadron's Phantoms in Yuma by 8 February, and an advance party having arrived on the 6th and 7th in the C-130s, training activities commenced on the 9th. For the next seven days, the "Thunderbolts" engaged in ACM training against TA-4 Skyhawks of Headquarters and Maintenance Squadron (H&MS) 31. Experience gained flying against the Skyhawks prepared the aircrews to fly against Navy Fighter Weapons School pilots and their F-5 Tiger II and A-4E Skyhawk Mongoose aircraft, which commenced on 17 February. It was on this day that the squadron lost an aircraft in a tragic accident.

Captains George Ladd (pilot) and Lamar Strickland (RIO) were briefed with another F-4J crew for a two-vs-one dissimilar engagement with Navy pilot Lieutenant Michael Garland flying an A-4E (BuNo 150009). No issues were encountered during take-off and the aircraft proceeded to the range designated for the ACM.

The engagement consisted of three head-on passes by Ladd's Phantom and the Navy A-4E. It was during the last pass that both aircraft collided. The port wing of the A-4E impacted the radome of Ladd's aircraft. Both aircraft broke apart with pieces streaming towards the ground. Both became uncontrollable with the Phantom entering a flat spin. Garland and Strickland were able to eject from their respective aircraft. Ladd could not; damage from the collision may have rendered his ejection system inoperable or he may have been injured and unable to eject. The Skyhawk hit the ground and exploded, as did the Phantom. Fires resulting from the impacts were so intense that nothing was left of either aircraft. Rescue units were dispatched from Yuma and, with the assistance of aircraft circling over the crash site, picked up Strickland and Garland. The two men suffered minor injuries and were lucky to be alive. Ladd's body was found less than 10 feet from the wreckage of the Phantom (BuNo 153838).[88]

While squadron aircrew gained valuable experience during the ACM portion of training, the only training objective not met was fighter interceptions, especially in a two-vs-one situation. The loss of Ladd's aircraft (leaving only nine Phantoms to complete the training), degraded radar systems, and the low number of maintenance phases were contributing factors. The program proved successful with aircraft readiness increasing by 27%, and unscheduled maintenance reduced by 30%. During the last five days of May and the first five days of June, aircraft readiness was 41% and 67% respectively. On 16 April, Captain R. D. Stearns and First Lieutenant Robert R. Pospischil departed for TOPGUN School at NAS Miramar. Three days later, the squadron began preparations to participate in Exercise *Solid Shield* and had flown 265 hours across 206 sorties by the end of the month.

The "Thunderbolts" began SATS qualification of aircrews at MCALF Bogue Field in preparation for *Solid Shield*. However, on 8 May, the squadron received word it would not be participating in the exercise. Sorties flown during the month of May totaled 183 with 225 flight hours earned.

In June, squadron personnel qualified with the M-16 at the Marine Corps Recruit Depot Parris Island firing ranges. A unit inspection also occurred, earning a satisfactory result. Ninety-five sorties were flown during the month for a mere 85 flight hours.[89]

No deployments were on the books for July, so standard training continued for the rest of the month. On 26 July, and ending on the 30th, squadron pilots flew DACM missions against fighters provided by the Navy Fighter Weapons School. As the DACM training began, the squadron was visited by Spanjer and his soon-to-be successor, Major General R. E. Carey. A rehearsal for the change of command ceremony was held two days later at MCAS Cherry Point, North Carolina. Elements from squadrons at MCAS Beaufort were to participate, including VMFA-251. Summer thunderstorms were notorious for popping up unannounced and one nearly killed Wuertz, the CO, during rehearsal on 28 July. Major John Cummings, who was with MAG-31 at the time, recalled:

> … [I] was in the que [*sic*] to join a squadron. '251 offered me a series of hops with their CO, Joe Wuertz, flying as part of the 2d MAW change of command ceremony. Gen Spanjer was being relieved by Vincent[90] and this was a BIG DEAL with every squadron in the wing, led by their COs, taking part.
>
> After LtCol. Wuertz and the other MAG-31 squadron COs flew our rehearsal, our plan was to fly back to NBC (MCAS Beaufort) to spend the night and return the next day for the following rehearsal. We were parked on the NKT (MCAS Cherry Point) transient line waiting for a fuel truck when a light rain began to fall. This rain soon turned into a deluge and the three of us (the plane captain was there too) took shelter under our plane. Sheets of water washed across the concrete and I, not wanting to get my ass wet, squatted. Col. Wuertz and the plane captain sat on the concrete. Then the lightning struck!

> I was conscious the whole time and I knew we were getting a shock like nothing I'd ever experienced … when the lightning turned us loose, I was out of breath and my right arm was stuck in a weird position. But I was alive! The plane captain and my pilot weren't moving! 122's plane was parked next to ours and they had been hit by a charge also but not as close as ours. LtCol. Allinder and "Dirt" Bolling were under the Crusader[91] plane.
>
> I picked the guy I knew best and started giving mouth-to-mouth to Col Wuertz. I hollered a couple of times to get their attention which finally worked because our plane captain was clearly not breathing. And I was having a hard [time] getting Col. Wuertz going … Bolling worked with our plane captain and probably saved his life. LtCol. Allinder prayed hard and somehow Joe Wuertz and our plane captain started showing signs of life. An ambulance showed up and the T-bolt CO and his plane captain were taken to sick bay.[92]
>
> The T-bolts sent another pilot up the next day, and I stayed there to help check the plane out and fly in the change of command.[93]

The change of command was successfully held on 30 July at MCAS Cherry Point with Carey assuming command of the 2nd MAW from Spanjer.

The first week of August kept the squadron busy. DACM training continued with a detachment of AV-8 Harriers from VMA-153 providing the aggressor aircraft. Preparations also began to support VMFA-122's participation in NATO exercise *Teamwork/Bonded Item 76* to be held in Denmark and Germany.[94] Aircrews previously selected began intensive training in aerial refueling with the aircraft configured for a ferry mission. Squadron representatives were sent to Yuma for a pre-deployment meeting. The deployment was scheduled for late September.

During the last few days of August, "Thunderbolt" Phantoms participated in electronic countermeasure (ECM) training with EA-6 Prowlers from Marine Tactical Electronic Warfare Squadron VMAQ-2 based out of Cherry Point.

Occupying squadron personnel for the month were plans to implement a new aircraft camouflage scheme developed by famed aviation artist Keith Ferris. One aircraft was to be painted in the scheme which was designed to disguise the aircraft's aspect rather than trying to conceal the whole aircraft. Unique to the scheme was the addition of a false canopy on the bottom of the aircraft. The F-4 paint design, shades of paint and authorization from Ferris were obtained.[95]

It appears though, the squadron never followed through with the repaint. Other Navy and Marine squadrons did try it out, but after repeated encounters with aircraft wearing the new camouflage, pilots began to recognize the scheme, decreasing its effectiveness.[96]

The squadron's advance party to assist VMFA-122 in its deployment to Europe arrived at Loring AFB in Maine on 6 September. The next day, the squadron launched 12 VMFA-122 Phantoms in addition to two of its own aircraft to be used as backups should any of 122's aircraft develop problems. In addition to the help provided to VMFA-122, the "Thunderbolts" flew nearly fifty sorties supporting MACS-23 during their annual training exercise.

On 24 September, the squadron deployed to MCAS Yuma for another round of air-to-air and air-to-ground training. Unlike the last deployment to Yuma, no major problems were encountered. The squadron's aircraft and personnel were all in place by 28 September, allowing the "Thunderbolts" to begin their training the next day.

From 29 September until the afternoon of 7 October, the squadron flew against TA-4 Skyhawks of H&MS-31 as fighters from the Navy Fighter Weapons School were committed elsewhere. "Thunderbolt" aircraft participated in a variety of fighter combat scenarios: one-vs-one, two-vs-one and two-vs-two. Low-level, overland intercept missions were also flown. During the period, the squadron flew 143 sorties.

At the conclusion of the air-to-air exercises on the 7th, the squadron ceased flight operations to allow ordnance personnel to reconfigure the Phantoms. While the Phantoms were being prepped, aircrews attended lectures covering ordnance preflight, weapons loading, arming and de-arming procedures, and the aircraft jettison system. Practice ground attacks were conducted from 8 October to the 16th. Missions with live ordnance began on the 18th and continued through to the 22nd. Seventy sorties were flown as aircraft dropped 80 MK-77 incendiary bombs, 500 MK-82 high-explosive bombs, fired 64 2.75-inch rockets, and expended 434 rounds of 20-mm ammunition.

Eleven aircraft returned to MCAS Beaufort on 23 October. All personnel and equipment were back at Beaufort by the 25th. One aircraft stayed behind for use by the officer in charge of the rear party and was back at Beaufort on the 26th.

Early in November, the squadron published a staff study headed up by Captain R. D. Stearns. The study proposed additions and revisions to the aviation Training and Readiness Manual and the Flight Readiness Data System (FREDS) pertaining to the Phantom. FREDS was designed to be an automated database with information needed to manage Marine Corps aviation assets. The study concentrated on a realistic approach to training with limited resources and was sent to VMFAT-101 at MCAS Yuma for their consideration and possible implementation.

Squadron aircraft flew in two small exercises during November. Two Phantoms were involved in fighter-intercept training with MACS-15 of the 4th MAW based out of Dobbins AFB near Atlanta, Georgia. Just before the

Thanksgiving holiday, the "Thunderbolts" flew 11 sorties in support of a MAG-31 operation dubbed *Turkey One*.

To conclude the year, the "Thunderbolts" participated in three exercises in December. Eight sorties were flown during a MAG-31 missile exercise from 8 through 10 December. Problems were encountered and only two Sparrows were fired. Each guided successfully to its target. In between the missile shoot, the "Thunderbolts" provided augmentation forces for the NORAD 20th Air Defense Region, launching four alert aircraft in support of Exercise *Vigilant Overview 77–1*. From 17 December, and concluding on the 22nd, the squadron conducted ECCM (electronic counter-countermeasures) sorties against Skyhawks from VAQ-33.[97]

January 1977 continued to be a slow month. Occupying the squadron in the middle of the month was ACM training with A-4M Skyhawks from VMA-331. As a result, two flyers were qualified as Aerial Combat Tactics Instructors. Planning also began for the eventual deployment to MCAS Iwakuni, Japan, scheduled to occur in July.

The pace picked up in February. DACM training was conducted on 3–5 February and 10–12 February. Flying against the "Thunderbolts" were F-14 Tomcats of VF-101 (the "Grim Reapers") based out of NAS Oceana. During the six days of training, the squadron flew 29 sorties.

A detachment of two Phantoms was sent to NAS Miramar from 15 February to the 19th to attend the Navy Fighter Weapons School Three G Course. The course consisted of numerous lectures and fighter weapons sorties. One aircraft was crewed by Colonel H. D. Bradshaw (MAG-31 CO) with Cluelow as his RIO. The second aircraft was crewed by Wuertz and his RIO, Captain K. A. Sloan.

Operation *Hatchett* occupied the squadron from the 22nd to the 24th. During the MAG-31 exercise, the squadron flew 16 sorties consisting of a mix of CAS, fighter escort and ECM fighter-intercept missions.

Flight operations were halted on 26 February in order to conduct basic training for the entire squadron. Officers qualified with the .38-caliber pistol, while both officers and SNCOs qualified with the .45-caliber pistol. Over a hundred Marines qualified with the M-16 rifle and completed their physical fitness test. Testing and inspections were held, and NBC (Nuclear, Biological, and Chemical) training was given to all personnel. The training lasted until 3 March.

Inspections by the 2nd MAW kept the squadron busy during the first two weeks of March. Flight training continued throughout the month, with ECCM exercises conducted against VMAQ-2 and DACM training flown against

USAF F-15 Eagles. The squadron flew 187 sorties, accumulating nearly two hundred sixty-seven flight hours for March.

Over the previous three months the squadron had to contend with a large turnover in personnel. Transfers and end of enlistment for many meant new personnel coming in that needed to be trained. With a deployment to Yuma soon to occur, and the upcoming deployment to Japan, getting the Marines to work together as a team would require time to accomplish.

The first day of April began with a change of command, Lieutenant Colonel Myrl W. Allinder Jr. taking over command from Wuertz. Allinder had little time to get up to speed on upcoming squadron activities. The next day, the squadron sent two of its Phantoms and an advance party to Yuma. The two aircraft flew five sorties as adversaries during Air Combat Tactics Instructor (ACTI) training of three VMA-131 pilots prior to the arrival of the main body of the squadron.

By 5 April, the rest of the squadron's Phantoms and the main body were in place to begin operations at Yuma. Training sorties flown consisted of ACM against Navy Fighter Weapons School and H&MS-31 aircraft, defense electronic countermeasures training, and air-to-ground missions. In addition to the flight training, a Training and Readiness Evaluation was conducted by the 2nd MAW in preparation for the deployment to Iwakuni. The squadron passed the evaluation and concluded the Yuma deployment on 27 April. By the 29th, the Marines were back at Beaufort and immediately began to ready themselves for the deployment to Iwakuni.

The new Marines who had joined the squadron received the training they needed, coming together as a team during the hectic pace of flight operations. During the Yuma deployment, the squadron had three reportable incidents and one ground incident. None resulted in damaged aircraft. Seven aircraft were also discovered to have fuel quantity indicator problems.

In May, a special assist team from the Naval Air Rework Facility (NARF) at Cherry Point began correcting the problems at Beaufort. One aircraft, BuNo 153856, resisting all efforts at being fixed, was transferred to the NARF facility. In late June, the squadron finally received a replacement aircraft (BuNo 155888). Despite the ongoing fuel indicator problem, squadron aircrews practiced aerial refueling with H&MS-31 TA-4s for the upcoming overseas tour.

Aerial-refueling training continued into June, this time with KC-130 tankers from VMGR-252. Maintenance personnel worked long hours, due to many of the Marines taking leave, in order to conduct tasks to prepare the squadron's 12 F-4Js for the 8,000-mile trip to Japan.[98]

Another issue the squadron had to contend with at the last minute was repainting its aircraft in a new scheme as dictated by the Navy. In the spring of 1977, the Chief of Naval Operations ordered that all aircraft would be painted an overall glossy dull gray.[99] The new scheme would replace the current gray on top/white on bottom scheme. A distinguishing feature of the existing paint scheme was the dark blue vertical stabilizer with a white cross and orange thunderbolt, with the letters DW in the bottom right, while the nose radome was painted white. Both of these also had to be changed. The radome would sport dull black on the top while the remainder of the radome would be the glossy dull gray, while the tail would feature a muted white cross and dark gray lightning bolt. The DW coloring went from white to dark gray. Despite the best efforts of the maintenance personnel, only about half of the unit's Phantoms sported the new paint scheme by the time the squadron departed for Japan. The remainder were given their makeover once the squadron arrived at Iwakuni.

The plan for the deployment to Iwakuni was dubbed Operation *Key Grove*. It was to begin on 7 July and end on 25 July. First to depart was the maintenance personnel of the squadron. They were divided into three groups: the Advance Party, the Enroute Support Teams (Orange and Blue Teams), and the Main Body. The Advance Party was assigned to leave on 7 July and once it arrived at Iwakuni it was to establish contact with MAG-15 to ensure adequate facilities were available to receive the Main Body, Enroute Support Teams (EST) and the 12 F-4Js.

The Enroute Support Teams were detailed to provide operational maintenance on the Phantoms en route to MCAS Iwakuni. EST Orange was to embark on a C-130 for MCAS Yuma on 7 July, followed by EST Blue on

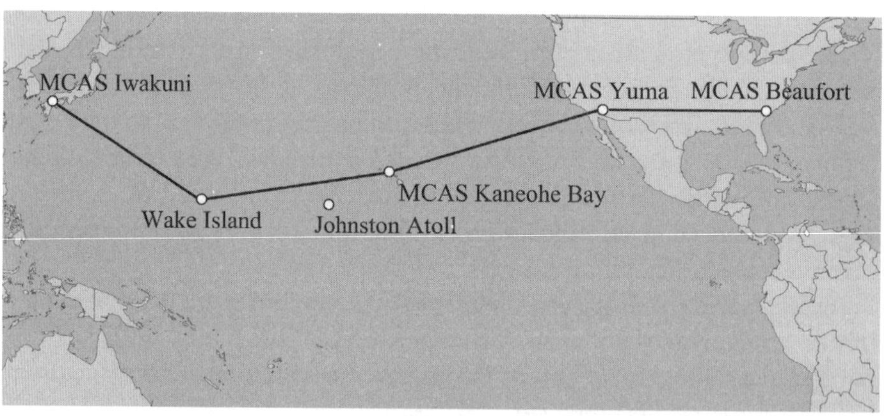

Deployment Route from MCAS Beaufort to MCAS Iwakuni, Japan, 8–26 July 1977

8 July. Each of teams would stay ahead of the aircraft providing support for the Phantoms at each stop along the route.

The Main Body was responsible for launching the aircraft from MCAS Beaufort and, once all aircraft were launched, they would fly via commercial airline to Iwakuni to recover the Phantoms set to arrive on 25 July. They were scheduled to depart Beaufort on the 18th.

In three flights of four aircraft, all 12 aircraft were to leave on 8 July for Yuma. Each would be carrying three external fuel tanks—one on each wing and one in the centerline position. They were to be refueled along the way by KC-130 tankers on each leg to MCAS Iwakuni. In addition, two spare Phantoms would also fly with each flight from Yuma to Iwakuni to be released at a predefined point on each leg if not needed. If all went according to plan, they would then depart Yuma in two flights of six on 10 July. Each flight would later rendezvous with a C-9 aircraft which provided navigation to MCAS Kaneohe Bay, Hawaii. On 19 July, the aircraft would depart Kaneohe, again in two flights of six aircraft, and head for Wake Island. As in the previous leg, a C-9 would rendezvous with them to provide navigation to Wake. Four days later, one flight of six aircraft would depart Wake on 23 July and head for Iwakuni. The second flight would follow on the 25th (see table on pages 147–8). In each case, the two flights would rendezvous with their C-9 aircraft for navigation assistance.

With MCAS Beaufort officials and families gathered nearby, the "Thunderbolts" departed as scheduled on the 8th. For the most part, all went according to plan. From Yuma to Kaneohe Bay, the two flights consisted of seven and five aircraft respectively, a slight change from the plan. As the first flight approached Kaneohe Bay, problems were encountered. The weather was expected to be Visual Flight Rules (VFR) along the route to Kaneohe Bay, yet the field was socked in due to lousy weather and required Instrument Flight Rules (IFR). Honolulu Center vectored the seven-plane formation 70 miles northwest of Kaneohe and then did not respond to further communications. The response from MCAS Kaneohe Bay approach control was slow and they were not prepared to recover the seven F-4Js in IFR. The senior watch officer was requested by the flight leader (Allinder) to rectify the situation. One F-4J had an external wing tank that did not transfer and because arrested landings were required due to rain and the wet runway, the wing tanks were jettisoned. VMFA-251 had previously coordinated with VMFA-212 to have a Landing Safety Officer (LSO) standing by in case of any emergency recoveries, and he controlled the trapping of the seven F-4Js in the rain.

The second flight leader (Major Jerry R. Cadick) obtained a debrief from Allinder by phone prior to departure on 11 July. The problems encountered on the 10th were corrected and the second flight of five F-4Js had no difficulties getting to and landing at Kaneohe Bay. Rather than accept the vector to the northwest given by Honolulu Center, the flight cancelled IFR and proceeded to the field VFR. The landing of all aircraft went smoothly.

After nearly a week at MCAS Kaneohe, the "Thunderbolts" were ready to proceed to Wake Island. The first flight of six F-4Js with two spare aircraft departed for Wake on 17 July. As the flight made its way to rendezvous with their assigned tanker, one aircraft was diverted back due to fluctuating oil pressure and a trim failure. This aircraft was replaced by an airborne spare and two aircraft (the diverted F-4J and the second spare) returned to MCAS Kaneohe Bay as planned.

The aircraft soon rendezvoused with their tanker and topped off their tanks. One F-4J lost its probe door upon retraction after refueling. The C-9 provided information to divert the aircraft, but it was able to proceed to Wake Island with the rest of the flight. Despite a serious bird hazard plaguing the base, the six Phantoms made an uneventful landing.

The second flight launched from Kaneohe Bay on 18 July. The C-9 crew took off at 1000, which was the scheduled take-off time for the six Phantoms. This delayed the F-4Js by 10 minutes. On the way to Wake Island, one experienced a PC-l hydraulic failure. The flight leader diverted the aircraft and his wingman into Johnston Island. The C-9 pathfinder provided the necessary clearance for the two aircraft. The remaining four F-4Js recovered at Wake Island. EST Blue followed the diverted aircraft into Johnston Island and performed field expedient repairs. On 20 July, the two Phantoms departed for Wake.

Although facilities were sparse at Wake, no effort was spared to provide support for the crews. The island was not the best environment to maintain aircraft; strong winds, hermit crabs, and deteriorating surfaces provided a rich FOD (foreign object debris) environment which made it difficult to keep the engine intake ramps clean. Turn-up screens were used on all ground run-ups.[100] Nevertheless, one engine was found to be damaged by FOD upon arriving in Japan.

On 24 July, the first flight (six F-4Js plus 2 spares) took off for MCAS Iwakuni. The spares returned unneeded. The flight to Iwakuni was uneventful. The advance party had 251's assigned area ready to go and all aircraft were recovered without incident.

The second flight took off two days later, following a delay that occurred as a result of a C-141 medical evacuation flight taking off at the same time from Wake. Once the second flight was airborne, the trip was routine except for weather, requiring course changes to get around several thunderstorms encountered along the way. All aircraft made it safely to Iwakuni.

Operation *Key Grove* (Planned)

Advance Party	*EST Orange*	*EST Blue*	*Aircraft*	*Main Body*
Departs MCAS Beaufort 7 July for MCAS Iwakuni	Departs MCAS Beaufort 7 July for MCAS Yuma	Departs MCAS Beaufort 8 July for MCAS Yuma	Departs MCAS Beaufort on 8 July for MCAS Yuma—three flights of four aircraft each	Departs MCAS Beaufort on 18 July for MCAS Iwakuni via commercial flight
	Departs MCAS Yuma 9 July for MCAS Kaneohe Bay	Departs MCAS Yuma 11 July for MCAS Kaneohe Bay	Six aircraft depart MCAS Yuma 10 July for MCAS Kaneohe Bay Six aircraft depart 11 July for MCAS Kaneohe	
	Departs MCAS Kaneohe Bay 17 July for Wake Island	Departs MCAS Kaneohe Bay 19 July for Wake Island	Six aircraft depart MCAS Kaneohe Bay 18 July for Wake Island Six aircraft depart MCAS Kaneohe Bay 19 July for Wake Island	
	Departs Wake Island 25 July for MCAS Iwakuni	Departs Wake Island 25 July for MCAS Iwakuni	Six aircraft depart Wake Island 23 July for MCAS Iwakuni Six aircraft depart Wake Island 25 July for MCAS Iwakuni	

Operation *Key Grove* (Executed)

Advance Party	*EST Orange*	*EST Blue*	*Aircraft*	*Main Body*
Departed MCAS Beaufort 7 July for MCAS Iwakuni	Departed MCAS Beaufort 7 July for MCAS Yuma	Departed MCAS Beaufort 8 July for MCAS Yuma	Departed MCAS Beaufort on 8 July for MCAS Yuma—Three flights of four aircraft each	Departed MCAS Beaufort on 18 July for MCAS Iwakuni via commercial flight
	Departed MCAS Yuma 9 July for MCAS Kaneohe Bay	Departed MCAS Yuma 11 July for MCAS Kaneohe Bay	Six aircraft departed MCAS Yuma 10 July for MCAS Kaneohe Bay Six aircraft depart 11 July for MCAS Kaneohe	
	Departed MCAS Kaneohe Bay 16 July for Wake Island	Departed MCAS Kaneohe Bay 18 July for Wake Island. Diverted to Johnson Island and did not reach Wake Island until 20 July	Six aircraft departed MCAS Kaneohe Bay 17 July for Wake Island Six aircraft departed MCAS Kaneohe Bay 18 July for Wake Island Two aircraft diverted to Johnston Island due to mechanical issues. Arrived Wake Island 20 July	
	Departed Wake Island 26 July for MCAS Iwakuni	Departed Wake Island 26 July for MCAS Iwakuni	Six aircraft departed Wake Island 24 July for MCAS Iwakuni Six aircraft departed Wake Island 26 July for MCAS Iwakuni	

Upon arrival in Japan, the squadron began to familiarize itself with its new home and took over duties from VMFA-115, which was heading back to MCAS Beaufort. The remaining days of July and the first two days of August were filled with lectures and tests. Some of the lectures included a brief on the Korea Buffer Zone procedures, air traffic control procedures, Korea Air Order of Battle, Peacetime Rules of Engagement, and an area brief on Iwakuni.

Flight operations began in earnest in August. From the 3rd to the 22nd, the "Thunderbolts" flew Basic Aircraft Maneuvering and fighter-intercept missions to become accustomed to local flying and working areas. The squadron's first exercise was *Readiness Check Alligator* on 23 August. At 1300 the same day, it was told to pack up and move out to a new destination. Twenty-four hours later, the squadron was ready for inspection by Lieutenant General Leslie E. Brown, Commanding General, Fleet Marine Force, Pacific (FMFPac). Having passed the inspection, the squadron unpacked all its gear and resumed operations. Also commencing on 23 August and lasting until the 26th, VMFA-251 participated in exercises *Cope Strike Mike* and *Cope Jade Charlie*. The two exercises involved the squadron flying CAS missions as well as escort for photo recon, and ECM missions into South Korea from Iwakuni. Nine sorties were flown for nearly twenty-five hours during the exercises. DACM against TA-4 Skyhawks of H&MS-12 and flying fighter intercepts kept the squadron busy for the remainder of August.

On 8 September, the squadron sent five aircraft to Clark AFB in the Philippines to participate in Exercise *Cope Thunder XI*. The detachment—designated Alpha—consisted of the five F-4J Phantoms, 10 aircrew and 37 support personnel. *Cope Thunder* was an air warfare exercise under control of the USAF. While the detachment was at Clark, it received another Phantom on 19 September. *Cope Thunder* ended on the 24th at which point the detachment packed up and moved to nearby NAS Cubi Point, located on the southern shores of Subic Bay. Waiting for them when they arrived was the rest of the squadron which had arrived on 21 September. For the remainder of the month, the Marines flew fighter weapons and fighter-intercept missions.

On 4 October, the squadron received a surprise when a team from 1st MAW arrived at Cubi to conduct an unscheduled Training and Readiness Evaluation (TRE). Over the course of four days, written exams were taken, and various missions flown: fighter attack escort, ground attack, night interceptions, missile shoots, and DACM missions—all done to determine the squadron's combat readiness.

Four days after the conclusion of the TRE, Exercise *Fortress Lightning* began and was completed on 21 October. The squadron's mission was to establish and maintain air superiority over a designated opponent, dubbed "Blue Forces." CAP, fighter intercepts, and scrambling aircraft from "strip alert" were flown to ensure the mission was accomplished.

While the schedule maintained at Cubi Point was hectic, there was time to relax. For most of the Marines in the squadron, time off was spent in the nearby town of Olongapo. There were bars, cheap beer, and plenty of women.

It was heaven for most of the Marines who spent their hard-earned money to kick back and enjoy themselves. There was a catch: a curfew from midnight to 0400. No one was allowed on the streets during those hours. If you were late coming back to the base, a visit with the legal officer was soon to follow. Ferdinand Marcos was still in power but losing his grip on the nation. Civil strife and a fear of a communist takeover gripped Marcos and his ruling party following bombings in Manila five years earlier. Political unrest had led to many arrests and executions. The curfew was imposed to keep opposition movement in check.

The day after the conclusion of the exercise, the squadron launched five aircraft from Cubi Point to Iwakuni, via a stop at Kadena AFB on Okinawa. On 23 October, five more aircraft were launched and followed the same route as the previous day's flight. One aircraft remained at Cubi Point since it was scheduled for a complete stripping, corrosion treatment, and repainting at the Fleet Aircraft Western Pacific Repair Facility.

The author recalled "upon return from Cubi, we got a three-day weekend. A bunch of us electricians and 'Gramps' from Ground Support took a trip to Hiroshima. We rented a room, visited the Peace Memorial (site of ground zero that fateful day in August 1945), and had many beers at a brewery. It was a well-deserved break after operations at Cubi. The weekend went by fast and back to work on Monday."

The first two weeks of November saw the squadron fly numerous night intercept missions. On 15 November and lasting until the 17th, the squadron participated in Exercise *Cope Jade Delta*. The "Thunderbolts" were scheduled to fly CAS, CAS CAP, and ECM missions over South Korea. Weather during the period was not conducive to flight operations. The squadron was scheduled to fly 24 sorties but 75% of them were cancelled due to the weather. Occupying the last day of November was exercise *Cope Strike 78-4* in South Korea. Squadron Phantoms conducted ground-attack training missions. The exercise concluded on 2 December.

The day before, the "Thunderbolts" observed the 36th anniversary of the squadron's foundation in 1941. Nothing special was held for the occasion; flight operations continued for *Cope Strike*. VMFA-251's next exercise was *Ssan Yong VII/LTX 1–78* in South Korea over the period 7–12 December. A detachment of six aircraft and support personnel was sent to Taegu Air Base to conduct operations in support of amphibious operations. While deployed to Taegu, the detachment flew 47 sorties consisting of air-to-ground and fighter-intercept missions for a total of nearly sixty-five hours. "Thunderbolt" aircrews gained experience operating from a Korean air base, working within

USAF command and control networks, and VFR navigation in South Korea. Supply for the squadron Phantoms was done via an F-4 fitted with a cargo tank and carrying the needed parts from Iwakuni. The supply issue delayed one jet from returning with the squadron due to a fuel leak. Four days after the return from South Korea, the squadron sent four Phantoms to Kadena AFB to participate in DACM against AV-8 Harriers stationed there. With the holiday season fast approaching, flight operations slowed down enough to allow the squadron and other MAG-15 personnel to treat children from a local orphanage with a Christmas party.[101]

The squadron spent most of its time in January preparing for Operation *Team Spirit 78*, to be held in South Korea. From 2 January to the 12th, MAG-15 ran an exercise involving all squadrons that tested all the tents and associated items that would be needed to support a MAG operating from a bare-bones base. Problems were identified and corrective measures taken prior to the squadron's departure in February.

An inspection by the FMFPac Inspection Team occupied the squadron from 16–21 January. Upon orders by the commanding general of the inspection team, on 18 and 19 January a detachment of six VMFA-251 F-4Js and six VMFA-235 F-4Js were deployed to Kadena to participate in (Operational Readiness Training Exercise) *Ortex 1-78*. The objective of the exercise was to determine MAG-15's ability to maintain air superiority over an assigned sector of airspace similar to the Korean scenario the squadron would be facing in February. With MACS-4 controlling the aircraft, the CAP missions and hot-pad scrambles intercepted all aggressor aircraft attempting to penetrate the assigned airspace sector. Upon returning to Iwakuni, the squadron received the remainder of the inspection with outstanding results.

The rest of the month had the Marines flying fighter-intercept missions and ACM missions against TA-4s and A-4Ms within the Iwakuni area; DACM missions were flown against TA-4s and AV-8s at Kadena AFB.

On 12 February, 46 maintenance personnel deployed to Yechon Air Base, Korea (K-58), for *Team Spirit 78*. Upon arriving at Yechon, the detachment assisted in erecting the tent accommodation, showers, maintenance tents, and mess tents that were to support the Marines participating in the operation. For many in the squadron, it was the first time they would be exposed to cold-weather field operations.

The day after maintenance personnel departed for Yechon, the squadron was awarded the FMFPac annual safety award. Just three days later, VMFA-251 completed its second accident-free year, flying nearly six thousand one hundred hours without an air or ground accident.

The squadron commenced training for *Team Spirit* on 20 February; this lasted until 6 March. A detachment of six aircraft flew to Yechon on 23 February to participate in training there. During this rotation, the squadron flew ground attack, fighter-intercept and fighter weapons missions.

Operation *Team Spirit 78* commenced on 7 March. The exercise consisted of an amphibious assault followed by the participation of the 9th Marine Amphibious Brigade and Republic of Korea Marine Corps units. VMFA-251 provided the fighter assets as part of the Marine Air/Ground Team. Operating from the base at Yechon, the squadron flew a variety of simulated combat missions and established air superiority.

"It was cold and muddy," recalled the author. "Walking to the shower and back to your assigned tent without getting muddy was a challenge to say the least. We were kept busy with maintenance, but for the most part the Phantoms held up pretty well. One thing that I vividly recall is the tents. The stoves used to keep them warm dated from World War II. I'd say the Corps got their money's worth out of those stoves."

Despite the rain, mud, and snow, the deployment was a success. The squadron was able to complete training in ground attacks, fighter weapons against adversary aircraft, scrambles, VID (visual identification, fighter intercepts), ECM, and communications security as well as gaining on-the-job experience in a cold-weather environment. The squadron's six aircraft flew all of their assigned missions.

Team Spirit 78 ended on 17 March and the detachment returned to Iwakuni. For the remainder of the month, the squadron flew fighter-intercept missions and ACM from Iwakuni. Cross-country jaunts were flown to Osan, Korea; Clark AFB in the Philippines, and Kadena AFB, Okinawa. First Lieutenant Robert Foley—a squadron RIO—recalled one of those cross-country flights.

> While the squadron was deployed to Iwakuni in 77–78 air crews had the occasional chance to get a weekend cross-country to Korea (ok), Okinawa (good), or the PI (great). On one such weekend, our two-plane [section] made it to Cubi Point, I guess on Friday afternoon. On Saturday it seemed like a great opportunity to fly a low-level (very low level) navigation training flight. I guess everyone involved knows who the crews were so the names are not important.
>
> Anyway, as we headed back to Iwakuni on Sunday afternoon, we landed at Kadena to refuel and have the planes given a once over by the small maintenance detachment we had semi-permanently stationed at Kadena.
>
> When we went back out to the flight line after filing, the ground crew was quite excited to show us the leaves they were finding, kind of wedged into the Sidewinder rails where they bolt up to the inboard wing pylons. As I recall that's 5–6 feet away from the intake and maybe a foot and a half under the bottom side of the wings.

> The crew was good about loosening up the bolts so we could get the well wedged leaves out of the pylons (and not documenting that maintenance event).
>
> I knew we were a "bit" low over the trees which were on some sort of farm or plantation. They were all very neatly aligned and growing in a nice, orderly fashion on what seemed like miles of rolling, undulating hills. This was somewhere south of Cubi: exactly where I don't recall.
>
> I know the story floated around but never made it back to higher ups (at least no one ever said anything during the deployment).
>
> I guess this was about as low as an F-4 will go without landing. And, it says a lot about the integrity and loyalty of the Marines with whom we served and kept our Phantoms flying.[102]

During April, fighter weapons training was conducted with VMA-214 and H&MS-12, both with MAG-12. The objective was to allow aircrews to gain experience in multi-bogey duels without the use of ground control intercept support. On 4 and 13 April, the squadron participated with the guided-missile cruiser USS *Oklahoma City* (CG-5) in anti-air warfare (AAW) training. The exercise provided the squadron with a unique opportunity to conduct AIM-7 simulated attacks against surface vessels and to conduct AAW training in support of that same vessel. Closing out the month of April, the "Thunderbolts" hosted MAG-15's Fighter Symposium. Attending the symposium were F-4E/Js of the 304th Tactical Fighter Squadron of the Japan Air Self-Defense Force based out of Tsuiki Air Base.

CAS missions as well as general bombing missions had to be conducted in either Korea or Okinawa, since there were no ranges in Japan to drop ordnance. To overcome the problem, the squadron established a turn-around crew at Kadena AFB on Okinawa towards the end of April and into May. The turn-around crew was used by other squadrons of MAG-15 as well as MAG-12.

Fighter weapons training and fighter intercepts over Japanese airspace, and ground attack and level bombing missions on Okinawa, kept pilots busy during May. The highlight of the month occurred on the 13th when MAG-15 executed a no-notice squadron recall in order to test its preparedness for combat. In less than five hours, all personnel were accounted for, aircraft loaded, crews briefed, and aircraft assigned. It was a marked improvement over *Check Alligator* held in August. The squadron's number of available aircraft was reduced by one when it had to ferry BuNo 153858 on 16 May for repair at the NARF at Tainan City on the southwest coast of Taiwan.

The squadron's luck of accident or incident-free hours ran out on 1 June. Captain Pospischil, flying BuNo 153911, recalled what happened:

> I was giving a section lead check to a squadron mate. We were doing a section go with me being on his wing. Right at liftoff I got an engine fire lite [*sic*] on my right engine. The tower was transmitting eject, eject! I did a quick secondary check and confirmed a fire.

> I shut down the right engine and declared an emergency. The aircraft began to settle so I ejected the centerline fuel tank which landed in the bay. I did a gentle left turn and landed the plane. The fire trucks were waiting for me, so I shut the plane down and we exited the plane at the end of the runway … An inspection revealed I took a 20 lb. bird down the intake (they estimated that by the size of the bones in the engine).[103]

Despite preparation for the squadron's redeployment back to MCAS Beaufort, the "Thunderbolts" were kept busy during June. DACM sorties were flown against A-4s and TA-4s at Iwakuni, and F-5s and AV-8s at Kadena. Night intercept missions were also flown against bogies dispensing chaff. When VMFA-122's advance party arrived on 20 June, the squadron initiated plans for the transfer of aircraft and facilities to the new unit. The transfer of the squadron's 12 F-4Js involved the inspection of each aircraft, as well as providing a detailed inventory. The transfer went smoothly and did not impact training and remaining flight operations. Near the end of the deployment, the squadron received word it had been nominated for the Hanson Award. Unfortunately, it did not receive the award, losing out to VMFA-531.[104]

At the beginning of July, operations ended as the unit began packing and transferring personnel for the trip back to Beaufort. Squadron strength was reduced as early leave was granted to many personnel and an advance party was sent home. All 12 of the squadron's F-4J Phantom IIs now belonged to VMFA-122. In return, the squadron took possession of eight VMFA-122 aircraft in Beaufort. The remaining personnel and equipment were transported home by MAC C-141 from 8 to 10 July. Their return journey took them to Anchorage, Alaska, before arriving at Beaufort.

Upon arrival at Beaufort, all men were granted a 10-day leave period except for a rear party consisting of eight officers and 12 enlisted men. Flight operations were reduced in July, flying slightly over 33 hours. On 14 July, Allinder relinquished command to Lieutenant Colonel Frederick J. Schober.

There was much work to be done once everyone returned from leave. Until the end of the year, the squadron was in a fluctuating state as those on leave returned, personnel transferred, and new men joined the squadron. From August to the end of year, the eight aircraft accepted from VMFA-122 were sent to several NARFs. In return, the squadron received eight F-4Js from VMFA-312. In December, the "Thunderbolts" received their first two F-4S jets from the NARF facility at North Island, San Diego. These aircraft had improved radars and other upgrades. Amazingly, the squadron had to maintain three different radar sets during the last half of 1978 due to the varied aircraft configurations. As the squadron received new Phantoms, they had to be repainted to replace any markings with VMFA-251 markings. The tail underwent another change; gone were the muted white cross and dark gray thunderbolt. An orange thunderbolt now adorned the vertical stabilizer.

During the last six months of the year, the squadron flew what missions it could to keep crews combat ready and trained. They participated in Exercise *Avelex* (Aviation Element Exercise) *4-78*, and flew ECM with EA-6B Prowlers, DACM against A-4Ms, AV-8As, and F-15s, intercept missions in all weather conditions, ACM, night sorties, ground attack, fighter weapons training, and escort missions. Despite the rebuilding state of the squadron, it racked up 1,327 flight hours.

Late in 1978, the Commandant of the Marine Corps (CMC) presented VMFA-251 with the Commandant's Aviation Efficiency Trophy for its "dedication, initiative, and overall excellence in the performance of its mission during the period of 1 July 1977 through 30 June 1978." The citation went on to say:

> Commencing with a highly successful TransPac, through a myriad of exercises from Fortress Lightning in the tropics to Cope Strikes in the Korean winter, and culminating with a most productive Operation Team Spirit, Marine Fighter Attack Squadron Two Five One (VMFA-251) has unequivocally established itself as the most professional, versatile, spirited and efficient Marine Aviation Squadron of 1978 ... Congratulations are sincerely extended for these accomplishments and the officers and men of VMFA-251 can be justifiably proud.[105]

The highlight for many Marines was the squadron's participation in the filming of Lewis Carlino's *The Great Santini*, starring Robert Duvall as the film's main character, Marine pilot Bull Meechum. The film was based on the novel of the same name written by the late Pat Conroy. Production began in Beaufort during the last week of September and continued through November. The squadron provided some of its Phantom IIs for aerial sequences shot for the film. Released in October 1979, it did not do well at the box office despite good reviews. Duvall and Michael O'Keefe, who portrayed his son in the film, both received Oscar nominations.

During the first half of 1979, in April, the squadron sent a detachment to the Navy Fighter Weapons School at NAS Miramar. Once the detachment completed its training, it joined the squadron in Yuma which had deployed there in late April for air-to-air and air-to-ground training. The Marines returned to MCAS Beaufort in late May, just before the Memorial Day weekend. During the Yuma deployment, it was discovered the F-4S aircraft were leaking a prodigious amount of fuel from the inner wing fuel cells. These aircraft would have to be repaired by NARF personnel. Apparently, it was also affecting other squadrons flying the F-4S.

Marines at MCAS Beaufort also received a look at their future when an F-18 Hornet proved what it could do with a demonstration flight. "I found it amazing," recalled the author. "The plane was nearly vertical and still moving forward just feet above the runway during one of its flights. I couldn't believe it. It was clear the aircraft was extremely maneuverable."

Tragically, the squadron lost one of its Phantoms and a pilot on 1 June. Just before noon on that fateful day, two aircraft were participating in fighter weapons tactics training about fifty miles off the coast of South Carolina when one of them may have suffered a compressor stall. The aircraft (BuNo 155828)—piloted by Captain Steve Anderson, with RIO First Lieutenant Jeffery Hill—could not be recovered and quickly plunged into the sea. Both Anderson and Hill ejected from the aircraft shortly before the aircraft hit the water. Whether they ejected at the same time is not known. It is possible Anderson ejected too late since his parachute was seen to deploy just as his seat hit the water.

The second aircraft may have sent a distress call to nearby rescue units. Hill was quickly recovered, aided by the second Phantom as well as a civilian vessel nearby that guided the rescue teams to the impact area. Hill was picked up by helicopter and transported to the naval hospital at MCAS Beaufort. He was shaken up but otherwise unhurt. Rescue units continued looking for Anderson's body for three days before the search was called off. The aircraft was not recovered, sinking upon impact to a depth of at least 100 feet.[106]

On 15 June, Schober handed over command of the squadron to Lieutenant Colonel Patrick Jones. The new CO had served two tours in Vietnam and had recently served as the commanding officer of H&MS-31 at Beaufort.

The squadron began the second half of 1979 with nine F-4S aircraft. Not all of them were available due to the fuel leak problem. With reduced aircraft availability, the squadron continued its training with air-to-air and ground-attack missions.

On 9 July, a detachment of four aircraft began operations as adversary aircraft for F-106 pilots assigned to the USAF Interceptor Weapons School. The deployment to Tyndall AFB, Florida, provided training in VID, fighter attack escort, and DACT for the eight aircrew. During the same period, VMFA-251 was assigned as the FMFLANT Augmentation unit to the 20th NORAD Region. Aircrews received briefings on NORAD systems and telecommunications, and alert equipment was installed at the squadron. The only problem incurred during the period was the continuation of the on-site NARF repair of the squadron's aircraft as they raced to correct the wing fuel cell issue.

Training shifted focus to air-to-ground missions for the month of August. Emphasis was placed on a high-threat environment and the tactics required to successfully execute the missions. On 5 August, Captain J. O. Marthiljohni (pilot) and Hill (RIO) departed for MCAS Yuma and Marine Aviation Weapons and Tactics Squadron (MAWTS) 1. Their attendance at the Weapons and Tactics Instructor (WTI) course was aimed at improving the squadron's training base as well as gaining current knowledge and tactics for use in training the unit's less-experienced aviators. *Avelex 3-79* was conducted at Beaufort on 9 August with briefings and rehearsals for two days before. The *Avelex* was a means to test all aspects of Marine Aviation. The squadron used two interceptor aircraft and two strike aircraft for the exercise, the importance of which was punctuated with the CMC attending the event. Two more F-4S aircraft left for Yuma on 17 August assigned to MAWTS-1 for use in the WTI course.

Aircrew combat readiness training was planned for the month of September with multiple mission types flown to update and refresh crew qualifications. On 2 September, tragedy struck as the squadron lost an F-4S while flying a mission during the WTI course at Yuma.

The aircraft carrying Marthiljohni and Hill (BuNo 155562), callsign *Saki 192*, was the wingman of a flight of two scheduled to conduct an escort mission for two CH-46 Sea Knight helicopters in the Chocolate Mountain range. *Yank 551* was a TF-15[107] assigned to be the aggressor aircraft for the mission.

The takeoff of *Yank 551* was delayed for 15 minutes due to minor maintenance problems. The lead F-4S, *Saki 191*, aborted due to maintenance issues. Marthiljohni and Hill continued the mission alone and set a course to rendezvous with the helicopters. Time of take-off was about ten minutes after the TF-15.

Three uneventful intercepts were conducted between the two aircraft before things went terribly wrong. The TF-15 conducted a high-to-low intercept of the F-4S and closed for a simulated missile shoot. The TF-15 called a long-range Fox-2[108] at two to three thousand feet above ground level (AGL), and about one nautical mile astern of the Phantom II. The F-4S was at an estimated 1,000 feet AGL at the time of the Fox-2. After the simulated missile shot by the TF-15, the TF-15 observed the F-4S commence a hard left turn and eject two flares. The TF-15 pulled off nose high and transmitted "break it off." The backseat pilot of the TF-15 continued to observe Marthiljohni and Hill's aircraft. He observed flames and objects streaming from the area of the right engine. This continued until the right engine exploded. Soon after the explosion, the F-4S slammed into the ground. No parachutes were seen by the TF-15.

After the F-4S crashed, the two CH-46s proceeded to the crash site where one landed and looked for the aircrew while the other returned to MCAS Yuma to aid the SAR effort.

Upon being notified of the crash, the SAR team from MCAS Yuma departed at 1555. The TF-15 went high to attempt to assist the inbound SAR team in locating the crash site. The SAR helicopter arrived 40 minutes later. Since the crash site was mountainous, the helicopter had to search for a nearby flat landing site. They found one at approximately seven hundred feet. A medical team and a small search party joined the effort to locate Marthiljohni and Hill. After climbing nearly fourteen hundred feet, the men reached the crash site. The remains of both men were found and moved to NAF El Centro.

An investigation was conducted and while some discrepancies were found with the fuselage fuel tanks and associated wires, none were deemed as causes for the crash. However, they were important enough to recommend changes to maintenance and inspection procedures for the F-4S. It is unclear what the cause of the crash may have been.[109]

Meanwhile, back at Beaufort, the squadron was contending with mother nature. The approach of Hurricane *David* forced the evacuation of four aircraft to MCAS Yuma on 4 September with the last aircraft returning to Beaufort on the 7th once the hurricane blew through. The squadron did realize a slight highlight during the month as the final F-4S was admitted to the NARF fuel leak rework program.

October was dedicated almost entirely to the preparation of crews for the MAWTS-l Air Combat Tactics Instructor certification course which was conducted at Beaufort during the final week of the month. Fighter weapons sorties of all types were flown against F-4, A-4, and F-15 adversaries. In addition to the fighter weapons workups, two "Thunderbolt" crews began Field Carrier Landing Practice workup and lectures with VMFA-115 in preparation for carrier qualification on board USS *Dwight D. Eisenhower* (CVN-69). During the period 22–26 October, the "Thunderbolts" provided four Phantoms which operated out of MCAS Beaufort in support of NORAD Exercise *Federal Indian/Amalgam Chief/Snowtime 80*. Night intercept missions were flown against ECM-capable aircraft.

The emphasis on fighter tactics was continued into November. The focus on fighter weapons sorties was aimed at the 25–30 November deployment of six Phantoms and eight aircrews to Tyndall AFB for DACT missions against F-106 Delta Darts assigned to the USAF Interceptor Weapons School. The two aircrews assigned to carrier qualifications aboard USS *Dwight D. Eisenhower* completed their assignment on 16 November. One crew was qualified but the second crew was not able to qualify due to lack of deck time. From 15 to 22 November, VMFA-251 provided support for 20th NORAD Region F-106s by flying as adversaries. By the end of the month, the squadron had received its first three F-4S aircraft modified with leading-edge slats (LES).

The squadron's detachment of six F-4S aircraft at Tyndall AFB began the month of December by moving to Eglin AFB, Florida, for fighter weapons missions with F-15s from the 33rd Tactical Fighter Wing. The deployment to Eglin ended on 8 December. Of note during the Tyndall–Eglin deployment was the initial employment of the F-4S with leading-edge slats (LES). Apparently, this was the first time LES-equipped Phantoms were involved in a Marine aviation training exercise. The upgraded Phantoms showed off their improved handling characteristics and increased turn performance during the deployment.

The squadron received its fourth F-4S with LES modifications on 11 December which brought the squadron to 12 aircraft assigned. VMFA-251 was well on its way to becoming the Marine Corps' first fully equipped squadron with the LES F-4S.[110]

The constant training continued through the first half of 1980. A close call for one aircrew occurred at MCAS Beaufort on 28 March. USAF Captain R. A. McNeese was attempting an arrested landing when the aircraft's lowered hook skipped, missing the cable, and the drag 'chute deployed from the rear of the aircraft.[111] In late April and May, the squadron returned to MCAS Yuma for air-to-air and air-to-ground training.

While the squadron was deployed to Yuma, the political thawing between Cuba and the United States took a turn for the worse despite efforts to normalize relationships. A humanitarian crisis soon occurred after six Cubans crashed the gates of the Peruvian embassy in Havana. Within days, over 10,000 Cubans were on the grounds of the embassy requesting asylum. Several countries agreed to accept the refugees, including the United States when then President Jimmy Carter decided to allow 3,500 of the refugees from the Peruvian embassy into the country. Aircraft and boats in Cuba and the United States began to transport the refugees. This mass exodus became known as the Mariel Boatlift, named for a port near Havana.

The boatlift soon expanded. When Cuba declared those that wanted to leave could do so, the crisis changed from a political crisis to a humanitarian one, especially in Florida. U.S. military units soon augmented the United States Coast Guard units trying to bring order to the chaos, as well as Cuba's growing aggressive actions. In May, Cuban MiGs began intercepting U.S. aircraft and sank a Bahamian patrol boat 400 miles east of Mariel. Perhaps as a response to this threat, VMFA-312 deployed from Beaufort to NAS Key West to provide fighter escort duty. VMFA-251 sent a detachment to Key West to augment VMFA-312 in early June and did not return to Beaufort until the 16th.[112]

The boatlift continued until September when Castro ordered all boats out of Mariel. In November, the last of the refugees stuck in Mariel were flown to Miami. Around 125,000 ended up in the United States.[113]

Rounding out the month, Lieutenant Colonel David A. Richwine assumed command from Patrick Jones. Richwine was also a combat veteran from Vietnam and earned his wings early in the 1970s.

As July began, attrition in personnel led to a shortage of assigned pilots. There was a good pool of trained aircrews and most of the aircraft were operational. For the next six months, training focused on air-to-air and air-to-ground; the primary focus, though, being air-to-air. However, before the training could get into full gear, the squadron prepared to support VMFA-333 and its upcoming deployment to Japan by providing two aircraft as back-ups. The two Phantoms took off on 5 July for MCAS El Toro. One returned to base four days later while the second remained at El Toro for repairs.

In an effort to optimize the training available for squadron crews, one aircrew was selected to attend the TOPGUN course at the Navy Fighter Weapons School. They departed with an aircraft on 11 July. Fourteen of the squadron's maintenance personnel followed to support the aircraft.

The next day, a Phantom was sent to MCAS Yuma for use in the MAWTS-l-sponsored WTI course which the squadron had one pilot attending. Local operations were directed at improving aircrew proficiency in VID and ACM scenarios.

The squadron also participated in the 2nd MAW Aviation Element Exercise for the period 14–16 July. On the 16th, it also provided four sorties in support of the Joint Chiefs of Staff-directed Joint Tactical Information Distribution System (JTIDS) evaluation with MACS-5. JTIDS is a network radio system used by the armed forces of the United States and allies to support data and communications needs, principally in air defense and missile defense. The network involved air and ground assets, as well as dedicated processing and control centers.

From 21 July, until the 25th, the squadron hosted two A-4Ms from VMA-223 and a T-38 from VF-43. Missions flown during the week were in support of the squadron's fighter weapons work up and provided training for the VMA-223 crews.

The aircraft that had been left at El Toro was flown to Yuma for use in the WTI course. The end of July also found the squadron's skipper participating in the WTI commander's course.

The first half of August had the squadron participating in local *Avelex* missions. The aircraft involved in the WTI course at Yuma returned with its support personnel on 2 August. The other aircraft was transferred to NAS Miramar to support the TOPGUN course. On 18 August, two squadron aircraft and three crews departed for NAS Roosevelt Roads to participate in a MAG-31 missile-firing exercise. Following the conclusion of the exercise, the aircraft returned on the 20th. On the same day, two squadron crews flew to NAS Oceana to assist in the evaluation of a Visual ACM Simulator. The two aircraft returned the following day. With the arrival of the two aircraft and support personnel from the TOPGUN school on 22 August, all squadron personnel and aircraft were back at Beaufort. Up until the closing days of August, the squadron focused on fighter intercepts in the air-to-air realm. On the 26th, the Marines changed gears as they prepared for another overseas deployment—this time to Norway.

The upcoming exercise was dubbed *Teamwork 80*. The NATO exercise would involve several member nations including the United States, Canada, Federal Republic of Germany, Denmark, Norway, and several others. Its intent was to test NATO assets and their ability to perform should a war break out.

The squadron continued its preparations for Norway during the first week in September. Once preparations were complete, the main body and equipment left for Orland Air Base, Norway, on 9 and 10 September. The maintenance chase crew for the Atlantic crossing operation—dubbed *Agile Martin*—also left for Goose Bay, Newfoundland, on 10 September. The next day, the squadron's 12 Phantoms departed for Goose Bay. Two days later, six of the F-4s left Goose Bay for Norway, followed by the remaining six on 14 September. One F-4S had to divert to Keflavik, Iceland, while the other five continued to Norway. The Phantom which diverted arrived at Orland on 15 September and, with the arrival of the chase crew on 16 September, the squadron was intact at Orland and ready to go. Acting as the fighter assets for MAG-40, the squadron placed aircraft on alert, flew combat air patrol, provided air defense, and other intercept operations in support of the *Teamwork 80* landing force for the period 17–24 September. At the conclusion of the exercise, the maintenance chase crew departed Orland for Lajes, Azores, on 25 September and 10 of the Phantoms arrived there on the 26th. The remaining two arrived at Lajes the next day. The deployment back to Beaufort continued on the 29th with the movement of 11 of the aircraft from Lajes to Loring AFB, Maine. On 30 September, the final F-4 left Lajes and arrived at Pease AFB, New Hampshire.

During the first four days of October, the squadron and its aircraft returned to MCAS Beaufort. There was no rest for the returnees as the "Thunderbolts" immediately prepared for another exercise. They were to participate in a Fleet Fighter ACM Readiness Program (FFARP) to be hosted by VF-43 at NAS Oceana. FFARP was a periodic training program which allowed a participating squadron to practice dogfighting techniques with a squadron designated as an adversary. An advance party consisting of two aircraft left on 17 October. On the same day, the squadron sent one of its officers—First Lieutenant N. J. Episcopo—to the Tactical Air Control Party (TACP) School as part of MAG-31's Augmentee Forward Air Controller program. The remainder of the squadron personnel and nine aircraft deployed to NAS Oceana on 19 October. The remaining aircraft was flown to the Naval Air Test Center at Patuxent River to be used in carrier suitability testing. At the end of the month, the squadron continued FFARP training at Oceana.

The training at Oceana continued until 6 November. The following day, nine of the Phantoms returned to MCAS Beaufort. Nearly all the maintenance personnel and squadron equipment returned on the same day. Two aircraft remained behind due to maintenance issues, with a small rear party repairing them; by 14 November, both aircraft were back at Beaufort. With three new pilots having joined the squadron, flight operations concentrated on familiarization and refresher training for them as well as those who missed the FFARP exercise. Just before Thanksgiving, the Marines participated in another MAG-31 Aviation Element Exercise.

With the squadron all present at Beaufort, and no deployments scheduled for the first time since October 1979, the "Thunderbolts" continued their routine training operations. Episcopo, who had returned from TACP School, left for four months on temporary additional duty to serve as a forward air controller. The squadron continued its NORAD commitments by flying sorties in Exercise *Federal Brave* on 2 and 3 December. From the 8th to the 12th, three pilots certified as air combat tactics instructors by completing the ACTI course hosted by MAWTS-1. Also on 12 December, the "Thunderbolts" went through personnel inspections, and a Christmas party for squadron Marines and their families was held. The squadron also participated in an anti-air warfare exercise held at Beaufort on 15 and 16 December. To round out the month, the majority of the unit's local operations focused on continued refresher training for newly arrived aircrews.[114]

The first half of 1981 was marked by two major deployments: the first to Roosevelt Roads and the second to MCAS Yuma in Arizona. From 8 January to the 23rd, three MAG-31 squadrons, including VMFA-251, participated in missile-firing exercises at the Puerto Rico air station. The exercise allowed crews to fire live missiles at target drones and also allowed ordnance personnel to gain experience loading the Sparrows and Sidewinders used.[115] On 20 March, the squadron departed Beaufort for Yuma to practice air-to-ground and air-to-air missions. Air combat training consisted of flying against Canadian F-5 aggressor aircraft while air-to-ground training consisted of dropping munitions with A-6 Intruders from MCAS Cherry Point. For the ground support personnel, they were treated to something rare. They were able to witness the results of their work by being flown by helicopter to an observation point to witness the aircraft drop their munitions on designated targets. The Yuma deployment concluded with a 2nd MAW combat-readiness inspection. The squadron returned to Beaufort on 10 April.[116]

On the last day of June, Lieutenant Colonel Norman G. G. Kerr took over command of the squadron from Richwine. Kerr had previously served with the squadron under Mavretic.

In early July, the squadron received five new pilots from VMFAT-101 (Marine Fighter Attack Training Squadron). Getting these pilots trained and combat ready was the emphasis for the rest of the month. On 11 July, two aviators, two aircraft, and a maintenance support team were deployed to Yuma to attend the WTI course. One aircraft (BuNo 153909) suffered minor damage when, on 23 July, a TA-75 towing tractor struck it.

Squadron flying in August focused on all-weather intercepts and preparing the new pilots for fighter weapons training. On the 5th, one of the Phantoms (BuNo 155899) at Yuma suffered engine damage. Apparently, it did not impact the WTI commitment. Two days later, at Beaufort, another aircraft (BuNo 155805) on the flight line was damaged when the aft canopy was punctured after failing to close properly. Kerr and another officer departed on 17 August for Yuma to attend the WTI commander's orientation course. By the 23rd, the aircraft and personnel had returned from Yuma following the completion of their course. From 24 August, running through the 28th, squadron pilots flew fighter escort and CAP sorties as part of exercise *Quick Thrust 2-81*, held by the Ninth Air Force headquartered at Shaw AFB, South Carolina.

For the month of September, VMFA-251 was on alert status as part of the Navy exercise *Sopwith Camel*. For the period 12–16 September, one aircraft and crew was sent to NAS Lemoore, California, as a component of the MAG-31 detachment for ACM training over land. During exercise *Seabat 4-81*, held from the 22nd to the 24th, the squadron participated in electronic warfare training. At the same time, its maintenance department was inspected by the 2nd MAW, receiving an "overall excellent" rating. The bulk of the squadron's training occurred from 15 September to 10 October during electronic warfare and CAS training at Nellis AFB in Nevada. Three aircraft were sent, along with two crews and a maintenance support team of 24 men. Nearly 170 flight hours were accumulated during the Nellis exercise.

The squadron underwent an operational test and evaluation safety stand-down from 12 October through the 16th. The stand-down affected all units of the 2nd MAW. Aircrews were lectured on basic and standard flying procedures, and all officers attended meetings presented by the commanding general of the 2nd MAW and the commanding officer of MAG-31. Immediately after the end of the safety stand-down, the squadron participated in MAG-31's anti-air warfare exercise. During the three-day event, the squadron flew 28 air defense sorties.

With another FFARP deployment to NAS Oceana to occur in February 1982, November saw the squadron training for the upcoming exercise by flying fighter weapons sorties and getting new pilots up to speed. It was also on alert status for *Sopwith Camel.*

Early in December, the squadron underwent another inspection by the 2nd MAW, this time its operations, intelligence and safety departments were scrutinized. Two pilots began their ACTI course, once again run by MAWTS-1. From the 12th to the 19th, the squadron participated in the 2nd MAW's aviation evaluation exercise. The first phase had the squadron defending MCAS Beaufort against an air attack. For the second phase, VMFA-251 led a simulated raid involving all MAG-31 units against the headquarters of the commanding general of the 2nd MAW. At the same time as the MAW exercise, the "Thunderbolts" were involved in *Seabat 1-82.* Flying was limited, but training in electronic warfare was accomplished.[117]

The new year opened with *Missile Exercise 1–82* at NAS Roosevelt Roads. Rather than deploying the whole squadron, elements left Beaufort, refueled en route and fired their missiles on arrival. The first six aircraft launched on 11 January and returned to Beaufort the next day. Before the exercise concluded, four additional aircraft completed the exercise, resulting in six successful AIM-7 launches and seven AIM-9 launches against target drones.

The first two weeks of February focused on air combat training while preparing for a deployment to the FFARP at NAS Oceana. On the 13th, the squadron deployed 10 aircraft and 164 Marines to the naval air station. During the remainder of the month, flight operations in Oceana involved ACM tactics against U.S. Navy F-5, A-4, and F-14 aggressor aircraft. Weather conditions were not the best but, despite unheated maintenance areas, squadron personnel worked above and beyond to keep the aircraft up and running.

On 6 March, the squadron returned to Beaufort. During the FFARP deployment, 104 air combat sorties were flown. Local flight operations for the remainder of the month focused on all-weather intercepts and aerial refueling as the "Thunderbolts" prepared for an April deployment to Iceland. To assist in aerial-refueling training, a USAF KC-135 was utilized to qualify squadron aircrew for the deployment.

On April Fools' Day, eight aircraft and two spares departed Beaufort, flying non-stop via aerial refueling to NAS Keflavik, Iceland, to participate in Exercise *Essential Warrior*. The next day, all aircraft, equipment, and personnel were in place and ready for flight operations. The Marines replaced the 57th Fighter Intercept Squadron (FIS) and assumed the duties of defending Icelandic airspace until the USAF unit returned. In addition to flying intercept and aerial-refueling training sorties, the squadron maintained hot-pad duty, with two aircraft and crews, 24 hours a day. The hot-pad aircraft scrambled 24 times and intercepted six Soviet Tu-95 *Bears*. On the 24th, the 57th FIS returned to Iceland and relieved VMFA-251. Squadron aircraft departed with KC-135 tanker support on the 26th and flew non-stop to MCAS Beaufort, a flight time of nearly eight hours.

Local flight operations in May emphasized training new aircrews. For 10–13 May, the squadron's maintenance department was inspected by the Commander, Naval Air Atlantic, and was given an outstanding result. *Anti-Air Warfare Exercise 2-82* was held from the 13th to the 14th. Flight operations for the exercise simulated NBC conditions. The squadron flew 15 sorties during the two days. While flying a training sortie on the 19th, Captain T. W. Thomas had to abort after suffering compressor stalls. He was able to bring his aircraft back to Beaufort without incident.

During the first four days of June, the squadron held its annual personnel training program which included qualifying with the rifle and pistol and conducting physical fitness tests. In addition to training sorties, VMFA-251 once again stood Commander-in-Chief, Atlantic Fleet contingency *Sopwith Camel* as well as preparing for an upcoming deployment to Patrick AFB. However, on 18 June, the squadron received word the deployment to Patrick was cancelled. Training operations for the deployment, which consisted of low-level and air-to-ground tactics, were also cancelled.[118]

Local flight operations continued in July with air-to-air and air-to-ground training missions aiming to increase aircrew combat readiness. On 9 July, two officers and two aircraft departed for NAS Miramar, California, to attend the Navy's TOPGUN school. Four days later, the squadron's record of 10,020 hours without an aerial mishap ended tragically. The F-4S (BuNo 153819) was participating in air-to-air combat training when an uncommanded ejection occurred, resulting in the Phantom crashing into the sea. The pilot, Captain William B. Hankins III, was pulled out of the water by rescue personnel. Upon examination, one of his legs was discovered to be broken. He was transported to Beaufort Naval Hospital. The RIO, Major John E. Daubert, was not recovered and presumed killed.[119] In addition to the lost aircraft, during a routine inspection of the engine intakes of one of its other jets, ground personnel discovered damaged compressor blades. The aircraft (BuNo 153828) was grounded until it could be repaired.

During August, the "Thunderbolts" participated in another MAG-31 Anti-Air Warfare exercise at Beaufort. The squadron flew 14 sorties during the two-day exercise. A post-flight inspection on 9 August found BuNo 155765 with bent compressor blades. On 12 August, Kerr relinquished command to Lieutenant Colonel Gary L. Elsten who became the squadron's 62nd commanding officer. The aircrew and aircraft sent to TOPGUN in July returned to Beaufort on the 13th. The rest of the month, except for 24–26 August, during which the squadron participated in Exercise *Seabat 4-82*, was devoted to flying intercept and aerial-refueling training sorties in preparation for the NATO exercise *Northern Wedding/Bold Guard* to be held in Denmark.

The entire squadron and its 12 Phantoms launched from Beaufort on 4 September for the Royal Danish Air Force Station at Vandel. The aircraft staged out of Goose Bay, Canada, for the final leg to Denmark. All 12 successfully crossed the Atlantic, arriving at Vandel in three echelons. By 10 September, all aircraft were in place at Vandel and ready to commence flight operations. During the exercise, VMFA-251 flew nearly four hundred hours in 172 sorties, which included the deployment to and from Vandel. Despite the stark working conditions, the squadron's maintenance crews ensured the "Thunderbolts" flew all of their assigned missions.

Northern Wedding/Bold Guard ended on 26 September. By 5 October, the entire squadron was back in Beaufort following a return trip via the Azores. Upon return, a 96-hour pass was given to all personnel. The squadron resumed operations on the 13th with an Operational Training Evaluation that ended two days later. On the 20th and 21st, the squadron participated in a small anti-air warfare exercise near Beaufort and ended up flying 24 sorties. October concluded with seven aircraft being sent to MCAS Yuma to participate in *Combined Arms Exercise* (*CAX*) *2-83*.

In addition to the flight operations at Yuma, the remaining Phantoms at Beaufort flew in Exercise *Quick Thrust*, overseen by the Ninth Air Force. The exercise was held over 11 days, ending on 11 November. On the 15th, aircraft, personnel, and equipment returned to MCAS Beaufort following the end of *CAX 2-83*. Continuing the rapid pace of operations, the squadron flew another aircraft to MCAS Yuma on 19 November for use in *WTI 1-83*. And in an unusual assignment, on the 20th, two Phantoms were flown to MCAS Iwakuni for transfer to VMFA-212 and VMFA-312. One aircraft was flown to Japan by a "Thunderbolt" crew while the other went with a MAG-24 crew.

There was no letup in operations for the squadron in December. Four F-4S Phantom IIs were flown to MCAS Cherry Point on the 6th to participate in an aviation element exercise held by the 2nd MAW. The detachment returned to Beaufort on 8 December. During the following two days, the squadron flew 60 sorties in another anti-air warfare exercise with the squadron commander acting as the tactical air commander for the exercise.[120]

January 1983 kicked off with the staff sections of the squadron (S-1, S-2, etc.) inspected by the 2nd MAW inspection team. Upon completion of the inspection the squadron received a satisfactory report. With that behind them, training was aimed at preparing aircrews for an air-to-air missile exercise and an upcoming evaluation under the guidance of the Marine Corps Combat Readiness Evaluation System (MCCRES). The system was designed to provide an accurate way to evaluate the ability of active and reserve forces to execute assigned combat missions under simulated conditions.[121]

VMFA-251 deployed seven aircraft to NAS Roosevelt Roads on 14 February to participate in a missile-firing exercise. Utilizing air refueling with Marine KC-130 tankers, the Phantoms flew non-stop to Puerto Rico from Beaufort with "live" AIM-7 and AIM-9 missiles on their rails. They then engaged target drones to fire their missiles. The exercise, ending on 17 February, was deemed successful. The very next day, the squadron deployed to MCAS Yuma for three weeks of air-to-ground training and the MCCRES evaluation. VMFA-251 aircrews flew a variety of missions including fighter escort and multi-plane coordinated strikes in simulated combat conditions. The MCCRES evaluation rated the squadron combat ready. The "Thunderbolts" returned to Beaufort on 10 March.

On 12 and 13 April, the squadron flew night intercept training missions while participating in NORAD exercise *Amalgam Chief.* Towards the end of the month, the squadron underwent another inspection, this time by the Marine Corps' Inspector General Team.

During the first two weeks in May, the unit participated in Exercise *Solid Shield*. Aircrews flew in a dissimilar combat environment against USAF F-15 Eagles and F-16 Fighting Falcons. The exercise provided a good foundation for exercise *College Dart* held at Tyndall AFB over the period 15–27 May. The squadron deployed to Tyndall and flew many air-to-air sorties against Marine AV-8A Harriers, and USAF F-106 Delta Darts and F-15s.

During June, VMFA-251 flew local intercept missions in all weather conditions, and air-to-ground training, to get newly arrived aircrews up to speed in preparation for another deployment to Tyndall in August.

Aircraft strength hovered between 10 and 12 aircraft during the first six months of 1983. The squadron lost no aircraft, but two required repairs following damage received in several incidents: one aircraft struck a flock of birds during take-off, and another lost an engine following a nozzle failure in afterburner. Fortunately, no one was injured. Repairs to these aircraft and required periodic inspections were no doubt the cause of the fluctuating aircraft strength.[122]

The Marines started July by sending two of their aviators to MCAS Yuma for the ACTI course. The rest of the squadron began preparations for a smaller *College Dart* to be held at Tyndall AFB. On the last day of the month, five aircraft and maintenance support personnel deployed to the Florida base to participate in the exercise.

Through 12 August, the squadron was occupied with the exercise at Tyndall. It provided much needed experience for new aircrews. Once the detachment returned to Beaufort, the "Thunderbolts" flew night air refueling operations with VMGR-252. At the same time, ECM training was conducted with VMAQ-2. August ended with the unit flying sorties for another anti-air warfare exercise.

Budgetary constraints curtailed flight operations in September. Despite the lack of funds, the squadron managed to send five aircraft to MCAS Cherry Point where air-to-air training took place utilizing a designated range (TACTS—Tactical Aircrew Combat Training System) near NAS Oceana. "Thunderbolt" aircrews tangled with A-6 Intruders, TA-4 and A-4 Skyhawks, and F-5 Tigers. The exercise ran from the 10th to the 17th. Ground training was the main focus for the month. Squadron personnel underwent leadership training, NBC training, ran their required Physical Fitness Test, and qualified with the pistol. One officer was sent to Yuma to participate in the WTI course.

For the month of October, the squadron concentrated on preparing for another FFARP exercise to be held at NAS Oceana, Virginia. With new aircrews continuing to join the squadron, and with the last week of the upcoming

FFARP exercise to include an MCCRES evaluation, the squadron held its own FFARP exercise at Beaufort beforehand. Flying one-vs-one sorties against VF-43 F-5s allowed the squadron to concentrate on two-vs-one, two-vs-two, and other engagements when it arrived at Oceana. On 12 October, the advance party deployed with two aircraft for Oceana. The next day, eight more aircraft and the main body arrived. For the rest of the month, the squadron was occupied with both exercises.

The FFARP and MCCRES continued into the first week of November. During the MCCRES portion of the deployment, a wide variety of ACM missions—which included two-vs-one through two-vs-four scenarios—were flown as well as ECM training missions. "Enemy" aircraft included TA-4 and A-4 Skyhawks, F-5 Tigers and F-14 Tomcats. Many of the squadron's pilots and RIOs completed the FFARP training. Others fell a few hours short of doing so. The squadron also fared well on the MCCRES evaluation. Once again, the maintenance personnel worked long hours to ensure the squadron met its given assignments, at times flying up to 16 sorties per day. The "Thunderbolts" arrived back at Beaufort on 5 November and the officer sent to Yuma for the WTI course also rejoined the squadron. For the rest of the month, routine training missions were flown.

December started off with the Marines participating in yet another anti-air warfare exercise. Throughout the month, aircrews were sent to Fort Ripley in Minnesota for cold-weather training and survival. In mid-December, the squadron began preparing two of its officers for the ACTI course to be held at Yuma.

The squadron continued its safe flying record with no aircraft losses reported. The total number of aircraft on hand continued to fluctuate between 10 and 12. Two were damaged: one aircraft lost its rear canopy soon after take-off and another had its nosewheel collapse on landing. By the end of December, the squadron had all 12 of its aircraft available for operations.[123]

Sometime during 1983, the squadron began repainting its aircraft to a new tactical paint scheme. Based on the directive issued the CNO early in 1982, a two-tone pattern using two shades of gray was adopted.[124]

VMFA-251 held a two-day safety stand-down to usher in 1984. Coinciding with the stand-down, the squadron prepared for an upcoming missile-firing exercise by having aircrews use flight simulators. Training on the simulators ran throughout January. The exercise was held from the 10th to the 19th of January. The officers sent to the ACTI course in Yuma to obtain their instructor certification began their journey home on the 26th. In preparation for a deployment to Norway, lectures on cold-weather training and aerial-refueling sorties took up much of the squadron's operations. At the end of the month, Elsten turned over command to Lieutenant Colonel D. L. Doyle.

With the Norway deployment scheduled for early March, training continued to emphasize aerial refueling. At the same time, all-weather intercepts and fighter intercepts were also flown. In addition, some low-level navigation training was also accomplished. Simulators continued to be used, with electronic warfare and radar training the priority. Aircrew on the simulators also familiarized themselves with European approaches and air operating areas.

Teamwork 84 was one of the largest NATO exercises held during the year, and the largest held above the Arctic Circle. Eight NATO member nations supplying ships, air assets, and ground troops were deployed with the objective of "preventing the exit of the Soviet Northern Fleet into the Norwegian Sea and the North Atlantic and to provide sea-based support to allied air and ground operations in Norway."[125] The air assets provided by the USMC would provide air support and cover for an amphibious operation in northern Norway.[126]

The scheduled route to Norway was through the Azores to Scotland and then to the Norwegian airfield at Bødø. The first aircraft departed MCAS Beaufort on 1 March. Significant crosswinds at the first stopover base, Lajes Field, Azores, required these aircraft to divert into Pease AFB, New Hampshire. Terrible weather conditions at the various airfields en route to Norway resulted in more delays. The squadron's first two aircraft arrived at Bødø on 9 March. The rest of the aircraft arrived the next day. One remained at Lajes after one of its engines developed a leak. The aircraft was repaired by having the faulty engine changed and was flown back to Beaufort when the squadron began its deployment home.

After arriving in Norway, the "Thunderbolts" participated in *Busy Eagle* and *Teamwork 84*. The exercise operating area was 160 nautical miles north of Bødø. The squadron flew in all weather conditions, participating in intercept missions and mock air-to-ground attacks. In order to accomplish the missions during the exercise, the Phantoms had to use KC-130 aerial refuelers from VMGR-252. By the time the exercise ended on 22 March, the squadron had flown 90 sorties while accumulating nearly two hundred flight hours. On the afternoon of the 22nd, VMFA-251 launched its 11 aircraft for RAF Machrihanish, Scotland, to begin the journey back to Beaufort. Once again, lousy weather conditions caused delays as the squadron returned home. The last of the Phantoms arrived at Beaufort on 3 April.

The "Thunderbolts" had more crews scheduled to attend the WTI course during April. As a result, two aircraft were sent to Yuma on the 13th. The aircraft were to be used to ensure the aircrews would receive the proper training in low-altitude tactics before going through the WTI course. Five days later, two more Phantoms were flown to Yuma for the course. Back in Beaufort, terrorist briefs were given to all hands. The squadron also hosted many educators and public officials for briefings and tours as part of a public relations drive. Near the end of the month, the squadron flew four missions at MCAS Cherry Point, North Carolina, and a single mission for *Sopwith Camel.*

May arrived with the squadron supporting a 2nd MAW simulated CAS event on three different days. Along with supporting 2nd MAW events, intercept and air-to-air training continued, and low-level training was intensified. The air-to-air training was geared toward the pending deployment to Nellis AFB. Departing on 4 May, and arriving home on the 13th, five aircraft and six crews successfully completed that deployment. Following graduation, the aircrew who attended the WTI course in April returned on 19 May. With all aircraft back at Beaufort, the squadron again concentrated on air-to-ground missions. On the 29th, two officers started their training to participate in the ACTI course. It was also the beginning of *Anti-Air Warfare Exercise* (*AAWEX*) *2-84.*

On 1 June, the anti-air exercise ended with the "Thunderbolts" completing all their assigned missions. The month was dedicated to air-to-ground, low-level navigation, and low-altitude tactics training. Despite the intensified training, the two officers assigned to the ACTI course in May, plus a late add-on of another officer, completed the course. Once again, the squadron flew simulated CAS missions per 2nd MAW orders on 4, 5 and 7 June. Aircrew training lectures continued throughout the month in preparation for another deployment to Yuma set for July. During an inspection on 18 June, one of the squadron's aircraft (BuNo 157245) was found to have a dent in the leading edge of the right wing. Whether the aircraft was flying or on the ground when the incident occurred is not known. From the 20th to the 22nd, a live-fire exercise had the squadron busy flying strike, CAP, and escort missions. MAG-31's flying budget hit zero on 26 June, forcing all group squadrons to halt all flying until July which was the start of the new fiscal year.[127]

July kicked off with air-to-ground and low-altitude tactics training for the deployment to Yuma. On 6 and 7 July, the squadron sent its 12 F-4S aircraft and support personnel to Arizona. The flights to and from Yuma utilized KC-10 tankers to refuel while en route. During the deployment, the squadron flew a mix of low-altitude tactics, air-to-ground ordnance delivery, CAS and deep air-support missions. Along with these missions, training with aerial tankers was also accomplished. Not all the assigned sorties could be flown, however. Strong afternoon thunderstorms that produced excessive winds, heavy rain, and blowing dust forced the squadron to cancel several missions. The deployment ended on 26 July and all aircraft and personnel had returned to Beaufort by the 29th. Upon return from Yuma, the "Thunderbolts" were assigned as the *Sopwith Camel* duty squadron for August.

As the month began, the squadron began training two crews for the ACTI course which involved many sorties practicing ACM. Coincidently, the squadron's training priorities shifted to ACM. In mid-August, five Phantoms were sent to Cherry Point for a tactical air combat and Display Debriefing System (DDS) training. The DDS system allowed for mission playback with the use of computers to allow aircrews to get instant feedback during mission debriefs. Squadron pilots flew one-vs-one, two-vs-one, and two-vs-two scenarios while gaining experience in DACM. At the same time, the ACTI crews began their evaluation. On 25 August, the DDS crews returned and both the ACTI crews successfully completed their training. To close out the month, and as the Labor Day holiday drew near, the entire squadron received safe-driving lectures before hitting the road.

A shift in training emphasis ushered in the month of September. Missions were flown to ensure bombing proficiency and fighter intercepts. Hurricane *Diana* slowed operations and on 9 September four aircraft were evacuated to Dallas, Texas. *Diana* soon passed by, allowing the aircraft to return to Beaufort three days later. Flight training immediately restarted and continued until the end of the month.

In October, the training emphasis once again shifted gears. This time flying consisted of all-weather intercepts and ACM. Tasked with numerous requirements from the 2nd MAW and MAG-31, the squadron was kept extremely busy. On 2 and 3 October, there was *Amalgam Chief*. For the period 15–21 October, there was a combined arms operation (CAO). During the CAO, newer aircrew were exposed to extended flight times to the aircraft operations area, simulated missile shoots, aerial refueling, and the Corps' Command and Control System. The last exercise was another anti-air warfare exercise from the 22nd to the 24th. As the month drew to a close, two more crews began training for another ACTI course.

In November, the squadron began training missions covering low-level intercepts over land and low-altitude tactical training. Crews received valuable training for an exercise with the USAF, dubbed *Red Flag*. The ACTI course was conducted from the 12th to the 17th and was successfully completed by both crews. Numerous missions dictated by the 2nd MAW were also flown. The last week of November involved one aircraft per day going to Eglin AFB, Florida, for a night to fly intercepts against F-15 Eagles. Near the end of the month, one aircraft (BuNo 155812) was temporarily put out of service when debris was sucked into the right engine.

In December, with a missile shoot and a major deployment drawing near, the squadron trained in all areas for the F-4S. The primary crews for the missile shoot were brought up to speed. On 3 December, through to the 7th, *Quick Thrust*, an Air Force exercise, was conducted with deep air support and CAP as the main missions. During the month, four aircraft were ferried to the Military Aircraft Storage and Disposition Center in Tucson, Arizona. For those four, their service lives were over.[128]

To start the new year, the "Thunderbolts" again drew duty for *Sopwith Camel*. Crews selected for an upcoming missile shoot in Puerto Rico began training and the squadron as a whole flew low-level intercepts and ACM to prepare for a *Red Flag* deployment. On 8 and 9 January, six aircraft took off for Puerto Rico to participate in a "shoot on arrival" missile-firing exercise. Crews participating in *Red Flag* flew to Nellis AFB on 18 and 19 January. During the course of the exercise, the crews flew strike escort missions and low-level intercepts, and new crews gained experience in aerial refueling. The deployment concluded on the 31st. The next morning, the squadron was set to return to Beaufort. The weather forecast between Nellis and Beaufort, however, was not good, making it a bit dicey to head home. Conversations with the *Red Flag* staff led nowhere. The squadron wanted to stay, but the Air Force denied permission; the Marines had to leave by 1300 to provide space on the ramp for other aircraft scheduled to arrive. Fortunately, the weather did not pan out as forecast and the Phantoms made it to Beaufort without incident.

February found aircraft and personnel still returning to Beaufort from *Red Flag*. The squadron's training regimen upon return involved fighter intercepts and ACM in preparation for a DDS deployment scheduled for March. The Marines participated in a *Seabat* exercise off the coast of Virginia near Norfolk. *Seabat* was an Air Force operation involving dissimilar air combat training. At end of the month, VMFA-251 flew CAP and fighter intercepts while participating in a local anti-air warfare exercise.

In early March, the squadron sent six aircraft, eight crews, and 29 maintenance personnel to MCAS Cherry Point for the DDS exercise. During the deployment, the Phantoms primarily flew DACM flights in a variety of situations: one-vs-one, two-vs-one, and two-vs-two engagements. The deployment successfully ended on 9 March. With the exception of the DDS, the squadron busied itself preparing for an upcoming wing inspection, which began on 18 March and concluded on the 28th. All aspects of the squadron were scrutinized, and personnel ran a scheduled physical fitness test. Prior preparation paid off. The squadron received excellent results at the end of the inspection. Flying during the 10-day inspection was limited to all-weather intercept sorties. March ended with a safety stand-down and two crews began preparing for another ACTI course.

With the inspection over, the "Thunderbolts" renewed their busy flight schedule for April with all-weather intercepts, fighter intercepts and ACM. The ACTI crews continued their training and passed the course near the end of the month. *Southeast Brave*, a USAF exercise, was conducted from 22 to 24 April. During the exercise, the squadron flew CAP and fighter intercepts. To end the month, the squadron held safety lectures for all personnel.

The fast pace of operations continued in May. The squadron participated in exercise *Solid Shield* for 11 days from 6 May, then deployed to NAS Oceana from the 20th to the 31st for another FFARP. In between the two exercises, the squadron participated in another anti-air warfare exercise. During *Solid Shield*, the Marine aircrews performed CAP, fighter intercept, and dissimilar air combat training. The heavy pace of operations took its toll when one aircraft (BuNo 155871) lost its right main wheel assembly.[129] The aircraft received minor damage and the aircrew were not injured in the incident. At Oceana, aircrews gained more experience in fighter intercepts and DACM against a variety of aircraft.

The FFARP exercise concluded on 8 June at which time the squadron returned to MCAS Beaufort. Upon return, two aircraft were launched for a missile shoot in Puerto Rico that ran for two days, concluding on the 12th. The squadron picked up *Sopwith Camel* duty again on 13 June and participated in the MAG-31 Commanding Officer's Change of Command the next day. After a NORAD exercise on the 16th, training shifted to air-to-ground and low-level missions as the squadron prepared for another deployment to Yuma in August.[130]

As July began, the squadron continued its training for the forthcoming Yuma deployment. Countless missions were flown including low-level navigation flights, low-altitude tactics, low-altitude weapons delivery, and aerial-refueling practice with KC-130 tankers. When not training for the deployment, the squadron flew dissimilar air combat training missions and all-weather intercepts as ordered by the 2nd MAW. One Phantom was damaged, however; it was the same aircraft that lost its right main wheel assembly in May. This time the left main gear caught fire as the aircraft was rolling out upon landing. Crash crews were called to the burning aircraft and the fire was quickly extinguished. The pilot and RIO suffered no injuries as a result of the mishap.

August began with the "Thunderbolts" participating in a local anti-air warfare exercise from the 6th to the 8th. During the exercise, the primary missions were CAP and fighter intercepts. As this concluded, the squadron began launching aircraft to MCAS Yuma with refueling by KC-10 tankers along the way. By 11 August, the Marines had established themselves at Yuma and begun flying missions. The primary missions flown were low-level tactics, dropping live air-to-ground ordnance, CAS using air and ground forward air controllers, escort tactics, and aerial refueling with KC-130 tankers. The "Thunderbolts" also flew night ordnance-delivery missions, assisted by KC-130s as flare ships and artillery marking the target. During one of the bombing missions, the Phantom (BuNo 155890) flown by P. K. Farra got a little too close to the ground as the aircraft was damaged by shrapnel from one of its own exploding MK-82 500-pound bombs. The exercise concluded on 28 August and the "Thunderbolts" began their return trip to Beaufort. The next day, two aircraft flew to the Military Aircraft Storage and Disposition Center at Davis–Monthan AFB in Arizona for decommissioning. The remaining aircraft returned to MCAS Beaufort on 30 August.

September had the squadron occupied with dissimilar air combat training. This was achieved against TOPGUN aircraft at Beaufort as well as another *Seabat* exercise. When not flying the DACM missions, the squadron flew all-weather intercepts and air-to-ground ordnance delivery as ordered by the 2nd MAW.

October marked the beginning of the end for the Phantom as the squadron's aircraft. On the horizon was the transition to the F/A-18 Hornet. Thus, the squadron began to stand-down in preparation for receiving the new aircraft. Training operations did not stop, but the number of flight hours decreased compared to previous months. Early in the month, the squadron sent two aircraft to the VMF-251 40th anniversary reunion in Albuquerque, New Mexico. At the reunion, Marine veterans from World War II got a close-up look at the modern Phantom II—a far cry from the F4F Wildcats and F4U Corsairs the squadron used while flying missions during the war. Aircrews participated in another DDS exercise at MCAS Cherry Point flying DACM, all-weather intercepts and aerial-refueling sorties. When the DDS exercise ended, the squadron participated in NORAD's *Amalgam Chief.* Missions for the exercise were flown out of NAS Pensacola, Florida. Squadron aircraft returned to Beaufort on 23 October.

By 22 November, all of the squadron's F-4S Phantoms had been transferred out. Up until the 18th, the squadron had flown all-weather intercept missions. Aircrews to transition to the F/A-18 began arriving at the squadron, along with enlisted maintenance personnel. The squadron ended the month preparing for a change of command ceremony.

More F/A-18 crews joined the squadron and began their first exercise by visiting the gas chamber for NBC training on 2 December. On 6 December, the "Thunderbolts" held an early Christmas party for all squadron members and their families. Doyle relinquished command to Lieutenant Colonel Thomas Wilkerson on 13 December. Thus, the Phantom II era came to an end after nearly twenty-two years of service with VMFA-251.[131]

CHAPTER 8

The Hornet and the End of the Cold War

In 1972, the United States Air Force began its quest to procure a new lightweight fighter (LWF), later called air combat fighter. Several companies sent in projects and two were chosen: General Dynamics and Northrop. The General Dynamics entry was the YF-16 Fighting Falcon, and the Northrop entry was the YF-17 Cobra. Two years later, the aircraft were put through their paces in a series of flight tests, flying hundreds of sorties by the time testing ended in December 1974. The following month, the USAF chose the YF-16.

All was not lost for Northrop. In 1971, the Navy became concerned at the high cost of its twin-engine F-14 Tomcat. It simply could not afford the Tomcats needed to equip its F-14 squadrons, as well as Marine and training units designated to receive the F-14. In addition, the Phantom II and A-7 Corsair II were getting old and would soon need replacing. Solutions were offered, most of which aimed at using existing aircraft redesigned to Navy standards. A group was formed and concluded a new aircraft was needed, one that could fulfill a fighter role and an attack role. They called it the VFAX, to be armed with both Sidewinders and Sparrows.

Congress had reservations about building a new aircraft from scratch and told the Navy to look at the LWF contenders. After looking at both the YF-16 (a Navy version was built by General Dynamics and Ling Temco Vought) and the YF-17 (modified by Northrop and McDonnell Douglas), and following months of design changes and computer simulations, the Navy chose the YF-17 in May 1975, deeming it better suited to Navy operations. The fact that it had two engines was a big safety factor. Several changes were necessary, one of which was making the aircraft easy to change over from a fighter role to an attack role.

After making changes to the YF-17 design, it was redesignated as the F/A-18 Hornet and made its first flight in 1978. It became a state-of-the-art aircraft with digital radar, carbon fiber wings, digital fly-by-wire controls, and HOTAS (Hands On Throttle And Stick) which allowed the pilot to control several systems without taking his hands off the throttle and stick. The aircraft was the first to be built from the ground up to carry out both air interceptions and ground-support missions. It could also be adapted for a photo-reconnaissance or electronic countermeasures role. Deliveries of the Hornet to the Navy began in 1981, with several versions delivered over the years. For the "Thunderbolts," it was the Hornet that would carry the squadron through the waning days of the Cold War.[1]

During the 1970s, the Cold War began to thaw as the U.S. normalized relations with China, highlighted by President Richard Nixon's trip to the country in 1972. Talks with Russia during the first half of the decade resulted in two treaties, SALT I and II (Strategic Arms Limitation Talks). SALT I froze the number of intercontinental ballistic missiles at then current levels but allowed each country to replace older missiles with newer models. SALT II was sent to the Senate for approval in mid-1979 but was not ratified. Despite the setback, the treaty was honored by both countries. In a rapid series of events, however, the Cold War began to heat up.

In November and December 1979, two events destroyed President Jimmy Carter's chances of a second term. First, revolutionary Iranians took over the U.S. embassy in Iran, holding over fifty U.S. citizens as hostages. Second, the Soviet Union invaded Afghanistan. Carter was soundly defeated in the 1980 election by Reagan who immediately took a hard line against the Soviet Union.

By 1980, the Middle East had begun to unravel yet again. Revolutionaries in Iran toppled the Shah's government and soon found themselves in a war with Iraq. The Soviet Union strengthened its border with Iran by increasing its military presence. In Africa, the Soviets backed Ethiopia while the U.S. supported Somalia in the ongoing conflict between the two nations.

To counter what the U.S. perceived as an expansion of communism, its military received a series of budget increases far exceeding what it had received in the past. The B-1 bomber program was reignited, the B-2 stealth bomber development began, and the MX missile deployment was put on a fast track. In 1983, Reagan announced the Strategic Defense Initiative—a missile defense system capable of shooting down incoming nuclear missiles. In the same year, nuclear missiles began to be deployed to Europe. The U.S. backed rebels in Nicaragua to counter a perceived communist takeover. In addition, the U.S. invaded Grenada to quell a government crisis by accepting an appeal for help from the Organization of Eastern Caribbean States. The U.S. backed out of the

1980 Olympics in Moscow while the Soviets and other Eastern Bloc nations boycotted the 1984 Olympics in Los Angeles.

Reagan's aggressive stance was meeting resistance within the U.S. and other nations. Following the *Able Archer* exercise in November 1983, which almost triggered a nuclear war, such a conflict was on everyone's mind and protests were held to seek a reduction or elimination of nuclear weapons by both nations. Coincidently, the film *The Day After*, which depicted a nuclear war with the Soviets and its aftermath, released in the same month, most likely did more than anything to raise public consciousness on the issue. By 1985, Reagan was meeting with Mikhail Gorbachev to work out a new nuclear arms treaty. After an unsuccessful first meeting, the two soon met again—this time the elimination of nuclear weapons was on the table.

The Soviet Union was not in good shape. Three of its leaders passed away within three years: Leonid Brezhnev, Yuri Andropov, and Konstantin Chernenko. Gorbachev took over in March 1985. The country was in the midst of an economic downturn, several of its Eastern Bloc countries were flexing their democratic muscle, and a series of questionable interventions, especially in Afghanistan, began to tear the Soviet Union apart. It simply could no longer afford its current path. The future looked promising but, until the Cold War ended, it was business as usual for the "Thunderbolts."

For the first six months of 1986, VMFA-251 continued its transition to the F/A-18 Hornet. In January, squadron pilots went through F/A-18 training with VFA-125 at Naval Air Station (NAS) Lemoore, California, and VFA-106 at NAS Cecil Field, Florida. Over seventy maintenance personnel received hands-on training on the new fighter attack aircraft with VFA-106.

In May, a pilot training at NAS Lemoore returned to the squadron. The following month, the pilots training at Cecil Field returned and the "Thunderbolts" finally received their first F/A-18 on 13 June. The second Hornet was received on the 17th. The next day, the commanding officer of the squadron, Wilkerson, flew the first sortie in a Hornet recorded by a VMFA-251 Marine. By the end of June, two more Hornets had been received.[2]

Throughout July and most of August, the "Thunderbolts" continued their transition to the Hornet. In a formal ceremony on 25 August, the squadron officially became the sixth Marine F/A-18 unit. By the end of August, the squadron had 10 Hornets assigned to it.

With eight aircraft, 12 pilots, and 54 senior non-commissioned officers and enlisted men, the "Thunderbolts" were deployed to Nellis AFB, Nevada, on 6 September to complete overland air combat maneuvering (OACM) training. The 12 new pilots gained valuable experience against USAF F-5s and F-4s flying in one-vs-one and two-vs-two scenarios. Aerial-refueling missions were also flown with help from a KC-130 tanker of VMGR-252. By the end of the eight-day exercise, the squadron had accumulated nearly one hundred fifty-five hours of flight time, including 31 hours at night.

In between local training sorties, on 20 October the squadron sent two pilots and three aircraft to NAS Miramar for instruction at the Navy Fighter Weapons School (TOPGUN). VMFA-251 supported a Ninth Air Force operation, dubbed *Quick Thrust*, for four days as well as a Marine Aircraft Group (MAG) 31 anti-air warfare exercise for a week. The squadron also sponsored a visit by World War II ace and Medal of Honor recipient Joe Foss. During his visit, Foss spoke with MAG-31 aircrews.

During November, six pilots were sent to four different schools (AIM-7 Sparrow School, EW/HARM (High-Speed Anti-Radiation Missile) School, TOPGUN CO's Course, and TOPGUN) while seven pilots began their training to receive recertification as air combat tactics instructors with the help of Marine Aviation Weapons and Tactics Squadron (MAWTS) 1. All flying for the Air Combat Tactics Instructor (ACTI) course was done locally. VMFA-251 also participated in a combined arms operation and began preparation for two inspections to be performed in December.

The squadron began the month of December with a missile shoot at NAS Roosevelt Roads, Puerto Rico; six aircraft fired four AIM-7 and two AIM-9 missiles and were certified as air-to-air capable. The two inspections were held mid-month. The maintenance department was scrutinized by Commander, Naval Air Force, Atlantic inspection teams and received excellent remarks. The entire squadron was inspected by 2nd Marine Aircraft Wing (MAW) inspection teams who ended up giving the unit an overall excellent grade. Everything from uniforms to aviation safety was looked at by the inspectors. The squadron also began holding tours for schools and businesses which had been halted during the first half of the year while the "Thunderbolts" transitioned to the Hornet.[3]

No aircraft were lost during the six-month period, but 20 other incidents were recorded. Of those, failure of the Inertial Navigation System accounted for 13 of the incidents. No injuries were reported.

There were no deployments or exercises on the books for the unit during January. All flight training was done locally as the squadron racked up close to 500 flight hours. The only event of note was another 2nd MAW inspection, but for Nuclear, Biological and Chemical Defense this time. At the conclusion of the inspection, the squadron earned a grade of outstanding.

From 14 February to the 28th, VMFA-251 deployed to Nellis AFB to participate in OACM. Within the same time frame, one pilot and two aircraft were sent to the Navy Fighter Weapons School. In addition, another pilot attended and graduated from the Naval Strike Warfare Center, Strike Leader Attack Training Syllabus (SLATS), at NAS Fallon, Nevada.

During March, the "Thunderbolts" continued support to the TOPGUN detachment sent the previous month. The squadron also completed a 2nd MAW-ordered squadron stand-down and embarkation evaluation. Once again it received an outstanding grade. One pilot graduated from the TOPGUN Senior Officer's Course and VMFA-251 hosted the officers and men of the 6th Marines from Camp Lejeune for an Aviation/F/A-18 indoctrination. Despite the lack of deployments, local training flights were numerous as the unit racked up more than 600 flight hours for the month.

Over the course of the next three months, most of the training flights continued to be flown locally. The squadron did send eight pilots to the McDonnell Douglas plant in St. Louis to undergo training on the HARM, known as the AGM-88. The HARM System was a relatively new weapons system designed to lock on to transmissions originating from surface-to-air radar systems and destroy them. Two pilots earned their ACTI certification with the help of MAWTS-1. Early in June, an anti-air missile exercise off the coast of North Carolina led to six aircraft being designated as air-to-air capable.

During the first six months of 1987, the squadron accumulated an impressive 2,647 flight hours despite being short on pilots and aircraft. It was still short one pilot of the 17 it needed by the end of June. The "Thunderbolts" started 1987 with 11 F/A-18s but by the end of June it was up to full strength with 12 Hornets.[4]

The continual flying did take its toll on aircraft. While none were lost, and no injuries were recorded, during the first six months of the year, the Inertial Navigation System problems continued to plague the squadron, accounting for 55% of the recorded incidents.

In July, the squadron sent two more pilots through the HARM training in St. Louis and three others started training for ACTI certification. In addition to local training flights, the squadron participated in Operation *Solar Flare*, a combined arms Marine exercise held near Camp Lejeune, North Carolina.

During the first week of August, the five pilots sent for HARM training ACTI certification completed their course. Seven more participated in an anti-air missile exercise held on 10 and 11 August off the Virginia coast; six Sparrows and one Sidewinder were fired. The next day, the squadron deployed to NAS Oceana for another Fleet Fighter ACM Readiness Program (FFARP) to hone their air combat maneuvering (ACM) skills against a variety of aircraft provided by VF-43. The "Thunderbolts" ending up flying 461 sorties while at Oceana, accumulating over 500 flight hours.

The squadron returned to Beaufort on 4 September. It then flew three Hornets to NAS Roosevelt Roads to participate in another missile exercise held from 18 to 20 September. During the exercise, the three aircraft fired three Sidewinders and dropped three laser-guided bombs. Five days after this latest evolution ended, the squadron sent a detachment to Nellis AFB for OACM and dissimilar air combat training. The nine aircraft and pilots flew a variety of tactical situations (two-vs-two, four-vs-four, six-vs-six, and eight-vs-eight) against USAF F-15s and F-16s provided by the 422nd TES (Test and Evaluation Squadron) and the USAF's Fighter Weapons School. After completing the training, the detachment returned to Beaufort on 11 October.

While the detachment was still at Nellis, the squadron sent its remaining three aircraft and two pilots to Marine Corps Air Station (MCAS) Yuma for the Weapons and Tactics Instructors (WTI) course on 1 October. They remained at Yuma for the entire month. Once the detachment at Nellis returned, local flight training resumed.

By 5 November, all personnel and aircraft were back at Beaufort. For the remainder of the year, the majority of the squadron's flying time was spent locally. It did participate in a MAG-31 exercise that simulated a wartime situation from 16 to 20 November and a 2nd MAW exercise from 7 to 11 December. During the wing exercise, the squadron flew offensive air support and air-to-air combat missions near Cherry Point, North Carolina. By the end of December, the squadron had its full complement of pilots (17) and 15 Hornets, three above its allowed number. Enlisted personnel numbers were increasing in anticipation of a WestPac (Western Pacific) tour in 1988.

For the entire year, the squadron flew 4,006 sorties and clocked up nearly five thousand four hundred twenty-nine flight hours. No aircraft were lost during the last six months of 1987, and the number of incidents decreased compared to the first six months of the year.[5]

Local flight operations continued during January. The squadron did participate in a missile-firing exercise off the coast of Virginia. However, because of drone shortages and lousy weather, only one AIM-7 Sparrow was fired. On 24 January, the squadron again surpassed 20,000 accident-free flight hours.

Most of February was dedicated to the squadron's participation in a combined arms exercise at Marine Corps Air Ground Combat Center Twentynine Palms in California. Eleven Hornets and nearly one hundred sixty Marines had arrived at the base by 8 February at which time the exercise commenced. While supporting the 3rd Battalion/6th Marines, the "Thunderbolts" dropped 250 MK-82/MK-83 bombs, 1,000 MK-76/BDU-48 practice bombs, fired 188 5-inch Zuni rockets, and more than 17,000 rounds of 20-mm high-explosive incendiary ammunition. During the 13-day exercise, the squadron accumulated nearly four hundred forty-nine flight hours. The Hornets and personnel were back at MCAS Beaufort by 25 February.

March and April kept the squadron in Beaufort with local flight operations and inspections. During March, pilots faced off against USAF pilots while flying dissimilar air combat maneuvering (DACM) sorties and participated in a MAG-31 exercise. An aerial gunnery exercise in early April kept the squadron busy for eight days. One incident was recorded that month when an aircraft began leaking liquid oxygen in the cockpit, injuring the pilot. He brought the aircraft back safely and was treated for his burns.

Inspections concluded during May. Since the squadron had been notified it would deploy overseas in the near future, the "Thunderbolts" passed a Marine Corps Combat Readiness Evaluation (MCCRE). In between the inspections and local flight ops, the squadron also participated in a 2nd MAW exercise. Several officers earned their ACTI certification while others completed the Naval Aviation Safety Officer's course, Landing Signal Officers Phase 1 course, and two completed the AIM-7 Sparrow school. For its excellent safety record over the previous year, the squadron received the Chief of Naval Operations Aviation Safety Award.

During June, the squadron participated in two exercises, one of which was an escort for an A-6E/EA-6B long-range strike to a target range in New Mexico from MCAS Cherry Point, North Carolina. At the end of the month, all pilots completed aerial-refueling qualifications as they prepared for another tour of duty in the Pacific.[6]

With a full complement of pilots, aircraft, and men, VMFA-251 departed MCAS Beaufort on 11 July for its new assignment—Yechon Air Base, South Korea. It was the squadron's second deployment under the Unit Deployment Program (UDP). The UDP was approved by the Commandant of the Marine Corps in late 1976 and, in July 1977, the "Thunderbolts" had become the first squadron to deploy under the UDP (to Iwakuni, Japan). However, the tour length then was 12 months instead of six months—the normal length of a tour for the UDP. The UDP was designed to reduce the number of unaccompanied tours (no dependents) and improve unit cohesiveness. Shortening the length of the tour eliminated the permanent change of station assignments for personnel involved in the deployment.[7] Within days of arriving at Yechon on 16 July, the "Thunderbolts" began strike training missions against several target areas including Pilsung and Noon Ni.

While at Yechon, the squadron's maintenance department identified an ongoing problem with the Hornet's ALR-67 system. The system warns the aircraft's pilot of possible enemy radar activity. The squadron notified MAG-15 who sent it up to the 1st MAW. An expert in the system was sent from Naval Air Weapons Center to help correct the problem. The repairs, once established, went through to all Hornet squadrons in the Western Pacific since they were having the same problems with the ALR-67.

A detachment of four aircraft was sent to Kadena Air Force Base (AFB) on Okinawa to participate in the 1st MAW's imaginatively named exercise *Wing Exercise 88*. During the eight-day program that began on 17 August, "Thunderbolt" pilots flew air defense missions against USAF and Japan Air Self-Defense Force units, and strike escort missions on Okinawa. Another detachment of six Hornets left Yechon on 26 August for Misawa Air Base, Japan. At Misawa, squadron pilots tangled with F-16s of the 432nd Tactical Fighter Wing (TFW) in DACM exercises. An F-16 mishap resulted in a one-week stand-down for the detachment. Flying day and night, the "Thunderbolts" also flew deep air support and airfield strike sorties. The deployment was hampered by poor weather, so the Hornets remained at Misawa until 15 September.

During September, the "Thunderbolts" also flew air combat tactics training missions with Korean-based USAF squadrons. They also flew strike and escort missions to designated target areas in Korea.

In early October, the squadron deployed to the Philippines and began operations out of NAS Cubi Point while participating in the latest iteration of Exercise *Cope Thunder*. Once again, "Thunderbolt" pilots honed their skills in vital area defense, deep air support, escort missions and simulated MiG sweeps against USAF and USN units. The squadron was scheduled to fly 11 days during the exercise, but only three days were flown due to Typhoons *Pat* and *Ruby* bringing in lousy weather. *Cope Thunder* ended on 27 October and the next day the Marines departed for MCAS Iwakuni.

Within days of establishing operations at Iwakuni, the squadron was participating in yet another exercise—*Valiant Blitz*. Flying from Iwakuni, "Thunderbolt" Hornets flew close air support (CAS), night intercept and DACM sorties over Korea. VMFA-251 and other Iwakuni-based squadrons also supported the 2nd Battalion/6th Marines with CAS training. The exercise, which began on 1 November, concluded on the 9th. Near the end of the month, the unit sent six Hornets to Kadena for Exercise *Beach Crest*. During the exercise, which lasted until 15 December, the "Thunderbolts" sharpened their skills by flying CAS, strike, and fighter weapons training missions. They were also able to certify three pilots as air combat tactics instructors with the help of MAWTS-1. Amid normal flying operations and the exercises, the squadron surpassed 24,000 flight hours without a mishap.

While the detachment was at Okinawa, an advance party departed Iwakuni for MCAS Beaufort on 8 December. Once the Kadena detachment returned to Iwakuni on the 15th, the remainder of the month was spent preparing its aircraft to be turned over to VMFA-333, which was replacing the squadron in the UDP program. While at Iwakuni, the squadron was assigned to MAG-15 and became the last unit to fly under that group. MAG-15 was deactivated on 30 December. VMFA-251 was then assigned to MAG-12.[8]

It was another mishap-free year for the "Thunderbolts." During the previous six months, one incident was reported—a bird strike while flying out of Iwakuni. For the year, the squadron flew over 3,200 sorties and accumulated more than 4,200 flight hours.

On 10 January, the squadron returned to MCAS Beaufort and began the task of rebuilding. Taking over VMFA-333's aircraft, flight operations were minimal. A massive turnover in personnel began which would take nearly a year to stabilize. By the end of June, 75% of the squadron's maintenance personnel and 85% of its pilots had been replaced. Training the new personnel became the primary focus of squadron activities for the next six months.

Despite this turnover in personnel, VMFA-251 did deploy for several exercises, although at a reduced strength during the first six months of 1989. The first of these small deployments occurred from 13 February to 15 April when the "Thunderbolts" sent one pilot, three aircraft and 25 maintenance personnel to support a WTI course at MCAS Yuma. From 17 March to 24 April, one pilot, two aircraft and 17 maintenance personnel were sent to NAS Miramar in California for TOPGUN School. In conjunction with the two deployments, the squadron flew ACM training against TOPGUN aircraft at Beaufort. The four ACM training evolutions ended on 24 February. Support was also provided to the 2nd MAW and the 2nd Marine Division with six Hornets flying missions out of Bogue Field, North Carolina. The exercise started on 9 April and concluded on the 24th. Once the deployments ended, the squadron's officers and enlisted men were sent to over 20 training schools.

Exercise *Solid Shield* occupied the squadron for most of May. The exercise took place along the east coast between Atlantic Field, North Carolina, and Parris Island, South Carolina. In support, the squadron flew air-to-air and air-to-ground missions from MCAS Beaufort and Bogue Field.

On the first day of June, VMFA-251 was recommended by the commanding officer of MAG-31 for the Commandant's Aviation Efficiency Trophy based on its accomplishments from 1987 to 1989. The yearly award recognizes a Marine aviation squadron for its performance and accomplishments in all tasks assigned to it. In October, the trophy was awarded.[9] The next day, a change of command ceremony was held as Lieutenant Colonel Robert Maddocks, Jr., handed over the colors to the squadron's new skipper, Lieutenant Colonel Richard Walker. Soon after, the Marines began the first of four deployments for the month. On 5 June, the squadron sent one pilot, two Hornets and 20 enlisted men to TOPGUN at NAS Miramar. The next day, four pilots were sent to NAS Fallon for a shortened version of the Navy SLATS course. This ended on 11 June. Two days earlier, the squadron had deployed to Nellis AFB, Nevada, to support the 422nd Test and Evaluation Squadron. It concentrated on division tactics in air-to-air missions against the 422nd's F-15 Eagles, but also conducted air-to-ground missions with MK-82 and MK-83 bombs (500 pounds and 1,000 pounds respectively) and deep air strikes with inert ordnance. The "Thunderbolts" departed Nellis for Beaufort on 25 June.[10]

Getting pilots and maintenance personnel trained and certified kept the squadron busy during July and August. Four pilots were designated as section leads, and on 10 July the new Pilot Training Officer returned after completing TOPGUN. Two pilots began preparing for ACTI certification scheduled to take place in August. Ground training sent squadron personnel to rifle and pistol ranges, and the NBC gas chamber—all yearly requirements for Marines.

On 1 August, six Hornets and requisite personnel deployed to Bogue Field, to participate in a Supporting Arms Coordination Exercise (SACEX). A SACEX integrates naval surface fire, artillery, and air support for ground units. For this exercise, the "Thunderbolt" detachment provided CAS for the 24th Marine Expeditionary Unit and Landing Force, Sixth Fleet. During the three phases of exercise, participants sought to identify the advantages of using the Hornet's flexibility in a Mediterranean scenario; the Hornets then trained with a Tactical Air Control Party at Camp Lejeune; and lastly supported the 2nd Marine Division with CAS and fire support aimed at improving command, control, and communications in a simulated combat environment.

Upon return from North Carolina on 18 August, the squadron began prepping for an upcoming missile exercise at Roosevelt Roads, Puerto Rico, and flew air-to-ground training sorties, dropping nearly four hundred fifty MK-82 and 64 MK-83 inert bombs.

The Marines completed their preparations for the missile shoot during the first two weeks of September, and an advance party was sent to Puerto Rico to prepare for the squadron's arrival. Mother nature once again forced them to change their plans. While the advance party was in Puerto Rico, Hurricane *Hugo* struck the island, forcing the cancellation of the missile shoot. Its course was predicted to hit the South Carolina area, so the "Thunderbolts" evacuated their Hornets to Tinker AFB in Oklahoma until the threat was over. The air station was not damaged. When the aircraft returned to Beaufort, the squadron began preparing for a 2nd MAW NBC inspection scheduled for the next month.

In early October, the squadron sent representatives to the Marine Corps Aviation Awards banquet in Pensacola where they were presented with the Commandant's Aviation Efficiency Award. Upon return, normal training operations resumed. The 2nd MAW NBC inspection was held during the third week of the month and the unit received an "Excellent Overall" grade upon completion. With the inspection concluded, the squadron began air-to-air gunnery practice that lasted for the rest of the month.

The pace of operations picked up for November. The "Thunderbolts" supported three different Air Force operations. First up was Operation *Sea Hugo* at Homestead AFB in Florida. There, they supported F-16s in an operational readiness exercise. This was followed by a short stint at Patrick AFB where the "Thunderbolts" supported a MAG-42 detachment. Next was Operation *Steep Hammer* at Langley AFB in Virginia where the Hornets worked with F-15 Eagles. These exercises started on 6 November and finished on the 15th.

Meanwhile, local aircrew training concentrated on air-to-air sorties. The majority of the sorties were flown on MCAS Beaufort's Tactical Air Control Training System Range, located off the coast of South Carolina and encompassing an area of more than 2,100 square miles. The range, and others similar to it, are able to provide real-time air and ground combat situations, allowing for a realistic evaluation of a pilot's combat skills and his use of weapons.

From 17 to 19 November, the squadron sent four Hornets to Gulfport, Mississippi, to support *Sentry Mudbug*. During the short exercise, the Hornets flew 32 sorties. Shortly after Thanksgiving, the squadron departed Beaufort for NAS Oceana for another FFARP with VF-43. During the deployment, which lasted until 22 December, the Marines flew numerous engagements against A-4F and F-16N aircraft which were using Soviet tactics. At the same time, the squadron was able to certify five pilots as air combat tactics instructors. Upon return to Beaufort, local training sorties resumed to round out the year.[11]

The squadron's impressive record of no mishaps continued, although one incident was recorded on 30 November. Hornet BuNo 161964 was found to have a damaged activating cartridge for the No. 1 engine fire extinguisher bottle.

After decades of training to face a Soviet threat, it appeared the "Thunderbolts" would not face their main adversary in battle. In the late 1980s, Gorbachev began to bring democracy to Soviet politics, basically acknowledging that Communism was a failure. Soviet-bloc countries in eastern Europe began to collapse with Gorbachev acknowledging their fall. Perhaps the most significant event defining the collapse of Communism occurred on 3 November when the East German government announced it would allow its citizens to cross its borders into West Germany and West Berlin.

As the Eastern Bloc crumbled, Soviet troops stationed in these countries began to pull out and return to the Soviet Union. In the Balkans, these withdrawals may have had an unintended consequence that would affect the region for years: the power vacuum left by the retreating Soviets allowed festering ethnic hatred among the many diverse groups to get out of control, resulting in a war of ethnic cleansing. In a few years, the "Thunderbolts" and numerous NATO allies would be involved in these wars.

With Soviet communism down, but not out, the Marines continued the daily grind of training and deployments as 1990 kicked off. In January, the squadron began preparations for a cold-weather exercise to be held in Wisconsin the following month. Training included classes on cold-weather operations and CAS in such an environment. The "Thunderbolts" also participated in an air-to-air missile shoot that was notable for the first successful firing against a Tactical Air Launched Decoy with infrared capability, a first in Marine aviation history. Two pilots were qualified as low altitude training instructors and one was designated as a division leader. On the last day of January, the squadron deployed to Volk Air National Guard Base in Wisconsin for the cold-weather exercise dubbed *Alpine Warrior*.

At the end of January, Marine VMFA squadrons operating the F/A-18 underwent an organizational change. The number of aircraft authorized remained unchanged at 12, but some departments were combined, and others eliminated. From 29 January, the squadron consisted of a Headquarters, Safety Department, S-1 (Administration), S-2 (Intelligence), S-3 (Operations), S-4 (Logistics) Departments, Medical Department, Aircraft Maintenance Department (Maintenance Control, Airframes, C/C, Flight Equipment, Ordnance, Avionics and Line/Ground Support Equipment), and a Marine Aviation Logistics Squadron. The fighter attack squadron primary mission was to intercept and destroy enemy aircraft under all weather conditions and to attack and destroy surface targets.[12]

During *Alpine Warrior*, which lasted until 20 February, the squadron supported the 4th Marine Expeditionary Brigade (MEB). Pilots and maintenance personnel gained experience in flying and maintaining the aircraft in cold weather. Sorties flown in support of the 4th MEB included deep air support, low-level aerial refueling, day and night CAS, and reconnaissance missions. All squadron personnel received training in rear area security and cold-weather survival. The survival training included an overnight stay in the field to put their new skills to the test. Following the conclusion of *Alpine Warrior* on 20 February, the squadron returned to MCAS Beaufort the next day.

No deployments were made during March but the first in a series of inspections in the coming months kept the squadron busy. The "Thunderbolts" received an excellent evaluation as a result of the commanding general's inspection of its NBC warfare program. The inspection fulfilled a required portion of the MCCRE. The squadron also sent two pilots and three aircraft to MCAS Yuma for a WTI course. With local training sorties and its participation in an anti-air warfare exercise, the unit flew slightly over 370 flight hours across 271 sorties.

In early April, the small detachment at Yuma for the WTI course returned to Beaufort. During a training sortie on 12 April First Lieutenant Douglas "Gunga" Denn was responsible for a milestone. During his sortie, the squadron surpassed 30,000 mishap-free flight hours, marking seven-and-a-half years without the loss of an aircraft.

In mid-April, the unit participated in a bombing competition sponsored by MAG-31. Four squadrons from MCAS Beaufort pitted their air-to-ground skills against Air Force units by dropping practice bombs at the Georgia Air National Guard Bombing Range near Townsend, Georgia. In addition to the Hornets from VMFA-251, VMFA-333, VMFA-115, and VMFA-451, USAF A-10 Thunderbolts from Myrtle Beach AFB and F-16 units from bases in Georgia, South Carolina, and Alabama also participated. Over the two-day competition, pilots were scored on how close they dropped their bombs to the marked target and how close to the scheduled time on target they were when they struck. When it was all over, VMFA-251's commanding officer, Walker, and Captain Paul. H. Supchak earned the best combined score for a flight (two aircraft) while the 346th Tactical Fighter Wing from Moody AFB won the best combined score for a unit.

With the competition over, the squadron's MCCRE began in earnest. First completed was the Maritime Prepositioning Force (MPF) inspection. This was performed to see how well the squadron responded to a rapid deployment. Following the MPF, the squadron commenced the air-to-ground and air-to-air portion of the inspection. The air-to-ground portion took place in the Beaufort area by flying raked-range bombing sorties, deep air strikes, and all-weather intercepts against a dedicated EA-6B Prowler. The final portion—air-to-air—required a deployment to Elgin AFB on 27 April.

With the help of F-15 Eagles of the 33rd TFW, the squadron completed its MCCRE. Over a two-week period, it flew a variety of sorties: DACM versus one, two or four aircraft, ship strikes and escort missions, and rescue combat air patrol to name a few. It was also evaluated on how it performed during a mishap exercise. The squadron successfully completed the extensive evaluation on 11 May and received its combat-ready status. The "Thunderbolts" returned to Beaufort the following day.

A week later, the squadron was awarded Fleet Marine Force, Atlantic, Annual Aviation Safety Award. The award was presented by the MAG-31 commander. The "Thunderbolts" also began preparing for the 2nd MAW internal inspection; it passed the inspection at the end of May.

Operations slowed down in June as the squadron regrouped after the inspections and began preparing for yet another to be held in August. Five pilots and two aircraft were sent to MCAS Cherry Point to support another Supporting Arms Training Exercise, while one pilot and aircraft were sent to NAS Miramar to attend TOPGUN.[13]

For the first six months of the year, the squadron lost no aircraft. One had a close call in January when it lost its right trailing-edge flap in flight. The pilot was able to bring the aircraft back safely and it was brought back into service following repairs.

With a new fiscal year in effect and flight hours cut back, the "Thunderbolts" had to work around less flying time for the remainder of the year. Planning for two future deployments—*Teamwork* and *Bold Guard*—which began sometime during the first six months of the year, continued in July. Three pilots earned their ACTI certification, and all pilots qualified in refueling with KC-135 tankers for the 4th MEB Norway deployment. Air-to-air training was highlighted by TOPGUN and support for VMFT-401 acting as aggressors for the school. Air-to-ground training was accomplished with divisions using inert ordnance.

Things changed on 2 August when Saddam Hussein's Iraqi forces invaded Kuwait. With war breaking out in the Middle East, and with the U.S. laying the groundwork for using coalition forces to push the Iraqis back, the squadron switched to a wartime footing and began training for a possible deployment. The *Teamwork* and *Bold Guard* exercises were cancelled. Squadron personnel were kept informed by MAWTS-1 and TOPGUN lectures, large strike missions and daily intelligence briefs. The squadron had been deemed combat ready in its last MCCRE, maintenance worked long hours getting aircraft ready, and flight operations were geared towards desert warfare and possible mission assignments. Despite this, the squadron was not selected to be involved in the initial strikes against Iraq. There was always the possibility of reinforcing coalition forces once they engaged the Iraqis and took back Kuwait.

Training during September continued to concentrate on the possibility of combat in the Middle East. Pilot training emphasized air-to-ground missions with the use of HARM and Walleye[14] smart weapons. Training sorties in electronic warfare were also flown that included missions against several electronic warfare capabilities such as jamming and deception. If the squadron was to deploy, it would appear it would go as part of the 6th MEB and be designated as VMFA-1 to reinforce units already committed. In addition to the heavy training schedule, the "Thunderbolts" sent a small detachment for TOPGUN training at Miramar.

With the possibility of being deployed as part of the 6th MEB, large multi-plane missions were planned and flown day and night. The squadron also participated in another MAG-31 bombing competition against Air Force units on 17 and 18 October. This time not only did the unit score the best for a flight, but it also earned best score overall. On 23 October, the "Thunderbolts" deployed to MCAS Cherry Point to work with MAG-26 as part of the 6th MEB. While at Cherry Point, missions concentrating on CAS were flown. At the same time, three pilots began preparing for ACTI certification. Pilots also flew missions for MAG-31 in support of the 2nd MAW and the 2nd Marine Division.

As much as the "Thunderbolts" may have desired to be deployed to the Middle East, it was not to be. All available units from the 2nd MAW were utilized to bolster the 3rd MAW which commanded Marine air assets in the Middle East. Other commitments had to be guaranteed besides the upcoming war in the Persian Gulf. At Beaufort, only three squadrons remained at the base and one of those was scheduled to be deployed. The "Thunderbolts" stayed Stateside for both *Desert Shield* and *Desert Storm*. For 3rd MAW reinforcements, 1st MAW units in the Pacific were to be used.[15]

The "Thunderbolts" returned from Cherry Point on 2 November and immediately began planning for an unscheduled Yuma deployment. During the month, training sorties concentrated on low-altitude tactics, raked-range bombing and live ordnance dropping. On 9 November, the squadron was awarded a Meritorious Unit Citation by the commander of MAG-31 for its accomplishments during the period 1 August 1987 through 1 July 1989. The day after Thanksgiving, the Marines deployed to MCAS Yuma. Two days later, missions commenced with low-altitude tactics training and raked-range bombing.

The Yuma deployment emphasized desert warfare and continued into December. Anti-air warfare, air support and bombing missions were flown. Missions were also flown to provide CAS to the 2nd Tank Battalion at Twentynine Palms, California. Lectures were also part of the deployment and covered desert survival and lessons learned from aviation units deployed to the Middle East. The Yuma deployment ended on 17 December. The following day, the squadron departed for Beaufort. All units were back home by the 21st, allowing the Marines to spend Christmas with their families.[16]

The squadron's record of consecutive loss-free flight hours remained intact. Two aircraft were involved in separate incidents, however. One Hornet ran into a maintenance work stand while taxiing into chocks and another suffered a bird strike; the pilot was able to bring the aircraft back safely.

January 1991 opened with a safety stand-down, but the pace picked up with the U.S. and coalition forces preparing for war with Iraq. Officers and staff non-commissioned officers received Casualty Assistance Calls Officer training. Pilots flew sorties over the Mid-Atlantic Electronic Warfare Range (MAEWR) in North Carolina, to hone their skills with the AGM-88 HARM, in addition to air-to-air training in the Beaufort area. All personnel were kept up to date on the situation in the Persian Gulf with weekly briefings.

On 17 January 1991, coalition forces launched their attack against Iraq. Striking first with air power, then launching a ground assault, coalition forces quickly began to rout Iraqi forces. With war now a reality, training took on a sense of urgency. "Thunderbolt" pilots cycled through the Weapon System Trainer (WST) at NAS Cecil Field, Florida, to practice using the AGM-65 Maverick, Walleye, Extended Range Data Link Walleye, and the Shrike anti-radiation missile.

Training continued into February. In addition, VMFT-401 deployed to Beaufort to assist the "Thunderbolts" in air-to-air training by providing F-5 Tiger IIs as adversary aircraft. Pilots also continued to use the MAEWR and the WST at Cecil Field. As they prepped for a possible deployment, the war ended on 28 February with a ceasefire agreement. Iraqi forces had been soundly defeated and Kuwait regained its independence.

With the war over, it was now clear the "Thunderbolts" would not deploy to the Middle East. In March, however, they did deploy, along with several units of MAG-31 to NAS Oceana to conduct normal training. Repairs to the runway intersection at Beaufort had to be made, hence the reason for the move. While at Oceana, the squadron flew in two MAG-31-directed practice strikes. The squadron was also informed it would be heading back to the Pacific with the deployment scheduled for July.

In April, three pilots began training for their ACTI course set for May. In addition to standard training, sorties for the ACTI training included one-vs-one, two-vs-two, and two-vs-an unknown number of adversaries, as well as lectures.

The ACTI certification began on 6 May. During one of the sorties on the following day, Captain Denn's aircraft (BuNo 163158) was involved in a mid-air collision. His aircraft was severely damaged, but he managed to bring it home. Denn was not injured but his Hornet required extensive repairs. With the WestPac deployment coming up, the "Thunderbolts" began preparing squadron families for the six-month separation. A host of administrative requirements had to be completed: allotments established or corrected; update beneficiaries for those with Serviceman's Group Life Insurance; emergency data for notifications had to filled out or corrected; Marines had to have their immunizations for overseas travel; and married Marines and their families attended a family readiness briefing. In mid-May, Lieutenant Colonel Norman G. Schlaich took over command of the squadron from Walker.

Early June saw the return of VMFT-401 to provide their F-5s as adversaries for the "Thunderbolts." Squadron pilots flew mostly one-vs-one engagements against the Tigers. At the same time the training was going on with VMFT-401, the unit participated in another MAG-31-sponsored bombing derby. It appears though, that this time the "Thunderbolts" did not take top honors in the competition. Soon after the derby, the squadron participated in a live missile shoot on 12 and 13 June. They expended 10 AIM-7F Sparrows and 10 AIM-9M Sidewinders. The Sparrows targeted air-launched decoys while the Sidewinders were fired at parachute flares due to the lack of available drones.[17]

Training began to wind down in early July. On 15 July, the squadron began its deployment to MCAS Iwakuni. Five days later, it was established at the Japanese base. Flight operations in the local area began on the 25th and continued for the rest of the month.

During August, the "Thunderbolts" split their flying time at Iwakuni and Curtin, Australia (a Royal Australian Air Force "bare" base). A six-plane detachment deployed down under to participate in Exercise *Pitch Black* on 9 August. Missions during the exercise were long-range night strikes that required aerial refueling. The strikes involved multiple aircraft and required detailed planning: A-6E, EA-6B, KC-130, A-4, Australian Boeing 707 tankers, and Australian F/A-18 Hornets. *Pitch Black* missions continued until 2 September. In Iwakuni, flight hours were curtailed but the squadron did send three pilots to participate in *Ulchi Focus Lens* in Seoul and Osan Air Base. *Ulchi Focus Lens* was a joint U.S.–South Korean computerized command and control exercise that focused on how U.S. and South Korean forces would defend the country if it were attacked.

On 7 September, the squadron participated in an air show at Misawa Air Base and at the same time the detachment in Australia returned to MCAS Iwakuni. With the squadron all present at Iwakuni, the "Thunderbolts" flew all-weather intercepts, low-level flights, and a few one-vs-one air combat sorties. Japanese F-15 Eagles from Tsuiki and U.S. Navy F-14 Tomcats from NAS Atsugi aided the Marines during their air combat training missions by flying as adversaries. The missions prepared the pilots for a deployment to Kadena AFB, Okinawa.

The deployment to Kadena began on 5 October and ended on 14 November. During the five weeks, the "Thunderbolts" flew against F-15 Eagles of the 13th TFW. Sorties started out as one-vs-one and progressed to two-vs-two, then three-vs-three, and ultimately culminated with four aircraft against an unknown number of adversaries. By the time the squadron returned to Iwakuni, more than 90 air-to-air missions had been flown.

Once the exercise at Kadena concluded, VMFA-251 moved directly to Osan Air Base, South Korea. For the next 30 days, the squadron concentrated on air-to-ground missions. Training sorties started with circular bombing patterns, and sorties with HARM, Walleye, and Forward Looking InfraRed (FLIR) pods. FLIR is a thermal imaging device that can detect heat sources and is especially useful in detecting and targeting enemy forces in low-visibility situations. Pilots then progressed to using pop-up tactics in CAS training sorties. During the stay in South Korea, the squadron sent two aircraft and three pilots back to Kadena for a four-day exercise that concluded on 6 December. By the 15th, the Marines were back at Iwakuni and began preparing their aircraft for transfer to VMFA-115. An advance party was sent to Beaufort to begin accepting VMFA-115's aircraft in return. In January 1992, squadron personnel returned to MCAS Beaufort.[18]

It is fitting the story ends here. As the squadron wrapped up yet another deployment, the USSR was no more. Following a failed coup in August 1991, a number of Soviet republics, particularly Russia, threatened to secede from the USSR. The Union of Soviet Socialist Republics formed The Commonwealth of Independent States on 21 December. With this act, the Soviet Union was no more and officially dissolved on 26 December 1991, officially ending the Cold War. But new challenges were in the making for the "Thunderbolts."

Epilogue

A typical day of flight operations usually began with all hands forming up in a line, shoulder to shoulder, to walk the length of the flight line. This was known as a FOD (foreign object debris) walk. Everyone scoured the flight line for objects that could potentially cause engine damage if sucked into the intakes. With the walk complete and aircrew briefed in the ready room, the aircrew suited up and walked to their assigned planes, which had been checked out during the course of the midnight shift and readied for flight.

The aircrew would walk around the aircraft, performing a pre-flight inspection. If something suspicious was found, maintenance crews would be called to look things over. If all was good, the aircrew strapped themselves in with the help of their plane captain. Once strapped in and the area around the aircraft cleared, the engine starting sequence began.

With the engines up to speed, the plane captain began a sequence of hand signals to direct the pilot to check various systems on the aircraft—nosewheel steering, flaps and ailerons, the horizontal stabilizers, and the rudder to name a few. Once the "all clear" was given, the chocks were removed, and the aircraft began to taxi to the runway.

Upon return, plane captains guided the aircraft to its position on the flight line. The wheels were chocked, and the engines shut down. Once the aircrew exited, they proceeded to maintenance control to file any reports that needed addressing by maintenance crews.

This process was repeated all day and into the evening until all assigned missions were completed. When on deployment, or a portion of the squadron was on temporary duty, the operational tempo picked up. Crews worked in three shifts, with the midnight shift responsible for having aircraft ready for the day's coming missions.

Of the thousands of missions and exercises the squadron flew, none were cancelled due to lack of aircraft availability. Maintenance men worked hard to ensure the aircraft were ready for whatever mission was called, be it a bombing mission, air-to-air combat simulations, missile shoots, navigation exercises, and, during the Korean War, dropping bombs on North Korean forces. In the background, however, there were issues that, on occasion, hampered the squadron's ability to carry out its orders.

Having the necessary parts to keep the aircraft up and serviceable is a constant thorn in the side of any squadron. VMFA-251 was no exception. Each type of aircraft required specific parts and, in some cases, these were lacking. The number of parts needed to be manufactured to maintain an adequate supply is daunting: everything from tires to indicators to circuit breakers to radar waveguides to fire warning elements—not to mention armament, ordnance, and electronics—had to be made and stocked for availability. Supply chain issues no doubt played a role when it came to a scarcity of parts, as did the ability of the manufacturer to keep up with Department of Defense requirements. To alleviate the supply issue, a "hangar queen" was usually a semi-permanent fixture in a squadron's hangar. The "hangar queen" itself was usually waiting on parts and until those came in, it was often stripped to get, or keep, other aircraft ready for flight.

In some cases, production errors led to problems with equipment. The company making the error sometimes caught them and notified the Navy. If these issues are not detected, incidents can cause an aircraft loss, or a severely damaged aircraft. Issues of this nature still occur. As an example, in 2022, the Navy was notified by ejection seat manufacturer Martin-Baker that some of its cartridge-actuated devices had problems. This affected, for example, several models of the F/A-18 Hornet, the EA-18 Growler, the T-45 Goshawk, and the F-5 Tiger II. Luckily, repairs could be made at the squadron level, but the affected aircraft were grounded until they could be inspected and approved for flight operations.[1] With fewer aircraft to complete assigned missions, other aircraft in the squadron had to take up the slack to meet training goals.

It takes money to run a squadron, and those costs continued to climb through the years. During the early 1970s, fuel shortages and the energy crisis forced squadrons to cut back on flight hours. In some cases, all flights were cancelled due to lack of funds. This occurred on occasion towards the end of a fiscal year, which ran from the month of July to the following June.

Advances in technology, combined with upgrades to aircraft, sometimes had an impact on availability. Squadron aircraft were modified on a regular basis. Sometimes updates were performed by the squadron, but a trip to a Naval Air Rework Facility was often the case. Once the modifications were made, the aircraft were then reassigned to squadrons needing them. In many cases, aircraft sent back to the squadron were not the same ones sent to be modified. Once again, aircraft on hand had to carry the load to complete assigned missions while others were away being modified.

Another issue squadron commanders had to deal with was the constant fluctuation in manpower. Men were constantly passing through the squadron either by transfer, discharge, or schooling. For all services, retaining trained personnel has always been difficult. The length of a tour of duty varied with enlisted men and officers. A tour of duty ranged from four to eight years.[2] Despite free medical and dental care, housing, and meals, take home pay was below that of a comparable job in the civilian world. Pilots often left for better pay flying for airlines, and enlisted personnel left for better-paying jobs or a college education. Of course, many left simply because they did not like the military way of life. It was rare that the squadron had the required number of personnel as stated by its Table of Organization. When an overseas deployment was in the works, and in order to get the squadron up to strength, personnel from other squadrons were usually transferred in to make up the shortfall. The constant change in personnel made it difficult to train the squadron in order to build morale and to work as a team to accomplish the mission. A shortage of personnel often forced commanders to have their men work longer hours to get the job done.

When things worked, operations went smoothly. Everyone knew their job and took pride in their accomplishments. Safety was enforced at all levels. Flight hours were accumulated without incident. And as things continued to go well over a period of time, that was when things could go sour quickly. Complacency had a habit of rearing its ugly head. No matter how often safety was pounded into each Marine, it was up to the individual Marine to ensure he did his part and help others do their part to enforce safety measures. Fatigue, a heavy workload, and schedules to maintain put pressure on all to make sure orders were executed. On occasion, safety stand-downs were ordered to reinforce safety procedures.

Lastly, the squadron shut down operations four times and went into a training mode as it acquired new aircraft. This happened with its transition to the Fury, Crusader, Phantom II, and Hornet. The process of acquiring the aircraft, and training pilots and maintenance personnel, usually took a year to accomplish. Once the training was complete, the squadron was declared operational.

For the "Thunderbolts," the cost of keeping the peace was high. During the period covered by this book (45 years), over two dozen aircraft were lost, and over 100 aircraft received various amounts of damage. At least sixteen pilots and radar intercept officers lost their lives. The number could be higher.

Official reports on aircraft losses and incidents I was able to obtain go back to 1951. As far as I have been able to determine, the years 1946 to 1950 are not available. For enlisted men, it is not known how many died during the course of their duties—enlisted men were rarely mentioned in official reports. As the years progressed, the number of aircraft losses (Class A accidents[3]) gradually decreased. The accomplishments made by the squadron, despite the issues it had to contend with, were remarkable. Each "Thunderbolt" can take pride in a job well done in doing their part to end the Cold War.

Following the end of the Cold War, the squadron continued its training. It wasn't long though before the squadron saw action.

In 1994, VMFA-251 deployed to Aviano Airbase in Italy, flying combat missions from January to April in support of Operation *Deny Flight* in Bosnia-Herzegovina. These were the first combat sorties made by a Marine squadron in Europe since World War I. *Deny Flight* began in April 1993 to enforce a UN no-fly zone over Bosnia and Herzegovina. The mission was later expanded to provide close air support missions and air strikes against targets in Bosnia. *Deny Flight* ended in December 1995.

Following its return to MCAS Beaufort, the squadron acquired the F/A-18C in May. After a year-long training period gearing up for a carrier deployment, they were assigned to Carrier Air Wing One (CVW-1) aboard the USS *America* (CV-66). The deployment began in August 1995 and ended in February 1996. During their stay on the USS *America*, the Thunderbolts flew missions in support of Operation *Deny Flight* and *Deliberate Force. Deliberate Force* was an air campaign conducted by the North Atlantic Treaty Organization (NATO), in concert with the United Nations Protection Force (UNPROFOR) ground operations. The purpose of these air strikes was to degrade the military capability of the Army of Republika Srpska (VRS) and force an end to the fighting. The operation was successful, eventually leading to a settlement. The operation began in August 1995 and ended the following month.

Two more deployments followed in in 1997 and 1999, aboard the USS *George Washington* (CVN-63) and USS *John F. Kennedy* (CV-67) respectively. Both cruises were to the Persian Gulf in support of Operation *Southern Watch*.

The next decade saw a host of carrier deployments in support of operations in the Middle East. In 2001 it deployed with CVW-1 aboard the USS *Theodore Roosevelt* (CVN-71). The Arabian Sea deployment established another record for the squadron—they were the first Marine squadron to participate in Operation *Enduring Freedom*. They returned to Beaufort in March 2002.

In September 2002, the squadron earned its second Hanson Award for the best Marine fighter attack squadron of the year.

In February 2003, the squadron deployed to Ahmed Al Jabar Air Base, Kuwait. There, they flew combat missions in support of operations *Southern Watch* and *Iraqi Freedom*. Following its return to MCAS Beaufort in May 2003, the squadron once again deployed to the Far East as part of the Unit Deployment Program. They departed in January 2004 and returned to Beaufort in June of the same year.

Early 2005 had the squadron preparing for a cruise on the USS *Enterprise* (CVN-61), scheduled to begin in May 2006. On the third of that month, the deployment began. Once on station in the North Arabian Gulf, VMFA-251 began combat operation in support of Operation *Iraqi Freedom*. They also flew a few missions for Operation *Sea Dragon*.

What followed next was another first for the squadron and Marine aviation. On 24 August, the Thunderbolts deployed from the USS *Enterprise* to Al Asad Air Base in Iraq. This was the first time the squadron forward deployed from a carrier to a forward air base. For the next two months, VMFA-251 flew combat missions in support of both operations *Iraqi Freedom* and *Enduring Freedom*. During this deployment, the squadron flew 100% of its assigned sorties. This marked the first time in Marine aviation history that a squadron supported two campaigns at the same time. Following its deployment to Al Asad, the squadron returned to the USS *Enterprise* on 25 October. The carrier made it to port on 18 November 2006.

By mid-2007, the squadron once again found itself on board the USS *Enterprise* for another deployment to the Persian Gulf. While there, the Hornets of VMFA-251 provided close air support for coalition forces on the ground in support of operations *Iraqi Freedom* and *Sea Dragon*. On 4 November, while flying combat missions over Iraq, the USS *Enterprise* received word to cease operations for *Iraqi Freedom* and begin combat operations in support of Operation *Enduring Freedom* in Afghanistan. The squadron made the first strike in Afghanistan on 6 November and continued striking Afghanistan for the next 10 days. Following the end of operations, the USS *Enterprise* began its journey back to the United States, arriving in Mayport, Florida on 16 December.[4]

Following the deployment, the squadron began to rebuild. This lasted from January to April of 2008. Following the rebuilding process, operations began to train new maintenance personnel and certify a new batch of pilots. Until its deactivation in 2020, the squadron deployed to numerous locations including Alaska and Finland, as well as making carrier cruises in 2011, 2012, and 2015. In 2013, the squadron earned its third Hanson Award as the best fighter attack squadron in Marine aviation.

Women have been serving in Marine units since 1948. In aviation this included maintenance, flight operations scheduling, and parachute rigging to name a few jobs. However, it wasn't until 1993 that the Marine Corps had its first female pilot. Since that time, a few women have served with VMFA-251, some seeing combat operations.[5] Of note, LtCol. Nicole Mann, who flew combat missions with the Thunderbolts, is now a NASA astronaut, and became the first female commander of a NASA commercial crew program.

In April 2020 the squadron was deactivated, ending nearly 74 years of continuous duty to the nation in a stellar way. If current Marine Corps air plans hold, the squadron is to be stood up in 2025 with the Lockheed-Martin F-35C, an aircraft built for carrier operations. Its new duty station is to be MCAS Cherry Point, North Carolina.

APPENDIX I

Commanding Officers

VMA-251, VMF-251, VMFA-251, July 1946–August 1994

Name	*Years*	*Squadron Designation*
Maj. Ralph G. McCormick	1 July 1946–30 Nov 1946	VMF-251
Maj. William A. Carlton	1 Dec 1946–31 Dec 1950	VMF-251
Maj. Donald P. Troyer	1 Jan 1951–27 Feb 1951	VMF-251
Capt. Carl C. Miles	27 Feb 1951–27 Apr 1951	VMA-251
LtCol. Gregory J. Weissenberger	27 Apr 1951–15 May 1951	VMA-251
LtCol. Philip L. Crawford	15 May 1951–31 Dec 1952	VMA-251
LtCol. Joe E. Warren	1 Jan 1952–3 Jan 1952	VMA-251
LtCol. Arthur M. Moran	4 Jan 1952–31 May 1952	VMA-251
Maj. Clarence E. Moore	1 June 1952–7 Nov 1952	VMA-251
LtCol. Sumner H. Whitten	8 Nov 1952–13 Feb 1953	VMA-251
LtCol. Harold A. Harwood	14 Feb 1953–15 Oct 1953	VMA-251
LtCol. Rufus D. Sams, Jr.	16 Oct 1953–9 Dec 1953	VMA-251
LtCol. Frank R. Porter, Jr.	10 Dec 1953–5 June 1954	VMA-251
LtCol. John D. Noble	6 June 1954–12 July 1954	VMA-251
Maj. Thomas B. Wood	13 July 1954–21 Nov 1954	VMA-251
LtCol. Robert J. Holm	22 Nov 1954–21 Sept 1955	VMA-251
LtCol. Joseph F. Quilty, Jr.	22 Sept 1955–21 Mar 1956	VMA-251
LtCol. Fred J. Frazer	22 Mar 1956–19 Oct 1956	VMA-251
LtCol. Elmer P. Thompson, Jr.	20 Oct 1956–20 Apr 1957	VMA-251
Capt. Paul S. French	21 Apr 1957–15 May 1957	VMF-251
LtCol. Harold G. Schlindering	16 May 1957–5 Oct 1957	VMF-251
LtCol. Wiley A. Green	6 Oct 1957–28 Apr 1958	VMF-251
LtCol. Thomas J. Saxon, Jr.	29 Apr 1958–23 June 1958	VMF-251

Name	*Years*	*Squadron Designation*
LtCol. Albert L. Clark	24 June 1958–31 Dec 1960	VMF-251
LtCol. Ernest E. Poor	1 Jan 1961–24 Sept 1962	VMF-251
Maj. Darold D. Parrish	25 Sept 1962–2 Dec 1962	VMF-251
LtCol. Kenny C. Palmer	3 Dec 1962–6 Jan 1964	VMF-251
LtCol. Robert D. Slay	7 Jan 1964–13 Nov 1964	VMF-251/VMFA-251
LtCol. Arthur O. Schmagel	14 Nov 1964–1 Sept 1965	VMFA-251
Maj. Darrel Bjorklund	2 Sept 1965–31 Jan 1966	VMFA-251
LtCol. Gordon H. Keller, Jr.	1 Feb 1966–18 Nov 1966	VMFA-251
Maj. Lawrence R. Hawkins	19 Nov 1966–29 Feb 1968	VMFA-251
LtCol. Edward C. Johnson	1 Mar 1968–18 Apr 1969	VMFA-251
LtCol. Rodney O. Lawrence	19 Apr 1969–31 Aug 1970	VMFA-251
LtCol. R. Plant	1 Sept 1970–8 Mar 1971	VMFA-251
Maj. James M. Mead	9 Mar 1971–31 July 1971	VMFA-251
LtCol. R. P. Lee	31 July 1971–23 June 1972	VMFA-251
LtCol. J. C. Byram, Jr.	24 June 1972–30 Apr 1973	VMFA-251
LtCol. J. C. Service III	1 May 1973–11 Dec 1973	VMFA-251
LtCol. Josephus L. Mavretic	12 Dec 1973–31 Jan 1975	VMFA-251
LtCol. G. E. Walsh	31 Jan 1975–31 Dec 1975	VMFA-251
LtCol. Joseph B. Wuertz	1 Jan 1976–1 Apr 1977	VMFA-251
LtCol. Myrl W. Allinder, Jr.	2 Apr 1977–12 July 1978	VMFA-251
LtCol. Frederick J. Schober	12 July 1978–15 June 1979	VMFA-251
LtCol. Patrick J. Jones	15 June 1979–5 June 1980	VMFA-251
LtCol. David A. Richwine	5 June 1980–30 June 1981	VMFA-251
LtCol. Norman G. G. Kerr	30 June 1981–12 Aug 1982	VMFA-251
LtCol. Gary L. Elsten	12 Aug 1982–27 Jan 1984	VMFA-251
LtCol. D. L. Doyle	27 Jan 1984–13 Dec 1985	VMFA-251
LtCol. Thomas L. Wilkerson	13 Dec 1985–3 July 1987	VMFA-251
LtCol. Robert A. Maddocks, Jr.	3 July 1987–2 June 1989	VMFA-251
LtCol. Richard W. Walker	2 June 1989–17 May 1991	VMFA-251
LtCol. Norman Schlaich	17 May 1991–Aug 1994	VMFA-251

APPENDIX 2

Squadron Carrier Assignments

1946–1991

Ship	*Designation*	*Dates*	*Area*	*Notes*
USS *Windham Bay*	T-CVE 92	9 June–2 July 1953	Japan	Transportation of squadron to Korea
USS *Oriskany*	CVA-34	1959	Pacific Ocean off west coast of U.S.	Carrier Qualifications
USS *Core*	T-AKV-41, formerly CVE-13	16 October 1959	Japan	Deployment to Atsugi, Japan
USS *Midway*	CVA-41	December 1959	Pacific Ocean	N/A
USS *Oriskany*	CVA-34	July 1960	Pacific Ocean	N/A
USS *Ranger*	CVA-61	July 1960	Pacific Ocean	N/A
USS *Franklin D. Roosevelt*	CVA-42	4–6 November 1961	Atlantic	Day Carrier Qualifications cut short by carrier arresting gear problems
USS *Shangri-La*	CV-38	11–15 December 1961	Atlantic	Refresher Day Carrier Qualifications and completion of Night Carrier Qualifications
USS *Shangri-La*	CV-38	7 February–28 August 1962	Mediterranean	Seven-month cruise
USS *Lexington*	CVS-16	June 1963	Not Known	Carrier Qualifications
USS *Saratoga*	CVA-60	April 1964	Atlantic	Carrier Qualifications

USS *Shangri-La* Itinerary, 1962

7 February	Departed Mayport
17 February	Passed Gibraltar, entered the Med
19 February	Anchored Mallorca—Relieved USS *Intrepid*
26 February	Arrived Cannes
5 March	Put to sea for operations
12 March	Arrived Palermo
14 March	Change of Command
21 March	Put to sea for operations
31 March	Arrived Rhodes
3 April	Put to sea for operations/movie making
7 April	Arrived Athens
11 April	Put to sea for operations
16 April	Arrived Istanbul
20 April	Put to sea for operations
28 April	Arrived Malta
2 May	Put to sea for operations
8 May	Arrived Genoa
14 May	Put to sea for operations
24 May	Arrived Livorno
1 June	Put to sea for operations
7 June	Arrived Cannes
25 June	Put to sea for three-carrier operations
2 July	Arrived Naples
9 July	Put to sea for operations
12 July	Arrived Naples
16 July	Put to sea for operations
21 July	Arrived Livorno
27 July	Put to sea for operations
3 August	Arrived Rapallo
9 August	Put to sea for operations
19 August	Golfo di Palmas—Relieved by USS *Enterprise*
21 August	Departed Mediterranean
28 August	Arrived Mayport

APPENDIX 3[1]

Close Air Support Controller Callsigns, July 1953

Call Sign	*Location*	*Attached to*
Redcap	CT-2711	I U.S. Corps
Input	CT-5327	IX U.S. Corps
Hitest	DT-1629	X U.S. Corps
Acme	CT-4528	2nd Infantry Division
Hatpin	CT-5631	3rd Infantry Division
Mailbox	CT-3427	7th Infantry Division
Oxcart	CS-1195	25th Infantry Division
Upgrade	DT-3231	40th Infantry Division
Plato	DT-1427	45th Infantry Division
Horseback	Unknown	1st Marine Division
Rupee	CT-2308	1st Commonwealth Division
Boatload	DT-5448	1 ROK Corps
Heatstroke	CT-8239	II ROK Corps
Diploma	DT-1916	III ROK Corps
Pushball	CT-7137	Capital ROK corps
Nightclub	CT-2913	1st ROK Division
Watchguard	CT-4427	2nd ROK Division
Man o war	CT-8454	3rd ROK Division
Headfirst	CT-8529	5th ROK Division
Taillamp	CT-8444	6th ROK Division
Witch hazel	DT-0736	7th ROK Division
Gasburner	CT-8843	8th ROK Division
Nugget	CT-6733	9th ROK Division
Blackbear	CT-7915	11th ROK Division

Call Sign	*Location*	*Attached to*
Lefthand	DT-3034	12th ROK Division
Bluster	DT-4963	15th ROK Division
Gyrate	DT-0729	20th ROK Division
Shoeblack	DT-4847	21st ROK Division

APPENDIX 4

Acronyms

ACM	Air Combat Maneuvering
ACTI	Air Combat Tactics Instructor
AFB	Air Force Base
AGL	Above Ground Level
AIM	Air Intercept Missile
AIRFMFPAC	Air Fleet Marine Force, Pacific
ASRT	Air Support Radar Team
AVELEX	Aviation Element Exercise
BAM	Basic Aircraft Maneuvering
CAP	Combat Air Patrol
CAS	Close Air Support
CINCLANTFLT	Commander in Chief, Atlantic Fleet
CNO	Chief of Naval Operations
CO	Commanding Officer
COMFAIRKWEST	Commander Fleet Air Key West
CUB	Construction Utility Battalion
DACM	Dissimilar Air Combat Maneuvering
DACT	Dissimilar Air Combat Training
DDS	Display Debriefing System
DECM	Defense Electronic Countermeasures
ECCM or ECM	Electronic Countermeasures
FASRON	Fleet Air Service Squadron
FFARP	Fleet Fighter ACM Readiness Program
FMFLANT	Fleet Marine Force, Atlantic
FMFPac	Fleet Marine Force, Pacific
FREDS	Flight Readiness Data System
GCA	Ground Control Approach

GCI	Ground Control Intercept
HMR	Marine Helicopter Transport Squadron
H&MS	Headquarters and Maintenance Squadron
HQ USMC	Headquarters, United States Marine Corps
IFF	Identification Friend or Foe
IFR	Instrument Flight Rules
JOC	Joint Operations Center
JTDIS	Joint Tactical Information Distribution System
LES	Leading Edge Slats
LSO	Landing Safety Officer
MAC	Military Airlift Command
MACS	Marine Air Control Squadron
MAG	Marine Air Group
MALS	Marine Air Logistics Squadron
MARS	Marine Aircraft Repair Squadron
MARTCOM	Marine Air Reserve Training Command
MAW	Marine Air Wing
MAWTB	Marine Aviation Weapons and Tactics Battalion
MAWTS	Marine Aviation Weapons and Tactics Squadron
MAWTULANT	Marine Air Weapons Training Unit, Atlantic
MCALF	Marine Corps Auxiliary Landing Field
MCAS	Marine Corps Air Station
MCCRE	Marine Corps Combat Readiness Evaluation
MCCRES	Marine Corps Combat Readiness Evaluation System
MCRD	Marine Corps Recruit Depot
MGCIS	Marine Ground Control Intercept Squadron
MLR	Main Line of Resistance
MPQ	Radar equipment used to control aircraft to bomb a target
MSG	Message
MSL	Mean Sea Level
MWSG	Marine Wing Service Group
NAAS	Naval Auxiliary Air Station
NAVSAFECEN	Naval Safety Center (now Naval Safety Command NAVSAFECOM)
NAP	Naval Aviation Pilot (enlisted rank)
NARF	Naval Air Rework/Refit Facility
NAS	Naval Air Station
NATO	North Atlantic Treaty Organization

NAVAIR	Naval Air Systems Command
NBC	Nuclear, Biological, and Chemical
NCO	Non-Commissioned Officer
NFO	Naval Flight Officer
NFWS	Navy Fighter Weapons School
NORAD	North American Air Defense Command
OPNAV	Office of the Chief of Naval Operations or Operational Navy
PC	Power Control Hydraulic System
PSI	Pounds per Square Inch
RAF	Royal Air Force
RESCAP	Rescue Combat Air Patrol
RIO	Report In and Out or Radar Intercept Officer
ROK	Republic of Korea (South Korea)
RPM	Revolutions per Minute
SACEX	Supporting Arms Coordination Exercise
SAR	Search and Rescue
SATS	Short Airfield for Tactical Support
SLATS	Strike Leader Attack Training Syllabus
TAC	Tactical Air Control
TACAN	Tactical Air Navigation
TACP	Tactical Air Control Party Specialist
TACTS	Tactical Aircrew Combat Training System
TADC	Tactical Air Direction Center
UDP	Unit Deployment Program
USAF	United States Air Force
USMC	United States Marine Corps
USN	United States Navy
VFAX	Fixed Wing Aircraft Experimental
VFR	Visual Flight Rules
VID	Visual Identification, Fighter Intercepts
VMA	Fixed Wing Marine Attack Squadron
VMAQ	Marine Tactical Electronic Warfare Squadron
VMAT	Fixed Wing Marine Attack Training Squadron
VMC	Fixed Wing Marine Composite Squadron or Visual Meteorological Conditions
VMF	Fixed Wing Marine Fighting Squadron
VMF(N)	Fixed Wing Marine Fighting Squadron (Night)
VMFA	Fixed Wing Marine Fighter Attack Squadron

VMGR	Marine Aerial Refueler Transport Squadron
VMO	Fixed Wing Marine Observation Squadron
VMSB	Fixed Wing Marine Scout Bombing Squadron
WTI	Weapons and Tactics Instruction
XO	Executive Officer

APPENDIX 5

Marine Corps Rank Abbreviations

Enlisted

Abbreviation	*Rank*	*Pay Grade*
PVT	Private	E-1
PFC	Private First Class	E-2
LCpl	Lance Corporal	E-3
Cpl	Corporal	E-4
Sgt	Sergeant	E-5
SSgt	Staff Sergeant	E-6
GySgt	Gunnery Sergeant	E-7
MSgt	Master Sergeant	E-8
1st Sgt	First Sergeant	E-8
MGySgt	Master Gunnery Sergeant	E-9
SgtMaj	Sergeant Major	E-9
SMMC	Sergeant Major of the Marine Corps	E-9

Warrant Officers

Abbreviation	*Rank*	*Pay Grade*
WO	Warrant Officer	W-1
CWO2	Chief Warrant Officer 2	W-2
CWO3	Chief Warrant Officer 3	W-3
CWO4	Chief Warrant Officer 4	W-4
CWO5	Chief Warrant Officer 5	W-5

Officers

Abbreviation	*Rank*	*Pay Grade*
2ndLt.	Second Lieutenant	O-1
1stLt.	First Lieutenant	O-2
Capt.	Captain	O-3
Maj.	Major	O-4
LtCol.	Lieutenant Colonel	O-5
Col.	Colonel	O-6
BGen.	Brigadier General	O-7
MajGen.	Major General	O-8
LtGen.	Lieutenant General	O-9
Gen.	General	O-10

APPENDIX 6[1]

Squadron Awards

1946–1991

Navy Unit Commendation Streamer

Korea 7–27 July 1953

Meritorious Unit Commendation Streamer

SU MAG-31 7 November 1983–31 March 1986
1 August 1987–1 July 1989

Marine Corps Expeditionary Streamer

Cuba, October–November 1961

National Defense Service Streamer

1 March 1951–27 July 1954
1 January 1961–15 August 1974
2 August 1990–30 November 1995

Korean Service Streamer

Summer–Fall 1953
5–27 July 1953

APPENDIX 7[1]

Aircraft Mishaps/Incidents

1946–1991

1946–1950

Documentation not available

1951–1955

Date	*Aircraft*	*BuNo*	*Pilot*	*Result*
12 September 1951	AD-1	9320	Frank L. Leister	A/C Destroyed
4 October 1951	AD-1	9202	Leo C. Aldon	Damaged
4 October 1951	AD-1	19152	Unknown	Damaged
28 October 1951	AD-1	9294	Frank L. Leister	Damaged
10 April 1952	F4U-4	81151	D. R. Annand	A/C Destroyed/Pilot Injured
13 May 1952	F4U-4	81218	J. K. Jensen	A/C Destroyed/Pilot Killed
15 August 1952	F4U-4	081040	Leonard C. Weatherwax	A/C Damaged
15 January 1953	F4U-4	080871	E. Belford	A/C Damaged
27 January 1953	F4U-4	081578	P. Kurfess	A/C Damaged
5 February 1953	F4U-4	080871	R. Barbour	A/C Damaged
5 February 1953	F4U-4	097125	Carpenter	A/C Damaged
25 March 1953	A-1C	122745	K. A. Lund	A/C Destroyed/Pilot Injured
25 April 1953	A-1C	122762	M. A. Wilson	A/C Damaged
31 December 1953	A-1D	123898	W. C. Durand	A/C Damaged
4 January 1954	A-1D	132279	W. C. Durand	A/C Destroyed/Pilot Killed
6 February 1954	A-1D	132275	S. Neblett	A/C Damaged

Date	*Aircraft*	*BuNo*	*Pilot*	*Result*
12 March 1954	A-1D	129008	D. W. Wright	A/C Damaged
25 March 1954	A-1D	122808	T. F. Miller	A/C Damaged
28 April 1954	A-1D	128989	D. H. Albert	A/C Damaged
16 June 1954	A-1D	123887	L. C. Barton	A/C Destroyed
27 August 1954	A-1D	129009	R. Gessaman	A/C Destroyed/Pilot Killed
10 March 1955	A-1D	123810	J. Kunzmann	A/C Destroyed/Pilot Killed
3 June 1955	A-1D	123900	L. Dillion	A/C Destroyed
30 June 1955	A-1D	123839	W. D. Thayer	A/C Damaged
25 October 1955	A-1D	132272	Blanchard	A/C Damaged
27 October 1955	A-1D	128952	P. T. Smith	A/C Destroyed/Pilot Killed
16 December 1955	A-1D	123791	R. S. Reed	A/C Damaged

1956

Date	*Aircraft*	*BuNo*	*Pilot*	*Result*
12 February 1956	AD-4	132352	1stLt. Lee E. Blanchard	A/C Damaged
14 March 1956	AD-4B	127860	2ndLt. John H. Taylor	A/C Destroyed
12 May 1956	AD-4	132341	1stLt. James D. Page	A/C Damaged
27 June 1956	AD-6	137492	1stLt. Jay E. Velie	A/C Destroyed
3 September 1956	AD-6	134573	1stLt. Joseph W. Hazen	A/C Damaged
23 November 1956	AD-6	134573	1stLt. William R. Rifino	A/C Destroyed/Pilot Killed
23 November 1956	AD-6	134631	1stLt. R. G. Morgan	A/C Damaged

1957

Date	*Aircraft*	*Bureau No.*	*Pilot*	*Result*
18 February 1957	AD-6	135299	2ndLt. Robert D. Kehs	A/C Destroyed
27 February 1957	AD-6	134568	1stLt. Robert N. Link	A/C Damaged

Date	*Aircraft*	*Bureau No.*	*Pilot*	*Result*
23 May 1957	FJ-3	135875	1stLt. Bruce G. Wanger	A/C Damaged
20 August 1957	FJ-3	135930	1stLt. Basil L. McCallister	A/C Destroyed
27 August 1957	FJ-3	136082	1stLt. Robert B. Stickel	A/C Damaged
4 September 1957	FJ-3	135806	1stLt. David C. Myers	A/C Destroyed
11 September 1957	FJ-3	135965	1stLt. Richard M. Irgens	A/C Destroyed
23 September 1957	FJ-3	135875	1stLt. Thomas J. Dumont	A/C Damaged

1958

Date	*Aircraft*	*Bureau No.*	*Pilot*	*Result*
12 February 1958	FJ-3	135868	2ndLt. John M. Burbank	A/C Destroyed
10 July 1958	F-8A	143765	1stLt. Harry Black	A/C Destroyed/Pilot Injured
23 July 1958	F-8A	145376	Capt. Edward J. Rutty	A/C Damaged
16 August 1958	F-8A	145355	LtCol. Albert L. Clark	A/C Damaged
20 August 1958	F-8A	145365	2ndLt. Glenn H. Downing	A/C Damaged
25 November 1958	F-8A	145452	2ndLt. Richard L. Chappelear	A/C Damaged

1959

Date	*Aircraft*	*BuNo.*	*Pilot*	*Result*
9 January 1959	F-8A	145434	MSgt. Harold G. Woodring (NAP)	A/C Damaged
17 March 1959	F-8A	145433	Maj. Edward H. P. Lynk	A/C Damaged
17 March 1959	F-8A	145444	Unknown	A/C Damaged
13 May 1959	F-8A	145475	Maj. Gordon K. Jackson	A/C Damaged

Date	*Aircraft*	*BuNo.*	*Pilot*	*Result*
27 May 1959	F-8A	145536	Capt. Joseph F. Mayfield, Jr.	A/C Destroyed/Pilot Killed
9 June 1959	F-8A	145435	Maj. Gordon K. Jackson	A/C Damaged
9 June 1959	F-8A	145441	Maj. Edward H. P. Lynk	A/C Damaged
9 June 1959	F-8A	145447	1stLt. Lawrence A. Whipple	A/C Damaged
9 June 1959	F-8A	145428	1stLt. Bernard H. Thomas	A/C Damaged
9 June 1959	F-8A	145449	MSgt. Harold G. Woodring (NAP)	A/C Damaged
3 August 1959	F-8A	145433	1stLt. John E. Kessler	A/C Damaged
24 September 1959	F-8A	145475	LtCol. Norman W. Gourley	A/C Damaged
28 November 1959	F-8B	145439	1stLt. Richard E. Alexander	A/C Damaged

1960

Date	*Aircraft*	*BuNo.*	*Pilot*	*Result*
13 May 1960	F-8B	145428	Capt. Leo J. Leblanc, Jr.	A/C Damaged
30 September 1960	F-8B	145474	1stLt. John M. Kretsinger	A/C Damaged
7 October 1960	F-8B	145436	1stLt. Glenn H. Downing	A/C Damaged
18 November 1960	F-8B	145436	Capt. Robert L. Leathers	A/C Destroyed/Pilot Killed

1961

Date	*Aircraft*	*BuNo.*	*Pilot*	*Result*
28 March 1961	F-8A	143732	Griffin	A/C Damaged
6 July 1961	F-8B	145540	Capt. Oliver H. McClelland	A/C Destroyed
12 December 1961	F-8B	145461	Capt. Melvin H. Sautter	A/C Damaged

Date	Aircraft	BuNo.	Pilot	Result
13 December 1961	F-8B	145488	1stLt. Myrl W. Allinder, Jr.	A/C Damaged
20 December 1961	F-8B	145468	1stLt. Myrl W. Allinder, Jr.	A/C Damaged

1962

Date	Aircraft	BuNo.	Pilot	Result
12 February 1962	F-8B	145480	LtCol. Ernest E. Poor	A/C Damaged
15 February 1962	F-8B	145462	1stLt. James N. Sabin	A/C Damaged
17 March 1962	F-8B	145454	1stLt. Myrl W. Allinder, Jr.	A/C Damaged
3 May 1962	F-8B	145468	Capt. Harry H. Grunwald, Jr.	A/C Destroyed/Pilot Killed
27 June 1962	F-8B	145461	1stLt. Peter Lyon	A/C Damaged
20 July 1962	F-8B	145462	Capt. William J. Knott	A/C Damaged
6 September 1962	F-8B	145467	O. J. Hines	A/C Damaged
3 November 1962	F-8B	145420	O. J. Hines	A/C Damaged

1963–1964

Date	Aircraft	BuNo.	Pilot	Result
24 January 1963	F-8B	145480	Maj. K. C. Palmer	A/C Destroyed/Pilot Injured
15 April 1963	F-8B	145512	R. A. Powers	A/C Damaged
18 April 1963	F-8B	Unknown	Unknown	A/C Damaged
18 April 1963	F-8B	145467	D. R. Bloom	A/C Damaged
2 November 1963	F-8B	145421	Unknown	A/C Damaged
26 November 1963	F-8B	145461	1stLt. William A. James	A/C Destroyed/Pilot Injured
24 December 1963	F-8B	145489	Unknown	A/C Damaged
6 May 1964	F-8B	145511	1stLt. William A. James	A/C Damaged
29 May 1964	F-8B	145467	Unknown	A/C Damaged

Date	Aircraft	BuNo.	Pilot	Result
3 June 1964	F-8B	145417	E. J. Sonntag	A/C Damaged
11 June 1964	F-8B	145467	Unknown	A/C Damaged
15 June 1964	F-8D	145481	Unknown	A/C Damaged
26 October 1964	F-8B	145518	Unknown	A/C Damaged

1965

Date	Aircraft	BuNo.	Pilot/RIO	Result
13 January 1965	F-8B	145467	2ndLt. Danny R. Slayden	A/C Destroyed/Pilot Injured
21 January 1965	F-8B	145432	E. R. Maag	A/C Damaged
17 July 1965	F-4B	149403	Unknown/Unknown	A/C Damaged
17 July 1965	F-4B	150630	Unknown/Unknown	A/C Damaged
17 September 1965	F-4B	150630	Unknown/Unknown	A/C Damaged
22 September 1965	F-4B	149417	Not Applicable	A/C Destroyed
27 October1965	F-4B	150430	Unknown/Unknown	A/C Damaged

1966

Date	Aircraft	BuNo.	Pilot/RIO	Result
24 June 1966	F-4B	149471	G. G. Sloman/ Unknown	A/C Damaged
30 June 1966	F-4B	151437	Unknown/Unknown	A/C Damaged
12 October 1966	F-4B	152230	Unknown/Unknown	A/C Damaged
11 October 1966	F-4B	150452	F. Hatton/Unknown	A/C Damaged

1967

Date	Aircraft	BuNo.	Pilot/RIO	Result
10 February 1967	F-4B	152217	Unknown/Unknown	No Damage
14 February 1967	F-4B	152230	Unknown/Unknown	A/C Damaged
3 April 1967	F-4B	152208	Unknown/Unknown	A/C Damaged
15 May 1967	F-4B	152217	Unknown/Unknown	A/C Damaged
26 June 1967	F-4B	150630	Unknown/Unknown	A/C Damaged

1968–1969

No reported mishaps/incidents

1970–1979

Date	*Aircraft*	*BuNo.*	*Pilot/RIO*	*A/C Result*
23 July 1970	F-4B	151437	Vance/Hagaman	Destroyed/Crew Killed
30 September 1970	F-4B	153048	Nolan/Kilpatrick	Destroyed/Crew Killed
4 June 1971	F-4B	148398	McLane/Woernle	Damaged
28 January 1972	F-4J	155821	Bond/Unknown	Damaged
22 February 1972	F-4J	153776	Unknown	Unknown
27 April 1972	F-4J	155836	Buckner/Unknown	Damaged
2 October 1973	F-4J	153774	Ayers/Lamers	Destroyed
28 November 1973	F-4J	153776	Unknown	Unknown
27 May 1974	F-4J	153770	R. Dwyer/ Van Esselstyne	Damaged
27 April 1975	F-4J	153770	Hynes/J. Cluelow	Destroyed/Crew Injured
16 September 1975	F-4J	153888	R. Dwyer/Cote	Destroyed
? November 1975	F-4J	Unknown	Daniels/Unknown	Unknown
29 January 1976	F-4J	Unknown	Unknown	Unknown
17 February 1976	F-4J	153838	Ladd/Strickland	Destroyed
2 April 1977	F-4J	153904	Not Occupied	Damaged
19 April 1977	F-4J	153896	Not Occupied	Damaged
1 June 1978	F-4J	153911	Pospischil/Unknown	Damaged
1 June 1979	F-4S	155828	S. J. Anderson/ J. J. Hill	Destroyed/Pilot Killed
2 September 1979	F-4S	155562	J. O. Marthiljohni/ J. J. Hill	Destroyed/Crew Killed

1980–1985

Date	*Aircraft*	*BuNo.*	*Pilot/RIO*	*A/C Result*
28 March 1980	F-4S	155521	R. A. McNeese/ Unknown	A/C Damaged
23 July 1981	F-4S	153909	Not Occupied	A/C Damaged
5 August 1981	F-4S	155899	J. R. Hedges/ Unknown	A/C Damaged
7 August 1981	F-4S	155805	Not Occupied	A/C Damaged
19 May 1982	F-4S	UNKN	T. W. Thomas/ Unknown	A/C Damaged
13 July 1982	F-4S	153819	W. B. Hankins/ J. E. Daubert	A/C Destroyed/RIO Killed
26 July 1982	F-4S	153828	Not Occupied	A/C Damaged
9 August 1982	F-4S	155765	Not Occupied	A/C Damaged
14 February 1983	F-4S	155812	Unknown	A/C Damaged
18 February 1983	F-4S	155747	Unknown	A/C Damaged
5 July 1983	F-4S	157257	Unknown	A/C Damaged
15 September 1983	F-4S	155833	R. A. White/ C. L. Moseley	A/C Damaged
18 June 1984	F-4S	157245	Unknown	A/C Damaged
28 November 1984	F-4S	155812	D. S. Johnson/ Unknown	A/C Damaged
7 May 1985	F-4S	155871	J. C. Pross/ Unknown	A/C Damaged
10 July 1985	F-4S	155871	Unknown	A/C Damaged
23 August 1985	F-4S	155890	P. K. Farra/ R. J. Smith	A/C Damaged

1986

Date	*Aircraft*	*BuNo.*	*Event Classification*	*A/C Result*
18 August 1986	F-18A	161970	FLT HZ*: GENERAL	Indications of INS (inertial navigation system) failure during flight.
26 August 1986	F-18A	161980	FLT HZ: GENERAL	INS failure during air combat maneuvering.

* Flight Hazard.

Date	*Aircraft*	*BuNo.*	*Event Classification*	*A/C Result*
10 September 1986	F-18A	161967	FLT HZ: GENERAL	While holding to begin an ACM engagement, INS* failed.
18 September 1986	F-18A	161980	FLT HZ: GENERAL	While engaged in ACM, INS failed.
2 October 1986	F-18A	161985	FLT HZ: GENERAL	While engaged in ACM, INS failed.
20 October 1986	F-18A	161970	FLT HZ: GENERAL	Aircraft experienced left engine fire during ACM engagement.
21 October 1986	F-18A	161965	FLT HZ: GENERAL	While straight and level CN1561/ ASN130 INS failed
22 October 1986	F-18A	161980	FLT HZ: GENERAL	While engaged in ACM CN1561/ ASN130 INS failed.
5 November 1986	F-18A	161985	C: FLIGHT	Engine fire in flight.
5 November 1986	F-18A	161985	FLT HZ: GENERAL	Aircraft experienced compressor stall followed by bleed air lights and right engine fire light.
15 November 1986	F-18A	161978	FLT HZ: GENERAL	On touchdown, aircraft veered to left on runway.
22 November 1986	F-18A	161965	FLT HZ: GENERAL	ASN/130 INS failed during maneuvering flight.
26 November 1986	F-18A	161965	FLT HZ: GENERAL	INS failed during straight and level flight.
1 December 1986	F-18A	161965	FLT HZ: GENERAL	INS failed immediately after take-off.
5 December 1986	F-18A	161965	FLT HZ: GENERAL	INS failed during climb immediately after take-off.

* Inertial Navigation System.

Date	*Aircraft*	*BuNo.*	*Event Classification*	*A/C Result*
5 December 1986	F-18A	161965	FLT HZ: GENERAL	Aircraft experienced series of engine chugs on final approach.
10 December 1986	F-18A	161967	C: FLIGHT	Engine fodded by lower aft UHF antenna.
10 December 1986	F-18A	161967	FLT HZ: GENERAL	During high-speed portion of an ACM sortie, aircraft experienced compressor stalls.
11 December 1986	F-18A	161970	FLT HZ: GENERAL	While straight and level, INS failed
22 December 1986	F-18A	161970	FLT HZ: GENERAL	INS failed during straight and level flight.

1987

Date	*Aircraft*	*BuNo.*	*Event Classification*	*A/C Result*
8 January 1987	F-18A	161980	C: FLIGHT	Engine compressor stall during flight caused by external foreign object damage.
8 January 1987	F-18A	161980	FLT HZ: GENERAL	After raising landing gear, aircraft experienced compressor stalls. Left engine damaged.
9 February 1987	F-18A	161965	FLT HZ: GENERAL	During climb, INS malfunctioned
10 February 1987	F-18A	161972	FLT HZ: GENERAL	INS malfunctioned
24 March 1987	F-18A	161969	FLT HZ: GENERAL	Section of afterburner liner failed causing engine bay fire and aft fuselage damage.

Date	*Aircraft*	*BuNo.*	*Event Classification*	*A/C Result*
24 March 1987	F-18A	161969	C: FLIGHT	Right engine fire light in flight.
12 May 1987	F-18A	161961	FLT HZ: GENERAL	INS malfunction.
13 May 1987	F-18A	161961	FLT HZ: GENERAL	INS malfunction.
9 June 1987	F-18A	161961	FLT HZ: GENERAL	INS malfunction.
19 September 1987	F-18A	161980	FLT HZ: GENERAL	MK-82 bomb tumbled & struck water one mile short of target.
22 September 1987	F-18A	161967	FLT HZ: GENERAL	Right variable exhaust nozzle stuck closed at cruise power setting.
22 September 1987	F-18A	161965	FLT HZ: GENERAL	Multiple flight control system failures.
18 November 1987	F-18A	161961	FLT HZ: BIRD/ ANIMAL STK	Aircraft struck bird while in landing pattern.
25 November 1987	F-18A	163159	FLT HZ: GENERAL	Emergency gear extension and short field arrestment made.

1988

Date	*Aircraft*	*BuNo.*	*Event Classification*	*A/C Result*
20 April 1988	F-18A	161986	FLT HZ: GENERAL	Pilot received burns to buttocks from liquid oxygen leak during flight.
29 December 1988	F-18A	UNK	FLT HZ: BIRD/ ANIMAL STK	Bird strike hazard in Japan operating area.

1989

List of Squadron Accidents/Incidents 1989				
Date	*Aircraft*	*BuNo.*	*Event Classification*	*A/C Result*
30 November 1989	F-18A	1619964	FLT HZ: GENERAL	Fire extinguisher bottle, #1 engine activating cartridge was found to be damaged.

1990

Date	Aircraft	BuNo.	Event Classification	A/C Result
8 January 1990	F-18A	161968	C: FLIGHT	Right trailing edge flap departed aircraft in flight.
6 September 1990	F-18A	161961	C: GROUND	Captive AIM-9 on Sta. 9 impacted B-1 maintenance work stand as aircraft taxied into chocks.
7 November 1990	F-18A	161981	C: FLIGHT RELATED	During low level, seeker head destroyed by bird strike.

1991

Date	*Aircraft*	*BuNo.*	*Event Classification*	*A/C Result*
7 May 1991	F-18A	163158	B: FLIGHT	Two aircraft had mid-air collision during DACT.
21 October 1991	F-18A	163162	C: FLIGHT	Engine failure on take-off roll.

Endnotes

1: Birth of a Squadron

1 Chapter condensed from Steven K. Dixon, *Photo Recon Became Fighter Duty: Marine Observation Squadron 251 in World War II* (Jefferson, North Carolina: McFarland & Company, 2016).

2 Henderson Field was named after Major Lofton Henderson, who was killed during the battle for Midway.

3 Cactus was a codename designating the objective area of the invasion. Bevy was Guadalcanal's actual codename, but it was little used. Cactus was favored by most. Bevy was later changed to Mainyard in February 1943.

4 Technical Sergeant was an enlisted rank used by the USMC until 1958.

5 The field was referred to as Green Island, however it was located on Nissan Island, largest island in the Green Islands group.

6 Both the F4U and the FG were Corsairs of the same model. However, the F4U was built by Chance Vought (the original manufacturer) and the FG was built by Goodyear.

2: Reactivation

1 "MacArthur speech Tokyo Bay, 1945," Sage American History, accessed 18 March 2019, https://www. http://sageamericanhistory.net/worldwar2/docs/Macarthurtokyo.html.

2 "Wernher von Braun," NASA, accessed 7 April 2019, https://history.msfc.nasa.gov/vonbraun/bio.html. For more information on the role German scientists played in the post-World War II United States and how they arrived, *Operation Paperclip* by Annie Jacobsen (New York: Back Bay Books, 2015) is an excellent source.

3 Robert J. McMahon, *The Cold War: A Very Short Introduction* (Oxford, United Kingdom: Oxford University Press, 2003), 21–2.

4 "Cold War History," Wilson Center, accessed 7 April 2019, https://digitalarchive.wilsoncenter.org/theme/cold-war-history.

5 "Freedom of Information Act Electronic Reading Room," Central Intelligence Agency, accessed 7 April 2019, https://www.cia.gov/library/readingroom/docs/1946-03-05.pdf.

6 USMC History Division, Email exchange with author, September 2018.

7 Major William J. Sambito, A History of Marine Attack Squadron 311, History and Museums Division, Headquarters USMC, Washington, 1978.

8 VMF-251 Historical Report, National Archives, July 1946.

9 Ibid, 1 August–30 September 1946.

10 Major Edna Loftus Smith, USMCR, VMA-251 History, USMC History Division.

11 A Link trainer is a ground training device used in instrument-flight training.

12 "Bombing of Pleasure Craft Probed," *Newark Advocate*, 26 August 1946.

13 Ibid.

14 "Marine Air War," *Naval Aviation News*, Bureau of Aeronautics, November 1947, 2.

15 Smith, USMCR, VMA-251 History.

16 "Marine Air War," 2.
17 Smith, USMCR, VMA-251 History.
18 VMF-251 Historical Report, National Archives, 1 July–30 September 1948.
19 "Marine Air Games Show Off Reserves," *Naval Aviation News*, Bureau of Aeronautics, October 1948, 20.
20 Ibid.
21 VMF-251 Historical Report, National Archives, 1 January–30 June 1949.
22 Ibid.
23 The date of arrival conflicts with several sources. The squadron report states 15 July, but the MCAS Cherry Point base paper for the period implies 16 July.
24 "Reserves Due Tomorrow for Two Weeks Training," *The Windsock*, MCAS Cherry Point, 15 July 1949.
25 VMF-251 Historical, National Archives, 1 July–31 December 1949.
26 "Marine Reserves Set Record," *Naval Aviation News*, Bureau of Aeronautics, November 1949, 26–7.
27 The McDonnell FH Phantom was the first all-jet aircraft to land on a US aircraft carrier and also the first jet to equip a Marine squadron.
28 Ibid.
29 Smith, USMCR, VMA-251 History.

3: The Korean War

1 Smith, Major Edna Loftus, USMCR, VMA-251 History, USMC History Division.
2 *The Marine Corps Reserve: A History 1916–1966* (Washington, D.C.: Division of Reserve, USMC, 1966), 164.
3 Ibid, 165.
4 VMF-251 Historical Report, National Archives, 1 June–31 December 1950.
5 *The Marine Corps Reserve*, 169–70.
6 Ibid, 171.
7 Ibid, 171–72.
8 Smith, USMCR, VMA-251 History.
9 Ibid.
10 Larry Davis and David Menard, *Douglas AD-1 Skyraider* (North Branch, MN, Specialty Press Publishers, 2002), 5–19.
11 Ibid.
12 VMA-251 Historical Report, National Archives, 1–30 April 1951.
13 Ibid.
14 "People v. McCracken," Justia, accessed 14 June 2019, https://law.justia.com/cases/california/supreme-court/2d/39/336.html; and "Day five: The kidnapping, rape and murder of a 12-year-old girl," The Orange County Register, accessed 1 June 2019, https://www.ocregister.com/2009/11/06/day-five-the-kidnapping-rape-and-murder-of-a-12-year-old-girl/.
15 VMA-251 Historical Report, National Archives, 1–31 August 1951; and VMA-251 Historical Report, National Archives, 1–30 September 1951.
16 The historical report for the period had his rank as T/Sgt which is not a USMC rank.
17 VMA-251 Historical Report, National Archives, 1–31 October 1951.
18 Herb Bibbee Questionnaire, 4 November 2019. Bibbee recalled the aircraft landed with the wheels up while the squadron Command Diary for the period reports the landing gear collapsed on landing.
19 VMA-251 Historical Report, National Archives, 1–30 November 1951.
20 Ibid, 1–31 December 1951.

21 Ibid, 1–31 January 1952.
22 VMA-251 Semi-Annual Report, National Archives, January–June 1952.
23 VMA-251 Historical Report, National Archives, 1–31 March 1952.
24 Ibid, 1–30 April 1952.
25 "Douglass Annand," delawareonline, accessed 20 March 2019, https://www.legacy.com/obituaries/delawareonline/obituary.aspx?n=douglass-annand&pid=145755077.
26 VMA-251 Semi-Annual Report, National Archives, January–June 1952; https://www.baaa-acro.com/crash/crash-boeing-b-29a-65-bn-superfortress-oceanside-11-killed, accessed 1 November 2022.
27 VMA-251 Semi-Annual Report, National Archives, January–June 1952.
28 VMA-251 Command Diary, National Archives, January–March 1953.
29 A FOIA Request for the accident report through the Navy History and Heritage Center was made but the report could not be located.
30 Ibid.
31 VMA-251 Command Diary, USMC History Division, June 1953.
32 LtCol. Pat Meid and Major James Yingling, *US Marine Operations in Korea 1950–1953: Volume 5: Operations in West Korea* (Washington, D.C.: Historical Division, Headquarters, USMC, 1972).
33 VMA-251 Command Diary, National Archives, January–March 1953.
34 Ibid.
35 Davis and Menard, *Douglas AD-1 Skyraider*, 20–28.
36 VMA-251 Command Diary, National Archives, April 1953.
37 "Mark 7 Nuclear Bomb," National Museum of the United States Air Force, accessed 27 June 2019, https://www.nationalmuseum.af.mil/Visit/Museum-Exhibits/Fact-Sheets/Display/Article/196744/mark-7-nuclear-bomb/.
38 Davis and Menard, *Douglas AD-1 Skyraider*, 33–34.
39 Also known as the Loft Method. In both cases, the aircraft pulls up at a high angle and releases its bomb. The bomb continues at a high-angle trajectory before arcing over to fall on the designated target. This allowed time for the plane to escape the area to avoid the effects of the nuclear blast.
40 VMA-251 Command Diary, Appendix 5, USMC History Division, April 1953.
41 VMA-251 Command Diary, USMC History Division, April 1953.
42 Ibid, June 1953.
43 The squadron report for July 1953 does not mention any reason why one aircraft was left behind.
44 Chapter 25, in *The Korean War, 1950–1953*, extract from American Military History, Offices of the Chief of Military History, United States Army, https://history.army.mil/books/AMH/AMH-25.htm, 568.
45 MAG-12 Command Diary, National Archives, July 1953.
46 Ibid.
47 The temperatures conflict in the MAG-12 and 1st MAW Command Diaries for the month of July.
48 1st MAW Command Diary, National Archives July 1953.
49 The coordinates were written with the Military Grid Reference System (MGRS) in use at the time. To get a precise location, 10 digits were needed. Using a four-digit combination is accurate to within one kilometer, six digits are accurate to 100 meters and 8 within 10 meters. The coordinates used in the After Action Report for the period ranged from four to eight digits. I then converted them to determine an approximate location using Google Earth. The original map consulted was Operational Navigation Chart (ONC-G-10) dated April 1972.

50 The squadron July 1953 command diary states a 0630 time over target, an 18-minute flight to the target from take-off. Given the distance from K-6 and comparing it to other target times for different missions, this appears to be incorrect. Best estimates put time over target 30–40 minutes after take-off.
51 Elree G. Barr video interview, Library of Congress, accessed 24 August 2019, http://memory.loc.gov/diglib/vhp/story/loc.natlib.afc2001001.58391/mv0001001.stream.
52 Ibid.
53 The takeoff times for one mission on this date differ between the diary date entry and the Aircraft Mission Log times in the VMA-251 Command Diary for July 1953. The second mission listed under the 21 July date has a take-off time of 1312 in the date entry, but on the Aircraft Log Sheet a take-off time of 1219 is listed. It appears this mission took off first, followed closely by the second mission. I have used the Aircraft Log Sheet time.
54 The MAG-12 Command Diary entry for 22 July noted the weather was marginal to non-operational in all target areas and K-6.
55 John P. Condon, *Corsairs to Panthers: US Marine Aviation in Korea* (Washington, D.C.: USMC Historical Center, 2002), 54.
56 1st MAW Command Diary, National Archives, July 1953.
57 Barr video interview.
58 Combat activity of the squadron comes from USMC History Division's VMA-251 Command Diary, July 1953; MAG-12 Command Diary, July 1953; and 1st MAW Command Diary, July 1953.
59 1st MAW Command Diary, USMC History Division, July 1953.
60 VMA-251 Command Diary, USMC History Division, July 1953.

4: Keeping the Peace

1 VMA-251 Command Diary, USMC History Division, September 1953.
2 Larry Davis and David Menard, *Douglas AD-1 Skyraider* (North Branch, MN, Specialty Press Publishers, 2002), 27.
3 Located about twenty miles south of Seoul.
4 VMA-251 Command Diary, National Archives, August 1953.
5 Ibid.
6 Ibid.
7 Ibid.
8 Ibid, September 1953.
9 MARine Landing EXercise
10 VMA-251 Command Diary, National Archives, October 1953.
11 Ibid, November 1953.
12 Ibid, January 1954.
13 Aircraft Accident Report, Naval History and Heritage Command, 21 January 1954.
14 Ibid.
15 Special weapons meant nuclear weapons.
16 VMA-251 Command Diary, National Archives, February 1954.
17 OY - O for observation and Y for Consolidated, the manufacturer.
18 HHS, 1st MAW Unit Diary, USMC History Division, 5 February 1954.
19 John P. Condon, *Corsairs to Panthers: US Marine Aviation in Korea* (Washington, D.C.: USMC History Center, 2002) 56.
20 VMA-251 Command Diary, National Archives, February 1954.
21 Condon, *Corsairs to Panthers*, 56.
22 VMA-121 Unit Diary, National Archives, 12 April 1954.

23 Ibid.
24 VMA-251 Command Diary, National Archives, March 1954.
25 1st MAW Command Chronology, National Archives, March 1954.
26 VMA-251 Command Diary, National Archives, April 1954.
27 The bureau number appears to be incorrect. The Navy lists the bureau number as belonging to an F2H-2N Banshee, built by McDonnell. Source is *United States Naval Aviation from 1910–1995*, 4th edition, and published by the Naval Historical Center, Department of the Navy.
28 VMA-251 Command Diary, National Archives, May 1954.
29 Ibid, June 1954.
30 Ibid, July–September 1954; and Aircraft Accident Report, File No. FF4-1/A23, BuNo 129009, Naval History and Heritage Command via FOIA.
31 VMA-251 Command Diary, National Archives, July–September 1954.
32 Ibid, October–December 1954.
33 Appendix F "Operations S-3 Section Diary" of the squadron command diary for the period January–March 1955 cites the Accident Board conclusion that the pilot failed "to use the take-off check-off list as he took off with full back elevator tab [hence the nose-high attitude noted]. An error in judgment was made when the pilot elected to continue the take-off run when it was apparent that something was wrong with the controls of the aircraft."
34 VMA-251 Command Diary, National Archives, January–March 1955.
35 Squadron records have the event occurring on 1 May. MAG-12 records say 26 May.
36 MAG-12 Command Diary, National Archives, April–May 1955.
37 VMA-251 Command Diary, National Archives, April–June 1955.
38 Combat Air Patrol. Squadron documents indicate a reconnaissance mission.
39 Clark was a second lieutenant.
40 The squadron was at K-3 at the time of the incident.
41 Squadron documents indicate the port wing was hit.
42 Personal account of 1stLt. Kenneth C. Sanguinetti, "Last Bombs Dropped in Korea," VMFA-251, accessed 4 January 2020, https://www.vmfa251.org/history_accounts_sanguinetti.htm.
43 MAG-12 Command Diary, National Archives, April–May 1955.
44 VMA-251 Command Diary, National Archives, April–June 1955.
45 "The Taiwan Straits Crises: 1954–55 and 1958," Office of the Historian, accessed 20 September 2020, https://history.state.gov/milestones/1953-1960/taiwan-strait-crisis.
46 Information on these accidents and the move to Japan were obtained from a list of squadron accidents provided by the Naval History and Heritage Command (NHHC) as well as squadron unit diaries for 27 and 28 October 1955 and 7–10 January 1956, National Archives.
47 The other pilot was Capt. Donald P. Plante, who was flying as Kibbe's wingman.
48 IFF—Identification Friend or Foe—enables military and civilian air traffic control interrogation systems to identify aircraft, vehicles, or forces as friendly and to determine their bearing and range from the interrogator.
49 The name of the tower in the report cannot be completely read.
50 Information from Aircraft Accident Report (AAR) 127860, Naval History and Heritage Command via FOIA, 14 March 1956.
51 The unit is referred to as Sub-Unit 1 in Aircraft Accident Reports of the period.
52 Ralph Sabroe questionnaire, 4 November 2020.
53 VMA-251 Unit Diary, National Archives, 22 April 1956.
54 Jay Velie papers courtesy of the Velie family.
55 Information from Aircraft Accident Report (AAR) 134573, Naval History and Heritage Command via FOIA, 3 September 1956.

56 Ralph Sabroe questionnaire.
57 NAS Atsugi was about three miles southeast of Camp Zama.
58 Information from Aircraft Accident Report (AAR) 134573, Naval History and Heritage Command via FOIA, 23 November 1956.
59 Information from Aircraft Accident Report (AAR) 135299, Naval History and Heritage Command via FOIA, 18 February 1957.
60 Information from Aircraft Accident Report (AAR) 134568, Naval History and Heritage Command via FOIA, 27 February 1957.
61 VMA-251 Unit Diary, National Archives, 20 April 1957.

5: The Jet Age Begins

1 VMA-251 Unit Diary, National Archives, 21 April 1957.
2 Steven Albright, "Lineage of VMFA-251," *The Hook*, Spring 1998, 51–3.
3 Steve Ginter, *North American FJ-3/3M Fury* (Simi Valley, CA: Self-Published, 2010) 1–4.
4 Aircraft Accident Report BuNo 135868, Naval History and Heritage Command via FOIA, 12 February 1958.
5 Aircraft Accident Report BuNo 135930, Naval History and Heritage Command via FOIA, 20 August 1957.
6 Aircraft Accident Report BuNo 135806, Naval History and Heritage Command via FOIA, 4 September 1957.
7 Aircraft Accident Report BuNo 135965, Naval History and Heritage Command via FOIA, 11 September 1957.
8 VMF-251 Unit Diary, National Archives, 28 April 1958.
9 Endorsement of MAG-31 Letter, National Archives, 8 January 1958.
10 VMF-251 Unit Diary, National Archives, 4 February 1958.
11 Ibid, 31 January 1958.
12 John Harold Johnstone, *A Brief History of the 2d Marines* (United States: Historical Branch, G-3 Division, Headquarters, U.S. Marine Corps, 1962), 17.
13 VMF-251 Unit Diary, National Archives, 31 January 1958.
14 Aircraft Accident Report BuNo 135868, Naval History and Heritage Command via FOIA, 12 February 1958.
15 VMF-251 Unit Diary, National Archives, 28 April 1958.
16 Ibid, 29 April 1958.

6: The Crusader Years

1 Peter Mersky, *Vought F-8 Crusader* (London: Osprey Publishing, 1989), 13–6.
2 Steve Ginter, *Vought's F-8 Crusader: Part Three, Marine Fighter Squadrons* (Simi Valley, CA: Self-published, 1989), 2.
3 Ibid.
4 VMF-251 Navy Speed Letter, National Archives, 23 December 1958.
5 Ginter, *Vought's F-8 Crusader*, 1.
6 Mersky, *Vought F-8 Crusader*, 16–8.
7 Ginter, *Vought's F-8 Crusader*, 2.
8 Ibid.
9 Correspondence with author, 18 September 2019.
10 This and the description of the accident from the VMF-334 AAR BuNo 143765, Naval History and Heritage Command via FOIA, 1 August 1958.
11 Personal recollection, "An Unfortunate FAM," VMFA-251, accessed 23 May 2020, https://www.vmfa251.org/history_accounts_black.htm.

12 VMF-251 AAR BuNo 145365, Naval History and Heritage Command via FOIA, 20 August 1958.

13 Aircraft Accident Report BuNo 145452, Naval History and Heritage Command via FOIA request, 21 April 1959.

14 Aircraft Accident Report BuNo 145536, Naval History and Heritage Command via FOIA, 27 May 1959.

15 This is purely guesswork. No documents could be located concerning the movement. It is a best guess based on the author's experiences in the USMC.

16 Timeline for events from the squadron cruise book provided by Steven Albright.

17 Truman R. Strobridge, *A Brief History of the 9th Marines* (Washington, D.C.: Historical Branch, G-3 Division Headquarters, U.S. Marine Corps, 1967), 17.

18 Aircraft Accident Report BuNo 145436, Naval History and Heritage Command via FOIA, 18 November 1960.

19 Ginter, *Vought's F-8 Crusader*, 26; and "Abbreviated Squadron History to 1994," VMFA-251 (USMC History Division, date unknown), accessed 18 January 2021, https://www.vmfa251.org/pdffiles/history_documents_abb_history.pdf.

20 The squadron earned a Marine Corps Expeditionary Streamer (Cuba) for the period of October–November 1961.

21 The aircraft could engage an arresting cable on the runway by lowering the tailhook, which allowed the aircraft to stop in a short distance.

22 Aircraft Accident Report BuNo 145540, Naval History and Heritage Command via FOIA, dated 6 July 1961.

23 Mediterranean Cruise, USS *Shangri-La*, National Archives, 7 February–28 August 1962. This report states 12 Crusaders in one paragraph, then 13 in another, then 12 again in another section. Official publications of the January, February, and March 1962 Allowances and Location of Navy Aircraft show the squadron with 20 Crusaders assigned. These reports are online at the Naval History and Heritage Command website: https://www.history.navy.mil/research/histories/naval-aviation-history/allowances-and-location.html. The cruise report further states that no aircraft and personnel were left behind for the cruise. If this is the case, then either the cruise report is incorrect, or the allowances and location reports are incorrect. If the squadron did bring only 12 aircraft aboard, where did the remaining eight Crusaders left behind end up?

24 Aircraft Accident Report BuNo 145488, Naval History and Heritage Command via FOIA, 13 December 1961. Allinder became the squadron commander in 1977.

25 "Odyssey 1962," USS *Shangri-La* Cruise Book, Fold3.com, accessed 24 January 2021, https://www.fold3.com/image/301463292.

26 Email correspondence with author, 14 June 2019.

27 "Club Members Remember their Fathers' Service to Our Nation," Rotary Club of North Raleigh, accessed 31 January 2021, http://northraleighrotary.org/club-members-remember-their-fathers-service-to-our-nation/.

28 "Abbreviated Squadron History to 1994," VMFA-251 (USMC History Division, date unknown), accessed 31 January 2021, https://www.vmfa251.org/pdffiles/history_documents_abb_history.pdf.

29 Mediterranean Cruise, USS *Shangri-La*, National Archives, 7 February–28 August 1962. For a complete list of the USS *Shangri-La* itinerary, see Appendix II.

30 Ginter, *Vought's F-8 Crusader*, 27.

31 Ibid, 28. Photo evidence suggests June 1963.

32 A SATS field is a rapidly constructed expeditionary airfield that can be erected near a battle area to provide air support for amphibious Marine forces.

33 "Abbreviated Squadron History to 1994," accessed 31 January 2021.

34 The Crusader had two Power Control hydraulic systems, known as PC 1 and PC 2. Each supplied the aircraft's hydraulic system with 3,000 psi. The systems were separate and operated independently. They operated the flight control surfaces. NAVAER Flight Manual, Navy Model F8U-1, revised 15 February 1959, 18–9. Author's Collection.
35 Aircraft Accident Report BuNo 145467, Naval History and Heritage Command via FOIA, 13 January 1965.
36 It is not known when the squadron began training its men in preparation for receiving the Phantom II.

7: The Phantom Years

1 Adapted from Steven K. Dixon, "Cold War Workhorse," *Modern War*, November/December 2012.
2 S/Sgt Steve Stibbens, "Phantom Flyers," *Leatherneck*, May 1965, 20.
3 "Abbreviated Squadron History to 1994," VMFA-251 (USMC History Division, date unknown), accessed 28 March 2021, https://www.vmfa251.org/pdffiles/history_documents_abb_history.pdf.
4 Recollection of Jerry Dorneker, VMFA-251, accessed 13 April 2021, https://www.vmfa251.org/history_accounts_dorneker.htm.
5 Dan Shinabery, email correspondence with author, 13 April 2021. FOD is an acronym for Foreign Object Debris. All personnel formed a line side-by-side and walked the flight line area picking up any objects which could have caused engine damage if sucked into the engine intakes.
6 Dan Shinabery, correspondence with author, June 2021.
7 VMFA-251 Command Chronology, National Archives, July–December 1966.
8 Ibid, January–June 1967.
9 Ibid, July–December 1967.
10 "Cherry Point Airspace Complex," GlobalSecurity.org, accessed 16 April 2021, https://www.globalsecurity.org/military/facility/moa-cherry-point.htm.
11 VMFA-251 Command Chronology, National Archives, January–June 1968.
12 The Naval Safety Center became Naval Safety Command on 7 February 2022.
13 VMFA-251 Command Chronology, National Archives, July–December 1968.
14 Ibid, January–June 1969.
15 The OV-10 Bronco is a twin-engine turboprop light attack and observation aircraft built by North American Rockwell. At the time, HML-267 also operated UH-1 helicopters, the ubiquitous "Huey."
16 VMFA-251 Command Chronology, National Archives, July–December 1969.
17 Aircraft Accident Report BuNo 151437, Naval Safety Center via FOIA, 23 July 1970.
18 Aircraft Accident Report BuNo 153048, Naval Safety Center via FOIA, 30 September 1970.
19 Ken Hanson, correspondence with author, December 2019.
20 Ken Hanson Collection. Used with permission.
21 VMFA-251 Command Chronology, National Archives, July–December 1970.
22 *USMC News* release, Release Number CAB-232-70, OX-4-1492, 20 November 1970. Ken Hanson Collection.
23 Ken Hanson Questionnaire, November 2019.
24 Ibid.
25 Aircraft Accident Report BuNo 148398, Naval Safety Center via FOIA, 7 October 1971.
26 VMFA-251 Command Chronology, National Archives, January–June 1971.
27 Ibid, July–December 1971.
28 Ibid, January–June 1971.
29 Ibid, July–December 1972.

30 The 21st NORAD was one of several air defense command regions covering the United States. Its main area of responsibility was the northeast U.S. 20th NORAD covered the southeast.
31 VMFA-251 Command Chronology, National Archives, January–June 1973.
32 John Bryson, online conversation with author, 8 October 2021.
33 Richard Lamers, email correspondence with author, 8 November 2021. Flight path taken from Lamers's logbook.
34 The aircraft accident report has their ranks as 1stLt., while newspaper reports of the accident had their ranks as captain. Example: *Williamsport-Sun Gazette*, Saturday, 29 September 1973, accessed at https://www.newspapers.com/image/41150622, 11.
35 Aircraft Accident Report BuNo 153886, Naval Safety Center via FOIA, 27 September 1973; and "Fatal Hard Landing," *Approach*, November 1974, 6–7.
36 Richard Lamers, 8 November 2021. Lamers did not specify the altitude.
37 Aircraft Accident Report BuNo 153774, Naval Safety Center via FOIA, 2 October 1973.
38 Richard Lamers, 8 November 2021.
39 VMFA-251 Command Chronology, National Archives, July–December 1973.
40 Personal Account from Tom Hens, VMFA-251, accessed 2 October 2021, https://www.vmfa251.org/history_accounts_hens.
41 LtCol. Josephus Mavretic (USMC Ret.), interview by author via Zoom, 5 November 2021.
42 Ibid.
43 "Status of Forces, June–December 1973," Marine Corps University, accessed 8 October 2021, https://www.usmcu.edu/Research/Marine-Corps-History-Division/Research-Tools-Facts-and-Figures/Status-of-Forces/, 21–9.
44 In October 1973, OPEC ceased exporting oil to the United States, quadrupling the price. Despite the embargo ending in March 1974, oil prices continued to climb.
45 VMFA-251 Command Chronology, National Archives, July–December 1974.
46 Mavretic, 5 November 2021.
47 Ibid.
48 Ibid.
49 Ibid.
50 Ibid.
51 Ibid.
52 Ibid.
53 Ibid, and VMFA-251 Command Chronology, National Archives, January–June 1974.
54 R. A. "Chick" Eldridge, "Instant Replay," *Approach*, January 1975, 6.
55 Mavretic, 5 November 2021.
56 Eldridge, "Instant Replay."
57 Mavretic, 5 November 2021.
58 Robert Dwyer, email correspondence with author, March 2019.
59 VMFA-251 Command Chronology, National Archives, January–June 1974.
60 This design was what eventually became the F-18 Hornet. The author witnessed a test flight of this aircraft in 1979 at MCAS Beaufort. As an aviation electrician, I was amazed by the aircraft's maneuverability.
61 VMFA-251 Command Chronology, National Archives, July–December 1974.
62 Lee Logan, email correspondence with author, 8 November 2021.
63 VMFA-251 Command Chronology, National Archives, July–December 1974.
64 Mavretic, 5 November 2021.
65 Logan, 8 November 2021.
66 Mavretic, 5 November 2021.
67 Logan, 8 November 2021.
68 Jeff Ethell died in 1997 while flying a restored P-38 Lightning. He was 49 years old.

69 VMFA-251 Command Chronology, National Archives, July–December 1974.
70 "Thunderbolts get new Commanding Officer," *Jet Stream*, 7 February 1975.
71 If command eject was selected, if either the pilot or RIO initiated an ejection, both would be ejected.
72 Aircraft Accident Report BuNo 153770, Naval Safety Center via FOIA, 27 April 1975.
73 The aircraft accident report notes that refueling was to occur at Warner Robbins Air Force Base.
74 Jay Cluelow, interview by author, 30 March 2019.
75 Ibid.
76 Ibid.
77 Ibid.
78 Aircraft Accident Report BuNo 153770, Naval Safety Center via FOIA, 27 April 1975.
79 Ibid.
80 Cluelow, 30 March 2019.
81 Cluelow Flight Log—Mishap Section.
82 VMFA-251 Command Chronology, National Archives, January–June 1975.
83 Ram Air Turbine. Connected to a hydraulic pump or electrical generator, it is deployed during an emergency to provide power to critical aircraft systems. Power is generated from the airstream by airspeed that in turn rotates the blades so the generator can produce power.
84 Aircraft Accident Report BuNo 153888, Naval Safety Center via FOIA, 16 September 1975.
85 "Bravo Zulu," *Approach*, October 1976.
86 VMFA-251 Command Chronology, National Archives, July–December 1975.
87 The C-141 Starlifter and C-5A Galaxy were USAF Military Airlift Command aircraft capable of carrying both troops and cargo. The C-130 Hercules is a multi-use aircraft used by the USMC, USAF, U.S. Coast Guard, and many air arms around the world. The C-9 Skytrain II was the Marine designation for the McDonnell Douglas DC-9 airliner.
88 Aircraft Accident Report BuNo 153838, Naval Safety Center via FOIA, 17 February 1976.
89 VMFA-251 Command Chronology, USMC History Division, January–June 1976.
90 As for Spanjer's successor, Cummings recalled it was a Vincent who took over. This is incorrect. MajGen. Carey did take over from Spanjer on 30 July 1976.
91 Nickname for VMFA-122.
92 Wuertz and the plane captain were hospitalized for observation and later released.
93 John Cummings, email correspondence with author, 26 April 2020.
94 "Status of Forces, September–December 1976," Marine Corps University, accessed 30 November 2021, https://www.usmcu.edu/Research/Marine-Corps-History-Division/Research-Tools-Facts-and-Figures/Status-of-Forces/, Tab B.
95 VMFA-251 Command Chronology, USMC History Division, July–December 1976.
96 Maj. John M. Elliott USMC (Ret.), *The Official Monogram US Navy and Marine Corps Aircraft Color Guide 1960–1993* (Sturbridge, Massachusetts: Monogram Aviation Publications, 1993), 34.
97 VMFA-251 Command Chronology, July–December 1976.
98 VMFA-251 Command Chronology, USMC History Division, January–June 1977.
99 Elliott, *The Official Monogram US Navy and Marine Corps Aircraft Color Guide*, 40.
100 Turn-up screens were placed on the engine intakes to prevent objects from being sucked into the engines on run-ups.
101 VMFA-251 Command Chronology, USMC History Division, July–December 1977.
102 "How Low Can You Go?" personal account from Robert Foley, VMFA-251, accessed 20 December 2021, https://www.vmfa251.org/history_accounts_foley.htm.
103 Robert Pospischil, email correspondence with author, 22 March 2020.

104 VMFA-251 Command Chronology, USMC History Division, January–June 1978.
105 Ibid, July–December 1978.
106 Aircraft Accident Report BuNo 155828, Naval Safety Center via FOIA, 1 June 1979; and *Beaufort Gazette*, 1 and 4 June 1979.
107 A two-seat training version of the F-15 Eagle.
108 Indicates a launch or simulated launch of a heat-seeking missile such as an AIM-9 Sidewinder.
109 Aircraft Accident Report BuNo 155562, Naval Safety Center via FOIA, 2 September 1979.
110 VMFA-251 Command Chronology, USMC History Division, July–December 1979.
111 The incident is listed on the Naval Safety Center list of incidents covering VMFA-251 aircraft. Based on the description, it's possible McNeese and his RIO were practicing SATS and utilizing Beaufort's MOREST system. The MOREST system allowed an aircraft to use its tail hook to land in a very short distance rather than utilizing the entire length of a runway. McNeese may have been an exchange pilot.
112 "Thunderbolts Return from Key West," *Jet Stream*, 20 June 1980.
113 Alex Larzelere, *Castro's Ploy–America's Dilemma: The 1980 Cuban Boatlift* (Washington, D.C.: National Defense University Press, 1988).
114 VMFA-251 Command Chronology, USMC History Division, July–December 1980.
115 "Puerto Rico Missile Shoot," *The Hook*, Spring 1981.
116 "VMFA-251 Returns from Yuma," *Jet Stream*, 17 April 1981.
117 VMFA-251 Command Chronology, USMC History Division, July–December 1981.
118 Ibid, January–June 1982.
119 Aircraft Accident Report BuNo 153819, Naval Safety Center via FOIA, 13 July 1982.
120 VMFA-251 Command Chronology, USMC History Division, July–December 1982.
121 Larkin E. Conatser, "Marine Corps Combat Readiness Evaluation System (MCCRES): three case studies for use in providing a more effective evaluator" (Thesis, Naval Post Graduate School, 1983).
122 VMFA-251 Command Chronology, USMC History Division, January–July 1983.
123 Ibid, July–December 1983.
124 Elliott, *The Official Monogram: US Navy and Marine Corps Aircraft Color Guide*, 60–2.
125 Jacob Børresen, "Alliance Naval Strategies and Norway in the Final Years of the Cold War," *Naval War College Review*, Vol. 64: No. 2, Article 7 (2011): 4. Accessed via https://digital-commons.usnwc.edu/nwc-review/vol64/iss2/7.
126 For a complete listing of USMC air assets for *Teamwork 84*, see Appendix 8.
127 VMFA-251 Command Chronology, USMC History Division, January–June 1984.
128 Ibid, July–December 1984.
129 Whether the incident happened during landing or take-off is not known.
130 VMFA-251 Command Chronology, USMC History Division, January–June 1985.
131 Ibid, July–December 1985.

8: The Hornet and the End of the Cold War

1 Mike Spick, *Modern Fighting Aircraft: F/A-18 Hornet* (London, England: Salamander Books Limited, 1984), 8–12; "F/A-18 Hornet Fighter Historical Snapshot," Boeing, accessed 1 February 2022, https://www.boeing.com/history/products/fa-18-hornet.page; and Enzo Angelucci and Peter Bowers, *The American Fighter* (New York, NY: Orion Books, 1985), 320–2.
2 VMFA-251 Command Chronology, USMC History Division, January–June 1986.
3 Ibid, July–December 1986.
4 Ibid, January–June 1987.
5 Ibid.

6 VMFA-251 Command Chronology, USMC History Division, January–December 1988.
7 Earl W. Hacker, "One Year UDP: A Cost Benefit Analysis" (Thesis, Naval Post Graduate School, December 1988), 6–7. The 12-month stay was necessitated by problems encountered by replacing the Phantom II GE-J79-10A engines with the GE-J79-10B engines.
8 VMFA-251 Command Chronology, USMC History Division, July–December 1988.
9 Awards, Marine Corps Air Association, *Naval Aviation News*, January/February 1990, 32.
10 VMFA-251 Command Chronology, USMC History Division, January–June 1989.
11 Ibid, July–December 1989.
12 Table of Manpower Requirements T/O 8830D, USMC, 29 January 1990.
13 VMFA-251 Command Chronology, USMC History Division, January–June 1990.
14 The AGM-62 Walleye was a TV-guided smart bomb for use against targets such as fuel storage tanks, bridges, and facilities. It was first used during the Vietnam War. It underwent several modifications until the weapon was withdrawn from service in the 1990s.
15 LtCol. Leroy Stearns, *US Marines in the Persian Gulf, 1990–1991: The 3D Marine Aircraft Wing in Desert Shield and Desert Storm* (Washington, D.C.: History and Museums Division HQS, USMC, 1999), 69–70.
16 VMFA-251 Command Chronology, USMC History Division, July–December 1990.
17 Ibid, January–June 1991.
18 Ibid, July–December 1991.

Epilogue

1 "Production Issue with Ejection Seat Cartridge Actuated Devices (CAD) Necessitates Replacement of CAD in some Navy, Marine Corps Aircraft," America's Navy, accessed 15 September 2022, https://www.navy.mil/Press-Office/Press-Releases/display-pressreleases/Article/3105635/production-issue-with-ejection-seat-cartridge-actuated-devices-cad-necessitates/.
2 "10 U.S. Code § 653—Minimum service requirement for certain flight crew positions," Cornell Law School, accessed 17 September 2022, https://www.law.cornell.edu/uscode/text/10/653. Enlisted men served a minimum of four years on active duty, and two years of inactive reserve duty. As of 1992, jet pilots serve eight years, while navigators and naval flight officers serve six years. Prior terms may have been shorter.
3 "Current Mishap Definitions and Reporting Criteria," Naval Safety Command, accessed 18 September, https://navalsafetycommand.navy.mil/Resources/Current-Mishap-Definitions/. The classification system changed over the years. Today a Class A accident is defined as suffering damage estimated to cost $2.5 million or more; Class B, Class C, Class D, and Class E are the other classifications in the current system.
4 VVFA-251 History, accessed 21 December 2018, https://www.mag31.marines.mil/MAG-31-Units/VMFA-251/About/.
5 "Female Aviators Spread Wings in Past, Present, Future," accessed 23 October 2022, Female aviators spread wings in past, present, future > United States Marine Corps Flagship > News Display (marines.mil).

Appendix 3

1 VMA-121 Command Diary, Appendix V, USMC History Division, July 1953.

Appendix 6

1 Information from USMC History Division.

Appendix 7

1 Information from Naval Safety Command and the help of Peter Greengrass.

Index

Page numbers in **bold** refer to illustrations and those in *italic* denote tables.